Proceedings of
The Fellowship of Catholic Scholars
Tenth Convention

THE CATHOLIC CHURCH'S MESSAGE TO UNITED STATES CITIZENS OF THE TWENTY-FIRST CENTURY

edited by
Paul L. Williams

Northeast Books

A division of the Cultural Society of Northeastern Pennsylvania,
a non-profit corporation
Pittston, Pennsylvania

THE CATHOLIC CHURCH'S MESSAGE TO UNITED STATES CITIZENS OF THE TWENTY-FIRST CENTURY

Published with ecclesiastical approval

ISBN 0—937374—04—0

Cover Design by Sandra Saks

Typeset by Ron Semian at Design Print, Inc.

Layout by Barbara Semian

Northeast Books Edition 1988
by special arrangement with the
Fellowship of Catholic Scholars

TABLE OF CONTENTS

CONTRIBUTORS

Benedict M. Ashley, O.P.	Dominican House of Studies St. Louis, Missouri
William Bentley Ball, Esq.	Ball, Skelly, Murren & Connell Harrisburg, Pennsylvania
Stephen M. Barr	University of Delaware
Gerard V. Bradley	University of Illinois
Msgr. Eugene V. Clark	St. John's University Jamaica, New York
Thomas A. Droleskey	St. Mark's School Hyattsville, Maryland
Father Patrick Egan	*Pastoral Renewal* Ann Arbor, Michigan
Robert George	Princeton University New Jersey
Gary D. Glenn	Northern Illinois University
Mrs. Helen Hull Hitchcock	*Women for Faith and Family* St. Louis, Missouri
Msgr. George A. Kelly	St. John's University Jamaica, New York
Leonard A. Kennedy, C.S.B.	University of St. Thomas Houston, Texas
Thomas Langan	St. Michael's College University of Toronto
Joyce A. Little	University of St. Thomas Houston, Texas
Archbishop Roger Mahony	**Of Los Angeles**
Mrs. Rita L. Marker	University of Steubenville Ohio
Father Marvin R. O'Connell	University of Notre Dame
Paul M. Quay, S.J.	Loyola University of Chicago
Herbert Ratner, M.D.	*Child and Family* Oak Park, Illinois
Mary F. Rousseau	Marquette University Wisconsin
Joseph A. Varacalli	State University of New York (Nassau)
Father Thomas Weinandy, OFM, Cap.	*Mother of God Community* Washington, D.C.

Introduction
Cardinal Wright Award
by
Archbishop Roger Mahony
Los Angeles

This year the Fellowship is conferring its prestigious Cardinal Wright Award on two of its members.

Father Joseph Farraher is a veteran moral theologian, whose name is linked with such outstanding Jesuit moralists as Gerald Kelly, John Ford and John Lynch. He has been a prolific writer of theological subjects for forty years and a leading defender of Catholic teaching during and after the controversy over Humanae Vitae. After Fr. Farraher retired from teaching diocesan seminarians at Menlo Park, he developed a Question and Answer section for Father Ken Baker's *Homiletic and Pastoral Review,* a section which he continues to produce monthly with intellectual vigor and doctrinal clarity.

It is with pleasure that I confer the Cardinal Wright Award on a distinguished Jesuit theologian: Father Joseph Farraher.

Father Joseph Fessio, a founder with Father Farraher of the Fellowship, was and is a student of Cardinal Ratzinger. He has in a few short years demonstrated remarkable creativity and determination. Fr. Fessio had not long returned to the United States when he established the St. Ignatius Institute on the campus of the University of San Francisco for the purpose of institutionalizing a source of authentic Catholic teaching. The St. Ignatius Institute remains a model for any school that bears the name Catholic. In addition, Fr. Fessio created the Ignatius Press, which now is the purveyor of Christian classics and the publisher of an outstanding list of new Catholic books that reinforce the faith for their readers. In recognition of these accomplishments the Holy See recently appointed Father Fessio an "expert" advisor to Archbishop Schotte for the forthcoming Synod on the Laity.

It is a pleasure to join with the Fellowship in conferring the Cardinal Wright Award on a distinguished Jesuit: Father Joseph Fessio.

I also want to thank John and Eileen Farrell, whose early and continuing help to the Fellowship has been an inspiration, especially in the creation of this Award.

PART ONE:
The Church's Socio-Economic Teaching

Natural Law, the Common Good, and American Politics

by

Robert George

Liberal political theory has long been concerned with the problem of individual rights and collective interests. Some liberals, most notably J. S. Mill, have taken a utilitarian approach to the problem.[1] Under such an approach, individual rights are themselves ultimately derived from a consideration of collective interests. The argument is that individuals have a right to, say, free speech because overall and in the long run permitting individuals to speak freely redounds to the net benefit of the community (or mankind) as a whole. Restrictions on speech may, of course, offer benefits in the short run, but these are outweighed by the greater benefits likely to accrue as fruits of liberty in the long run.

Most contemporary liberal political philosophers, however, are wary of the utilitarian approach. Their chief concern is that it does not provide a sufficiently secure foundation for individual rights. They worry that many individual rights could be overridden if they were left to stand or fall on the basis of considerations of utility. Claiming to reject utilitarianism, they have developed liberal political theories based on principles of what Mill called "abstract right." The idea here is that basic individual rights are not derived from a consideration of what makes the community better off; on the contrary, such rights exist and should be honored even when their exercise makes the community genuinely worse off.[2]

What alternative account of the moral foundations of individual rights is available once the utilitarian account has been rejected? Here a division exists among contemporary liberal political philosophers. Orthodox liberals, e.g., John Rawls, Robert Nozick, Ronald Dworkin, and David Richards, argue against the inclusion of "perfectionist" principles in political theory. They maintain that individual rights and other principles of justice must be identified, and political institutions designed, without employing controversial ideas about human nature or conceptions of the human good. In Dworkin's crisp statement, "Political decisions must be, as far as possible, independent of any particular conception of the good life, or of what gives value to life."[3]

The anti-perfectionism of orthodox liberalism has been challenged, however, by a number of contemporary political philosophers who understand themselves to be working broadly within the tradition of liberalism. Vinit Haksar, Joseph Raz, William Galston, and others defend versions of liberalism in which they seek to ground basic human rights in conceptions of human well-being. They eschew value neutrality in the design of political institutions and the identification of principles of justice and individual rights.

In this essay I will criticize a liberal view of individual rights and collective interests and defend an alternative understanding drawn from the tradition of natural law theory. I will focus my critical attention on anti-perfectionist liberalism, and, in particular, on the work of Ronald Dworkin. I maintain that Dworkin's liberalism embodies a distorted understanding both of individual rights and collective interests (or what natural law theorists call the "common good"). Once these distortions are brought to light, the superficial appeal of Dworkin's sharp distinction between the role of courts, as concerned with upholding individual rights, and that of legislatures, as concerned with advancing collective interests, vanishes. So too does the apparent plausibility of Dworkin's argument for an individual "right to moral independence" against governmental regulation of "private" morality.

As Dworkin understands the matter, individual rights constrain the government's pursuit of collective interests. Rights specify things that the government cannot do to persons even when the collective welfare could thereby be advanced.[4] Thus, individual rights and collective interests are viewed as potentially (and, often enough, actually) in con-flict. Dworkin endorses what he understands to be the characteristically liberal position that, except in cases of extraordinary emergency, individual rights "trump" collective interests.

Let us first attend to Dworkin's understanding of the realities which, we are told, (ordinarily) trump collective interests. Where do individual rights come from? How are they derived? On these questions Dworkin's anti-perfectionism leaves him ultimately without a satisfactory answer. He holds that the specific political rights to which liberals are committed, e.g., rights to free speech, religious liberty, "privacy," etc., are derived not from considerations of what is truly good for human beings, nor, for that matter, from what other anti-perfectionist liberals have con-ceived of as general rights to liberty or autonomy, but rather from an abstract right to *equality,* viz., the right to be treated by the government with equal concern and respect.[5]

Whether the specific political rights favored by Dworkin and other liberals can plausibly be derived from this abstract right is questionable. Later on I will attack Dworkin's proposed derivation of one such right, i.e., the right to "privacy" or "moral independence." For now, I simply wish to observe that the abstract right to equality appears to be foun-dational in Dworkin's theory of political morality — he makes no effort to derive it from more fundamental principles. But this is problematic insofar as the proposition it states appears to be neither a self-evident practical principle nor a necessary truth. Tracing back a chain of prac-tical reasoning from the moral decision to recognize a specific political right, one does not ultimately arrive at a grasp of the self-evident intelligibility of an abstract right to equality which terminates the chain by leaving no relevant questions unanswered. Nor does one contradict oneself in denying the abstract right. The right to equality itself, then, stands in need of a demonstration that would appeal ultimately to self-evident practical principles or necessary truths. Otherwise the assertion that there is such a right states nothing more than a not-so-widely shared intuition.

Let us turn now to Dworkin's view of collective interests. How ought we to conceive of the interests of the community which are, we are told, (ordinarily) trumped when in conflict with individual rights? According to Dworkin, they should be conceived of as the community's general background goals which would, but for the existence of the right, justify governmental interference with the individual's choice and action (e.g., by requiring him to do something he might not wish to do, or by impeding or preventing him from doing something he might wish to do). These goals are variously referred to by Dworkin in summary fashion as the "aggregate collective good,"[6] the "general benefit,"[7] the "general interest,"[8] the "collective general interest,"[9] the "public interest,"[10] the "public's welfare,"[11] the "general welfare,"[12] and "general utility."[13] Ought these terms to be taken as implying a utilitarian conception of collective interests? The references to *"aggregate* collective good" and "general utility" notwithstanding. Dworkin has consistently maintained that they *need* not be thus taken.[14] Nevertheless, utilitarian conceptions of collective interests are the only ones Dworkin has ever taken seriously.[15]

It could be argued that this is a result of Dworkin's stated belief that a form of utilitarianism, one he calls "neutral utilitarianism," represents the working conception of collective interests in American politics. He maintains that "it has supplied, for example, the working justification of most of the constraints on our liberty through law that we accept as proper."[16] What is "neutral utilitarianism?" It is the version of utilitarianism that "takes as the goal of politics the fulfillment of as many people's goals for their own lives as possible"[17] and is "neutral between all people *and preferences.*"[18]

Now, it does seem to me that American legislators and judges frequently adopt a utilitarian approach to political decision-making. (Consider, e.g., the defense policy of nuclear deterrence or, rhetoric about women's rights aside, the judicially mandated policy of legal abortion.) But Dworkin grossly overstates the case in alleging that a form of utilitarianism which is neutral *among preferences* supplies the working justification for *most* of the laws accepted by Americans as proper. Very many preferences are frustrated by the law not merely because lawmakers consider them to be "outweighed" by competing preferences, but because they judge them to be the sorts of preferences which should in principle be excluded from consideration from the start.[19]

In any event, lawmakers err to the extent that they understand collective interests in *any* utilitarian sense. Twenty years and more of intense philosophical criticism of utilitarianism (and consequentialism generally) has established that the strategy of resolving practical (including political) problems by appeal to a principle of optimizing consequences is utterly hopeless. The constitutive "principle" of utilitarianism cannot *rationally* guide choice and action because it fails to state a coherent proposition. One could choose in such a way as to optimize consequences only if the various forms of good, and the various instantiations of particular forms of good, constitutive of human well-being were commensurable in such a way as to make possible the weighing and comparison of states of affairs required by the utilitarian principle. But, as critics of utilitarianism have conclusively shown, such commensurability is an illusion.[20] Thus, no one can accurately say, for example, that so much friendship is worth so much knowledge; or that this one man's life is worth less (or more) than the lives of these two (or ten, or ten thousand) others.

Beyond this, however, the fact of incommensurability undermines any aggregative conception of collective interests. This means that "collective interests" are, in reality, the interests of *individuals*.[21] There simply are no "collective interests" not reducible to concrete aspects of the well-being of individual members of the collectivity. Does this insinuate the sort of "individualism" characteristic of libertarian political theories? No. This is because among the concrete interests of every individual human being is living in harmony and friendship with others. Moreover, an appreciation of the values of interpersonal harmony and friendship helps to bring into focus the moral requirement that the benefits and burdens of communal life (including rights and duties) be distributed fairly and with a due regard for the particular needs and abilities of different persons

Now, Dworkin's practical juxtaposition of individual rights with an aggregative conception of collective interests gives an air of plausibility to his distinction between the role of courts, as concerned with upholding principle, and that of legislatures, as concerned with advancing policy. For Dworkin, "[p]rinciples are propositions that describe rights; policies are propositions that describe goals."[22] To say that rights trump, e.g., the general welfare, is to say that principle should prevail where it conflicts with policy. Courts, according to Dworkin, offer a "forum of principle,"; they are responsible for protecting individual rights. Legislatures, on the other hand, are concerned with matters of policy; they are responsible for advancing collective interests. Under an aggregative conception of collective interests, the best policy would be the one that yielded the "most" good — individual interests and rights notwithstanding. If individual rights nevertheless existed independent of collective interests, it would indeed make sense to provide a political forum with broad powers countervailing to those of legislatures to which individuals could appeal for their protection. The idea of courts as such a forum is by no means unreasonable.

But if we conceive of collective interests in a non-utilitarian, non-aggregative way, the neat contrasts between matters of principle and policy and individual rights and collective interests blur. An appreciation of incommensurability brings to light the profound senses in which legislative responsibilities for policy implicate matters of principle. To advance collective interests (conceived in a non-utilitarian way) is, among other things, to respect the requirements of practical reasoning which structure choice — including legislative choice — in respect of the range of incommensurable aspects of individual and communal human flourishing. These moral requirements may often be expressed in terms of entitlements of individuals not only to particular liberties, but to a great many other opportunities and goods. These entitlements (negative and positive) are the "individual rights" which legislatures must not only respect but protect and advance if they are to fulfill their *policy* responsibilities under a non-aggregative conception of collective interests.

Under a non-aggregative conception of collective interests, no individual's interests may be left out of account by policymakers, nor may any individual's rights be trampled (by legislators, judges, or anyone else), without thereby *damaging* the common welfare. Incommensurability means that it is impossible to say that the state of affairs produced by a violation of individual rights is "better" for the community than the state of affairs which would have obtained had individual rights been respected. Where rights are conceived of as constraints on the pursuit of collective interests, it is assumed that sometimes collective interests actually could be advanced by violating rights (although it would, ordinarily, be wrong to do so). But this could only be true under an aggregative conception of collective interests. And such a conception cannot be justified in light of the problem of incommensurability.

The non-aggregative conception of collective interests I have been sketching out closely resembles the traditional natural law theory of the common good. While talk of "rights" does not figure prominently in the classical and medieval statements of that theory, its perfectionist concern for human well-being provides ample grounds for the derivation of human rights by its modern exponents. These rights are understood by contemporary natural law theorists not as constraints on the pursuit of the common good, but as constitutive aspects thereof. Thus, for natural law theorists, legislatures are not properly designed or understood as institutions devoted to advancing aggregate good constrained by the power of courts to enforce individual rights. Rather, legislative responsibility for preserving and advancing the common good includes an obligation to honor and protect rights. Courts — even those which do not enjoy the power of judicial review of legislation — share this obligation, albeit in a more or less circumscribed way. But it is certainly not a peculiarly (or even primarily) judicial obligation.

Natural law principles of political morality frequently require the government to refrain from interfering with individual choice and action.[23] Sometimes, the unimpeded individual will choose to act in such a way as to damage not only himself but others as well. This need not imply a view of morality which sacrifices collective interests to individual rights. The goods of individual liberty, autonomy, authenticity, etc. are themselves incommensurable aspects of human well-being. But *this* does not mean that individual choice and action may never be impeded — only that the legitimacy of governmental decisions to interfere with individual choice and action depends upon the consistency of those decisions with the requirements of practical reasoning that structure human choosing in respect of the range of incommensurable human values. Where these requirements exclude governmental interference with individual choice and action, any loss in terms of goods foregone by governmental respect for individual rights is simply not properly understood as a sacrifice of collective interests. Again, regardless of the goods to be gained by a disregard for rights, the incommensurability of goods means that the common good, since it is non-aggregative, simply cannot be advanced by governmental action which infringes rights. Such action *only* damages the common good.

The natural law theory of individual rights and collective interests has the advantage over anti-perfectionist liberalism of providing a rational account of the moral foundations of rights by understanding them as implications of intrinsic human goods and basic moral principles which rationally guide and structure human choosing in respect of such goods. Its thoroughgoing rejection of aggregative conceptions of collective interests makes it possible, moreover, to understand rights not as constraints on the pursuit of such interests, but as constitutive aspects of the common good.

Now, what has any of this to do with American politics? Liberalism is not only a political theory; it is a political movement. As a movement, it has an agenda which has been prosecuted vigorously and, on the whole, successfully in the United States. Liberals have achieved many of their goals by effectively capturing the terms of American political debate. These terms typically juxtapose individual rights with collective interests. The "liberal" position is depicted as the one favoring individual rights; the conservative position as the one favoring collective interests.

American conservatism has, by and large, left the liberal understanding of individual rights and collective interests unchallenged. Indeed, in at least some respects, American conservatives seem willing to accept this understanding flat out. In economic matters, for example, conservatives have simply tried to turn the tables on liberals by depicting government regulation as unjustly (and shortsightedly) favoring collective interests over individual rights. Those libertarian-minded conservatives who denounce governmental interference with "capitalist acts between consenting adults" rightly claim to be not so much "conservatives" as "classical liberals." In non-economic matters, e.g., matters of criminal justice, conservatives have made their own play for the rhetorical advantage, juxtaposing "the rights of the criminal" with the "rights of society."

Over the past forty years liberals in the Western democratic nations have campaigned to obtain legal immunities for controversial activities they believe to be matters of individual right. Among the most controversial claims of right they have advanced are those having to do with human sexuality and reproduction. Liberals maintain that these are (for the most part) "private" matters. They must, therefore, be left to individuals to decide for themselves. The government violates individual rights when it bans or unduly restricts abortion, contraception, pornography, and sodomy.

The political strategy American liberals have found most effective has not involved persuading legislators to repeal such legislation; rather, it has involved persuading judges to invalidate it under their power of constitutional judicial review. State laws restricting abortion,[24] contraception,[25] and pornography[26] have been struck down by the federal courts as unconstitutional violations of a putative "right of privacy."[27]

Now, Dworkin has attempted to provide a theoretical justification for something very like the liberal notion of the "right of privacy." He calls it the "right to moral independence."[28] The central premise from which he argues is the abstract right to equality.

In his early work, Dworkin argued that government violates this right whenever it restricts individual liberty on the ground that one citizen's conception of the good life is nobler or superior to another's.[29] This claim, however, came in for stinging criticism. It is far from obvious that a legislative concern for the morality of members of the public is necessarily indicative of contempt for those persons whose preferred conduct is banned or restricted. On the contrary, as John Finnis has argued, morals legislation "*may* manifest, not contempt, but a sense of the equal worth and human dignity of those people, whose conduct is outlawed precisely on the ground that it expresses a serious misconception of, and actually degrades, human worth and dignity, and thus degrades their own personal worth and dignity, along with that of others who may be induced to share in or emulate their degradation."[30]

Some liberals reply to Finnis' argument by denying that conduct typically regulated by morals legislation, e.g., various forms of consensual sexual activity, can ever be inconsistent with human worth and dignity.[31] In their view, there can be nothing morally wrong with such "autonomous" and purely "self-regarding" conduct.[32] Dworkin, however, offers no such rejoinder. He does not suppose that the right to moral independence exists because "private" choices are never subject to moral standards. Rather, he argues that the right protects the individual from interference with such choices even where he may choose wrongly. Indeed, such choices are, in his view, immune from governmental intrusion as a matter of moral right even where the decision involves conduct which is demeaning, degrading, or destructive.

But where such conduct is involved, there certainly need be nothing inegalitarian in legislative action aimed at preventing it. Such action certainly (but not arbitrarily) prefers some types of *conduct* over others; but it just as certainly need reflect no preference of one *person* over another. It condemns some conduct as unworthy of persons; but it need condemn no person as less worthy than any other. The paternalism involved in a decision to intervene in persons' lives to prevent them from demeaning, degrading, or destroying themselves by their own wrongful choices might very well, as Finnis suggests, be motivated precisely by an appreciation of their equal worth and dignity.[33]

In his more recent work, Dworkin has revised his argument from equality. He still maintains that individuals have a moral right to be free from governmental intrusion in "private" matters, but his argument is more complex. He says that the principle of equality requires that government

> "... must impose no sacrifice or constraint on any citizen in virtue of an argument that a citizen could not accept without abandoning his sense of equal worth ... [But] no self-respecting person who believes that a particular way to live is most valuable for him can accept that this way of life is base or degrading."[34]

But additional complexity fails to afford Dworkin's argument additional cogency. Whether or not the individual whose preferred conduct is proscribed or restricted accepts the argument grounding the proscription or restriction, or even thinks about the matter at all, is irrelevant to whether those exercising authority over that conduct are treating that individual with equal concern and respect.

If he happens to think about it and accepts the argument, he in effect agrees that the conduct in question is indeed unworthy of him. He still might find it difficult to conform his behavior to the law; and insofar as he continues to indulge in the unworthy conduct he will likely find it difficult to retain his self-respect. Now, self-respect is a genuine human good; the loss of self-respect is a genuine evil. But in this event damage to the individual's self-respect is not properly attributable to the law, but to his own moral failings. His self-respect will be restored to the extent that he reforms his character and conforms his conduct to the standard required not only by the law but also by his own revised understanding of the morality of the conduct in question.

But what if he does not accept the argument? In this event there will be no damage to self-respect at all. He will regard the law as backward, stupid, insensitive, unjust. He might express anger towards, and/or sorrow for, those responsible for, or supportive of, the law. He might *feel* as though he is being treated as a second-class citizen for engaging in conduct which he believes to be acceptable or even enriching. He might work for the repeal of the law, and even practice civil disobedience. He cannot, however, reasonably maintain that the law fails to treat him as an equal. To the extent that the law embodies a legislative concern to prevent individuals from demeaning, degrading, or destroying themselves, it treats his welfare as just as important as everyone else's. In seeking to uphold public morals, it favors the moral well-being of each and every member of the public. No one's interest in living a worthy and dignified life is singled out as more or less important.

In a carefully constructed article, Dworkin has attempted to apply his view of individual rights and collective interests to the problem of pornography.[35] Therein he straightforwardly (and accurately) identifies certain significant respects in which the availability of pornography damages collective interests. He says that a decision to recognize a right to use pornography, even in private,

> "... would sharply limit the ability of individuals consciously and reflectively to influence the conditions of their own and their children's development. It would limit their ability to bring about the cultural structure

Nevertheless, he argues, such a right exists and should be recognized by law. Despite the fact that legal restrictions on the availability and use of pornography might very well advance collective interests in such true human goods as dignity and beauty in human sexual relationships, such legal restrictions would be unjust. They would violate the right to moral independence, and, ultimately, the right to equality, of those individuals wishing to use pornography.

I have already attacked Dworkin's attempt to derive the putative right to moral independence from the right to equality. Good faith legislative efforts to combat, e.g., pornography, even where such efforts go awry (as when valuable non-pornographic materials are prudishly or squeamishly banned or restricted), imply no denial of the equality of persons. I now want to conclude my case against Dworkin's view of individual rights and collective interests by challenging him on the specific question of a right to pornography, and demonstrating that anti-pornography legislation need not violate anyone's rights, nor sacrifice anyone's interests, for the sake of advancing collective interests.

The human interest in dignity and beauty in sexual relationships — and in the creation and maintenance of a "cultural structure" which supports these ideals — is a "collective" interest (only) in the sense that it is an interest shared by each and every individual member of the collectivity. It is a "common" interest, and a matter of the common good, in the sense that it is shared by all and may be preserved and advanced by common endeavor. What is worth noticing is that among those whose interests are preserved and advanced by anti-pornography legislation are those individuals who would be inclined to use pornography. Dignity and beauty in sexual relationships (and a supporting cultural structure) are no less goods for them than for anyone else. To the extent that it serves these (truly common) goods, anti-pornography legislation preserves and advances, rather than harms, their interests as well as the interests of everybody else.

This would not be the case, of course, if human interests were ultimately matters of desire-satisfaction. In this event, anti-pornography legislation would represent a favoring of the desires of those who happened to like dignity and beauty in sexual relationships over those who happened to like pornography. A genuine *conflict* of interests would then exist. Collective interests really would be an aggregative matter: whatever satisfied the most desires (or the desires of most people) would be in the collective interest. Individual rights, if they existed, would constrain the collective pursuit of desire-satisfaction. They would specify immunities which would, in effect, entitle the individual to certain types of desire-satisfaction of his own — even at a cost to the overall desire-satisfaction of the collectivity.

But once we understand interests as having to do with human goods *not* reducible to desire-satisfaction, apparent conflicts of interest of this sort should not trouble us. Anti-pornography legislation, to the extent it is effective, frustrates the desires (or potential desires) of persons inclined to use pornography, but it does so precisely in the interests of, among others, those very individuals. Insofar as it does not treat their interests as in any sense inferior to those of anyone else, it does not fail to treat them with equal concern and respect.

NOTES

[1] See J. S. Mill "On Liberty" in Mary Warnock, editor, **John Stuart Mill, Utilitarianism, On Liberty, Essay on Bentham** (New York: Signet, 1974), p. 136.

[2] See Ronald Dworkin, **A Matter of Principle** (Cambridge: Harvard University Press, 1985), p. 350.

[3] **Ibid.**, p. 191.

[4] Dworkin, **Taking Rights Seriously** (Cambridge: Harvard University Press, 1977), p. 198.

[5] **Ibid.**, pp. 266-278.

[6] **Ibid.**, p. 91.

[7] **Ibid.**, p. 198.

[8] **Ibid.**, p. 269; and Dworkin, **Law's Empire** (Cambridge: Harvard University Press, 1986), p.221.

[9] **Law's Empire**, p. 311.

[10] **A Matter of Principle**, p. 11.

[11] **Ibid.**, p. 387.

[12] **Ibid.**, p. 11.

[13] **Taking Rights Seriously**, p. 191.

[14] See **ibid.**, pp. 169 and 364-365; **A Matter of Principle**, pp. 370-71; and Dworkin, "A Reply by Ronald Dworkin" in Marshall Cohen, editor, **Ronald Dworkin and Contemporary Jurisprudence** (Totawa: Rowman and Allanheld, 1983), p. 281.

[15] At one point Dworkin briefly considers, but then abruptly dismisses, a non-utilitarian conception along the lines of the one I defend *infra*. He labels this conception, which understands collective interests as including the creation and maintenance of "conditions... in which it is most likely that people will in fact choose and lead the lives that are the most valuable lives for them to lead," "Platonist." While he acknowledges that this conception "does not necessarily justify brainwashing or the other techniques of thought control that we have learned to fear," he excuses himself from further consideration of it on the ground that he "doubt[s] that it appeals to many people." **A Matter of Principle**, pp. 414-415.

[16] **Ibid.**, p. 370.

[17] **Ibid.**, p. 360.

[18] **Ronald Dworkin and Contemporary Jurisprudence**, p. 282 (emphasis supplied).

[19] For some examples, see J. M. Finnis, "A Bill of Rights for Britain? The Moral of Contemporary Jurisprudence," The Maccabaean Lecture in Jurisprudence, Proceedings of the British Academy, London, Volume LXXI (1985), p. 318; and Vinit Haksar, **Equality, Liberty, and Perfectionism** (Oxford: Clarendon Press, 1979), pp. 260-261.

[20] See especially Germain Grisez, "Against Consequentialism," 23 *American Journal of Jurisprudence* 21 (1978); John Finnis, **Fundamentals of Ethics** (Oxford: Oxford University Press, 1983) pp. 86-93; Finnis, Grisez, and Joseph M. Boyle, Jr., **Nuclear Deterrence, Morality and Realism** (Oxford: Clarendon Press, 1987), ch. IX; and Joseph Raz, "Value Incommensurability: Some Preliminaries," *Proceedings of the Aristotelian Society* 86 (1985-86), pp. 117-134. Also of interest: Anselm W. Muller, "Radical Subjectivity: Morality versus Utilitarianism," 19 *Ratio* 115-132 (1977); Philippa Foot, "Utilitarianism and the Virtues," *Mind*, Volume xciv (1985), pp. 196-209; and "Morality, Action and Outcome" in Ted Honderich, editor, **Morality and Objectivity** (London: Routledge and Kegan Paul, 1985), pp. 23-28.

[21] See Finnis, **Natural Law and Natural Rights** (Oxford: Clarendon Press, 1980), p. 168.

[22] **Taking Rights Seriously**, p. 90.

[23] See Finnis, **Natural Law and Natural Rights**, pp. 218-223.

[24] *Roe vs. Wade,* 410 U.S. 113 (1973).

25 *Griswold v. Connecticut*, 381 U.S. 479 (1965); and *Eisenstadt v. Baird*, 405 U.S. 348 (1972).

26 *Stanley v. Georgia*, 394 U.S. 557 (1969).

27 While the Supreme Court of the United States continues to permit the strict regulation of "obscenity," it has so defined that term as to render only the nastiest forms of pornography "obscene." The Court appears, however, to have drawn the line on "privacy" at homosexual sodomy, recently upholding a Georgia law making sodomy a crime constitutionally valid, at least insofar as applied to homosexual acts. *Bowers v. Hardwick*, 106 S. Ct. 2841 (1986).

28 **A Matter of Principle**, p. 353.

29 **Taking Rights Seriously**, p. 273.

30 Finnis, "Legal Enforcement of 'Duties to Oneself': Kant v. Neo-Kantians," 87 *Columbia Law Review* 433 at p. 437.

31 See, e.g., David A. J. Richards, **Sex, Drugs, Death and the Law** (Totawa: Rowman and Littlefield, 1982), pp. 96-116.

32 Richards understands moral principles as "constraints. . . that free, rational, and equal persons could offer and accept as universally applicable constraints on their *interpersonal* conduct." "Kantian Ethics and the Harm Principle: A Reply to John Finnis," 87 *Columbia Law Review* 457, at 461 (emphasis supplied).

33 See, in addition to the passage quoted *supra* at note 30, **Natural Law and Natural Rights**, pp. 222-223.

34 **A Matter of Principle**, pp. 205-206.

35 "Do We Have a Right to Pornography?", 1 *Oxford Journal of Legal Studies* 177-212 (1981); reprinted in **A Matter of Principle**, pp. 335-372.

36 **A Matter of Principle**, p. 349.

PART TWO:
The Church and United States Politics

The Church's Message To Government and Institutional Leaders
by
William Bentley Ball

If in 1973 the Supreme Court had held that ownership of slaves was a constitutional right, and if the Bureau of the Census were to report that, in this year 1987, 1,847,000 human beings were now in slave status, each subject to the absolute will of someone else in the nation, I wonder whether we would now be celebrating the 200th birthday of the American Constitution.

I did not write that sentence as a mere attention-getter. Quite obviously it is meant to cause one to react: "How then dare we think of constitutional birthdays in a year of death days for 1,847,000 human beings aborted just this year?" But that is only part of my purpose, the rest being to call attention to other illnesses of our Constitution which, added to Roe and Wade's Disease, may mean that there will be no 300th birthday.

The Supreme Court of the United States, to which Article III of the Constitution awards jurisdiction in cases involving the Constitution, is today an institution at once vastly powerful and incredibly weak. Within the space of two terms of the Court we can see dramatic examples of its power for evil or good — for evil in 1973, in its abortion decision; for good, in 1972 in its decision upholding the religious and parental liberties of the Amish. But we see its weakness in every recent term of Court, because its decisions follow few channels of fixed principle. The Court, is, frankly, all over the lot in its opinions.

Up to the middle of the 19th Century, the Court could be said to have a philosophy which reflected the Protestant Christian ethos. Even as late as 1892, the Court, in a unanimous opinion, felt comfortable in stating that "this is a Christian nation."[1] Today the justices are not only without a Christian philosophy, but appear (except probably for Justice Scalia) to lack even a theistic philosophy. It is for this reason that I am little excited by commentary on the Court typically given in the media today — that is, that the Court is split between "liberals" and "conservatives," that the justices are divided as between Justice Brennan's view espousing a "living Constitution" and Attorney General Meese's view espousing adherence to the "original intent" of the Founding Fathers.

Has the Church a message with respect to American constitutional jurisprudence? *It* has; but the message has not been delivered. I do not suggest that the National Conference of Catholic Bishops has the message typed up and ready to go. At least I have not heard that this is so. But the nomination of Judge Robert H. Bork to the Supreme Court makes us wish, not only that the message had been prepared but that the message had been delivered at the Senate hearings and everywhere else that it might be heard. The message would not be a statement for or against Bork, but a statement of Christian fundamentals of jurisprudence. I find it difficult to understand the silence. The Bork situation is at any rate well worth our attention at this important conference, for the ideas being debated concerning Bork are ideas unhappily *not* being discussed at the hearings and are yet pregnant with fate. Turning to the hearings, let me isolate ideas on the following three topics which should be part of the Church's message to government and public leaders: (1) Judicial Review; (2) Subsidiarity; (3) The Bearing of Public Witness.

1. JUDICIAL REVIEW

A. The Pointless "Liberal" - "Conservative" Debate. Nothing but confusion is added to the constitutional scene by insisting that at stake in the Bork matter is the choice between judicial "liberalism" and judicial "conservatism." If the former means so-called "abortion rights" (now being masked under the Aesopian word "privacy") or a regime of secularism in education, I cannot call that "liberal"; it is instead oppressive. If the latter means that the courts are powerless to enjoin enforcement of a state law requiring Amishmen to violate their religious conscience by enrolling their children in public high schools, I cannot call that "conservative"; it is instead extremist.[2] Let me turn to more graphic examples of each.

B. Liberal Oppressivism. I turn to the opinion of Justice Brennan (joined in by seven justices) in *Edwards v. Aguilard*[3], the so-called "Creationism Case." Our national media have reacted to that decision with the same bias they accorded the lower federal court decisions in the Tennessee and Alabama cases challenging the promotion of "Secular Humanism" in the public schools. In the *Edwards* case, we see a Louisiana statute, enacted in 1982, which forbade the teaching of the theory of evolution in public elementary and secondary schools unless accompanied by instruction in what the Act called "creation science," or scientific evidence that man and the universe were in fact created. Media comment have called this the "Second Scopes Trial," albeit there was no trial. The federal district court refused to let the case come to trial, instead holding that the Act, on its face, violated the Establishment Clause. The Fifth Circuit agreed. On appeal, the Supreme Court affirmed, with Chief Justice Rehnquist and Justice Scalia dissenting. Justice Brennan wrote the opinion of the Court.

The Brennan opinion rests chiefly upon the holding of the 1971 decision in *Lemon v Kurzman,* viz., to avoid violation of the Establishment

Clause, a statute must have a secular purpose and not a religious purpose. The purpose of the Louisiana act, Brennan said, "was to restructure the science curriculum to conform with a particular religious viewpoint." He based this conclusion upon his belief that the proponents of the legislation were motivated by a religious belief in creation, and that "[t]he preeminent purpose of the Louisiana legislature was clearly to advance the religious viewpoint that a supernatural being created humankind." This would sponsor in the public school curriculum "...the giving of persuasive advantage to a religious doctrine that rejects the factual basis of evolution..." (Justice Brennan seems not to have read Michael Denton's brilliant **Evolution: A Theory in Crisis**.)

Brennan based his decision, even more fundamentally, on the old myth first stated in the 1948 *McCollum* opinion of Justice Frankfurter:

> [t]he public school is at once the symbol of our democracy and the most pervasive means for promoting our common destiny. In no activity of the State is it more vital to keep out divisive [by which he meant "religious"] forces than in its schools.[4]

Justice Scalia, castigating the majority opinion in the *Edwards* case, said that no statute could be struck down merely because of the religious motivation of its sponsors. "[P]olitical activism by the religiously motivated is part of our heritage ... Today's religious activism may give us the [Creationism] Act, but yesterday resulted in the abolition of slavery, and tomorrow may bring relief for famine victims." Nor, he said, is a law invalid merely because it happens to coincide with the tenets of some religions. Scalia decried the majority's ignoring of the chief justification which the legislature had made for its enactment: (1) that there are two and only two scientific explanations for the beginning of life — evolution and creation, (2) that scientific evidence of creation is educationally valuable but is being censored in the public schools. "The legislature," he said, "wanted to ensure that students would be free to decide for themselves how life began, based on a fair and balanced presentation of the scientific evidence ... free of any coercive pressures from the State." Scalia concluded that the Act had a secular purpose within the meaning of the *Lemon* test. However, he believed that *Lemon* was wrongly decided, at least as to the idea that the Establishment Clause requires that legislation have a secular legislative purpose.

The Creationism decision of the Court is a lamentably anti-intellectual, repressive, reactionary piece of unalloyed secularist fundamentalism. It perpetuates the gross errors of the *McCollum* and *Lemon* cases.

C. Conservative Extremism. I turn to the recently famous 1971 article of the then Professor Robert H. Bork in *Indiana Law Journal*.[5] Bork here made two statements which are taken as unexceptionable by the judicial conservatives who have supported Bork's candidacy but which (in the calm eye of that real conservatism which sees tradition as the matrix out of which good change is generated) is extreme. The first is his apparent denial of natural, or higher, or God-given rights. Here is how he put it:

> The judge can have nothing to do with any absolute set of truths existing independently and depending upon God or the nature of the universe.

> If a judge should claim to have access to such a body of truths, to possess
> a volume of the annotated natural law, we would, quite justifiably, suspect
> that the source of the revelation was really no more exalted than the
> judge's viscera. In a system there is no absolute set of truths, to which the
> term 'political truth' can refer.

In the name of good sense and the common weal, do we want even one justice on the Supreme Court who will tell us that his vote in a particular case was based on what God told him in the back yard? Similarly, do we want even one justice on the Supreme Court who will say that there is *no* such thing as a God-given, or natural, right if not spelled out in the constitutional text? Bork in 1971, would probably have replied that, to the judge sworn to uphold the Constitution, it is the *Constitution's* words about life, liberty, property and due process of law, and not any statement of God, whereby the judge is commanded to protect what some choose to call their "God-given" rights. Tested, however, that answer does not satify. Bork, in the same *Indiana Law Journal* article, said that he would have voted against the majority in the landmark case of *Pierce v. Society of Sisters* which held unconstitutional an Oregon law requiring all children to attend public schools. He based this upon his conviction (shared by Chief Justice Rehnquist) that (a) the legislature is the most democratic branch of government because it is closest to the people, (b) enactments of legislatures are not to be overridden unless such enactments conflict with *express* constitutional prohibition. Finding no black-letter print in the Constitution that prohibited states from monopolizing education, and refusing to invoke any unprinted "natural," or "God-given," or "higher" law, of parental rights in determining the education of their children, or of churches' rights to conduct educational ministries, he said he would uphold governmental monopoly of the education of the young.[6]

Bork's 1971 view denying natural rights and pledging so great a deference to legislatures is particularly extreme when we consider what was really involved in the Oregon statute considered in *Pierce.* It was the product, not even of normal legislative procedures, but of a popular referendum carried through on a wave of xenophobic hysteria at the close of World War I. The hysteria was promoted by a Masonic Order called the Imperial Council, A.A.O. Nobles Mystic Shrine, which professed shocked alarm over (as they put it) "people forming groups," Popery, and the having of private schools. The Nobles Mystic wanted every child molded into being a "true American" in a single public school system. These noble and mystical characters, befezzed, armed with scimitars, and bright with bigotry, propagandized and paraded in the towns of Oregon — jackasses riding on camels — and inflamed Oregonians to vote for a referendum requiring every child to be enrolled in an institution of the state.

It is painful to think that, especially in the extreme situation where not even normal legislative processes had yielded up a statute, and where all religious schools would be shut down, and where, against the conscientious convictions of their parents, the children would be shunted into government institutions, Judge Bork would feel obligated to vote on behalf of the enforcement of that statute. It was to be hoped that, at the Senate hearings, Judge Bork would have been asked if he still holds that view, but a remarkable feature of the Senate hearings was that religious liberty got almost zero focus and parental rights none.

D. The Church's Message. The essential Church, that is, the Church in its tradition, must regard the American Constitution as providing a singularly beneficent ordering of government. But the Constitution, like the Supreme Court itself, is still but an instrument, and, unless informed by Scriptural principles, it can become an instrument of oppression. That is the ever present danger when the courts forsake the view of a higher law while yet pursuing the alternative of a barren secularism. The Benthamite view that legislative acts are binding in the absence of direct conflicts with *express* prohibitory language in the Constitution is deadly in terms of human liberty.

In this hour of total national attention both to the Supreme Court and the Constitution, we seem to have forgotten even the higher law teaching in which the Supreme Court itself has indulged in past years. The Court, in 1898, in *Holden v. Hardy*[7], spoke of "certain immutable principles of justice which inhere in the very nature of free government." In *Twining v. New Jersey*[8] the Court referred to "fundamental and inalienable rights of mankind" some of which might or might not be listed or defined in the text of the Constitution. Justice Cardozo, in *Palko v. Connecticut*[9], in 1937, said there are immunities not spelled out in the Constitution which are "implicit in the concept of ordered liberty." In *Rochin v. California*[10], the Court, holding that due process of law was violated by a conviction based on evidence obtained by stomach-pumping, based its holding on its belief that such a conviction violated rights which exist simply because "so rooted in the traditions and conscience of our people as to be ranked as fundamental."

These, and cases before and after these, are familiar enough law and stand central in our constitutional tradition born in the "unalienable rights" language of the Declaration of Independence. It is against this background that I find the Bork-Berns-Will view of constitutional liberty to be stultifying, and the Church's silence mystifying.

2. SUBSIDIARITY

There can be no doubt of the need in America today for the involvement of government in areas of societal life where, in earlier days, it had not been seen. Catholics, in principle, do not regard "government" as an alien thing. Ideally, it is nothing other than "we, the people" engaged in helping the human community. It is also true that governmental agencies sometimes fail to serve the common good and develop attitudes — indeed policies — which render them truly alien, self-aggrandizing and financially burdensome.

Unhappily, in the last decade in the United States there have appeared at some levels of Church endeavor a false conception of "common good" which in fact militates against the common good. That consists of the denial of the principle of subsidiarity in favor of an unthinking statism. This has been manifest in two ways: (a) the embracing of government aid in *substitution* for Christian charitable sacrifice in welfare and educational work, and (b) increasing acceptance of governmental controls which impede the carrying forward of religious ministry.

A message by the Church respecting the first cannot be sent at present, because, first of all, *within* the Church, there needs to be a realization of *why* it is that we no longer have the flow of religious vocations and the intensity of sacrificial spirit to maintain Catholic ministries to children, the poor, the sick, here and in missions abroad as they flourished in the past. It is simply foolish to imagine that substituting governmental funding for the sacrificial services of Christ-dedicated men and women is desirable. Surely the immediate result of such dependency is the pull toward the secularization of ministries; and the end result will be the end of the ministries. The once-Catholic colleges, of course, have no trouble with secularization.[11] But I would hope that our other institutions do. So, then they (and all the Church) must ask *why* it is that Catholic institutions were flourishing twenty years ago and are declining today.

This situation brings to mind the old German fable about the emperor's new clothes. Do not our Church's leaders *know* that the disarray and decline taking place are due to but two things: (1) loss of belief that the Catholic Church is the one true Church, (2) loss of belief that the Catholic faith is the most important thing in a Catholic's life? Today the orthodox Catholic is disgraced by the polls which show the "80% Catholics," the "60% Catholics," the "cafeteria Catholics," and the timorous or genial official toleration of dissidence.

Until there is a candid reckoning with the causes of decline, there can be readied no message by the Church with respect to how far Church dependency upon government shall proceed or the future of the Church's ministries.

As to the second aspect of the denial of the principle of subsidiarity — namely, increasing acceptance of governmental controls which impede carrying forward the religious ministry, I have noted in many situations which arise in dioceses an unfortunate proneness to accept regulatory measures. This proneness is caused in part from a lack of simple American self-respect — a legitimate love of independence and a proper pride. It contrasts with habits borrowed from some foreign countries in which servility to "the authorities" is bred, and the making of corrupt bargains a way of life. Another way to put it is a lack of the spirit of constitutionalism. This attitude one sees, for example, in unthinking or abject acceptance of arbitrary governmental regulation of education. In the 1970's, when the National Labor Relations Board began attempting to exercise jurisdiction over Catholic schools, there were dioceses which accepted this unquestioningly (to their great credit the Archdiocese of Philadelphia and the Dioceses of Scranton and Gary sponsored injunction actions against NLRB to block its jurisdiction at the outset). Dioceses refusing to fight jurisdiction seemed not to care that NLRB's jurisdiction would make government agents the judges of anything within the schools that pertained to "terms and conditions of employment" — a term which, when thought through, will be seen to cover virtually everything in the school. In the early '80's I observed with horror the director of a state Catholic Conference returning from a government-conducted Title IX (sex discrimination) briefing session in Washington proclaiming that the dioceses of his state must not only comply with the mass of extravagant and unconstitutional new regulations but, by golly, must "show good faith" by going beyond them!

Or take the situation where the state educational bureaucracy has, by statute or otherwise, imposed upon private schools state prescriptions of curriculum, or state teacher certification, or even the licensing of schools. In one state, in the 1980's, Catholic school superintendents refused to challenge a state law which required *all* private schools to conform themselves to any and all programs or activities prescribed by the State Board of Education — a blank check to government giving it total power over Catholic schools — schools which the state did not found and does not fund. The superintendents initially *supported* the statute, saying (a) that to oppose it might jeopardize the nonpublic school aid programs (though that was not so), (b) that Catholic schools must not appear to be out of the "mainstream" (should they not be proud to *not* be?), (c) that the state hadn't yet threatened specific trouble under the statute (but the blank check *power* was the danger), (d) that obedience to the statute would help Catholic schools to be (as they put it) "up to standard" (in heaven's name: the *public* school standard?).

The Church's message on subsidiarity, when given, should be as follows:

1. The ministries constitute a religious exercise and thus come within the purview of the Free Exercise Clause of the First Amendment. (But if not deemed a religious exercise, why should the Church be involved?) That being so, government may not impede or suppress the life or activity of the ministry in the absence of, not a mere "public interest," but a *supreme* societal interest, or what the courts have called a "compelling state interest," an interest absolutely essential to the common good. Further, it is government, not the ministry, which must bear the burden of proof that such an interest justifies its action.

2. The ministries are protected by the doctrine of "Unconstitutional Conditions" — *i.e.,* government may not condition receipt of a public benefit upon the giving up of a First Amendment right. Most existing government programs by which aid directly or indirectly flows to religious institutions involve no such conditions. Those Catholic college presidents who say that their choice is to die (for want of government aid) or to secularize are dead wrong and should be called dead wrong.

I see church leaders too often failing to deliver this message. They either seem to fear the tax-paid public bureaucracy or else appear to say that their ministries are really not all that religious. Just read the muted, equivocal statements on religion in some of the "Catholic" college catalogs!

3. THE BEARING OF PUBLIC WITNESS

What I have said in connection with subsidiarity has an obvious relationship to the bearing of public witness — or Christ-bearing before the world, in spite of the world, or even against the world. Christ-bearing under the steeple, or within the sacristy, is still generally considered acceptable conduct. Christ-bearing out of doors, so to speak, is too often considered suspect conduct and is sometimes considered illegal conduct.

James Madison — who was no atheist — believed in religious pluralism as a deterrent: a multiplicity of sects would prevent a religious establishment or religious monopoly. Professor Paul Freund, of Harvard Law School, persuaded the Supreme Court, in the 1970's, to make this a constitutional principle. The Court, in *Lemon v. Kurtzman,* to which I have referred, invented out of whole cloth (or Freund's cloth) a remarkable variant of the Establishment Clause: parochial schools must be denied aid because lobbying by Catholics for such legislation would cause, as the Court said, "religious division along political lines." This new doctrine of the Supreme Court was a hard slap to the face of the Catholic public, but while Church leaders grumbled about the denial of the public aid, they made no strong unified outcry denouncing the insulting "divisiveness" statement made by the Court.

It is little wonder, then, that the Church has made no significant statement attacking Section 501(c)(3) of the Internal Revenue Code. That all-important section of the Internal Revenue Code defines tax exempt status of charitable organizations (including religious organizations) and makes their exemption depend upon restriction of their free speech, free exercise and free press rights as given in the First Amendment.

Section 501(c)(3) of the Internal Revenue Code says, in effect, that an organization operated exclusively for religious, charitable or educational purposes will be exempt from income taxes if (among other things) it "does not participate in, or intervene in (including the publishing or distribution of statements), any political campaign on behalf of any candidate for public office." This same section also contains a restriction against "substantial" lobbying activities.

This section of the Internal Revenue Code is, on its face, extremely stultifying, but has been expanded administratively by the IRS to include the following:

1. The providing of advertising space, or the provision of free advertising space, in Church publications only to those candidates whose views the Church endorses.
2. Posing for photographs with only those candidates whose views are endorsed by the Church.
3. Publication or distribution of statements which characterize a particular candidate's views in a favorable or unfavorable manner, *e.g.,* "pro-abortion."

And so the IRS goes on for 13 such paragraphs all of which are restrictive of liberty of speech, and press, and basic political liberties. As to all 13 of those activities, it is my firm opinion that if the activity is a necessary expression of the moral teaching of the Church, it is constitutionally protectible, though barred by the IRS and even if barred by Section 501(c)(3). I well recognize the dangers of the loss of the material advantage of tax exempt status. But before she would suffer the tongue of Christian witness to be silenced, the Church should be willing, if failing to protect her liberties in the courts, to engage in massive, universal, passive resistance to tax enforcement.

There are three perspectives which the question of Church involvement in political processes must be examined: (1) the moral imperative, (2) the constitutional right, and (3) the preservation of material advantages — *e.g.,* tax exempt status.

The constitutional right was well summoned up by the Supreme Court, in *Thornhill v. Alabama,* in 1940:

> Freedom of discussion, if it would fulfill its historic function in this nation, must embrace all issues about which information is needed or appropriate to enable the members of society to cope with the exigencies of their period.[12]

This message of this report in summation is as follows: first, the need to declare against legal positivism and in favor of judicial review rooted in the natural law; second, the need to state the constitutional principles which must be followed for the protection of religious ministry; third, the need to insist that the taxing power shall not be used to inhibit the free exercise of religion.

Dear friends in this Fellowship: I think that the twin problem of being an orthodox Catholic today is that first, of necessity, we must on occasion question our leaders over the dissidence on the part of some, and the timorousness of others in the face of evil. Secondly, that out of love and fidelity we honor and revere their office, and we respect and love them, if not in all cases as shepherds, certainly always as brothers. We therefore, in our present crisis, experience pain — the pain not of anger, not of vanity, not of irritation or vexation — but *the pain of caring*. That is one of the burdens which love and fidelity impose.

FOOTNOTES

1 *Church of the Holy Trinity v. United States,* 143 U.S. 457, 471 (1892).

2 Such a case was *Wisconsin v. Yoder,* 406 U.S. 205 (1972). This decision in favor of the Amish has been vehemently criticized by "conservatives" Walter Berns, of American Enterprise Institute, the journalist George Will and twice recently by Judge Robert H. Bork.

3 __U.S.__, 55 U.S.L.W. 4860 (U.S. June 19, 1987).

4 *McCollum v. Board of Education,* 333 U.S. 203, 231 (1948).

5 47 Indiana L.J. 1 (1971).

6 On the exact same basis, Bork later states that he would have dissented in *Roe v. Wade.* He would have dissented, that is, not because he is "pro-life." Nothing in his record to date shows that. His dissent would have been based upon his unwillingness to disturb state legislation absent contradicting black-letter constitutional provisions.

7 169 U.S. 366, 387 (1898).

8 211 U.S. 78, 110 (1908).

9 302 U.S. 319, 325 (1937).

10 342 U.S. 165, 169 (1952).

11 See my article in *Crisis,* "Faith and Freedom", March, 1987, p. 8.

12 *Thornhill v. Alabama,* 310 U.S. 88, 101-102 (1940).

Tensions Between the Social Teaching of the Church and the Constitutional Framework of the American Regime

by

Thomas A. Droleskey

Can the Church, founded upon the Rock of Peter and charged by Jesus Christ with the responsibility of guiding all souls to the glory of the Beatific Vision, maintain the allegiance of the members of Christ's Mystical Body in the framework of a democratic government? Is it possible for the Church to authentically communicate the transcendent truths of Truth Himself, Jesus Christ, in an atmosphere where a premium is placed upon the values of pluralism, dialogic discovery of truth, indifferentism, and egalitarian majoritarianism as the bases of legitimate public policy?

Compunding these questions are rampant misconceptions — most of which are popularly accepted as beyond question — concerning the nature of politics, government, democracy, law, majority rule, equality, and the whole purpose of the Church of Christ. We have reached a situation — largely as a result of the progression of events since the Reformation and the Age of the Enlightenment — where the Magisterium of the Church has been replaced by the Magisterium of a Supreme Court (constituted, of course, by Justices "enlightened" with the ethos of the Twentieth Century).

The question for our consideration here, however, concerns the framework of the American regime as it relates to the social teaching of the Church. It is clear to see that part of the tensions currently extant have their origin in the fact that there is no source of moral authority within the United States. The Constitution has become, for some, the *source* of human rights rather than the *guarantor* of God-given rights. The Church is therefore seen as an illegitimate actor when her members attempt to call society to a moral order which is at the basis of authentic social justice and an enduring sense of order in society. However, the obvious fact of a lack of a moral authority accounts for only part of the tensions between the social teaching of the Church and the framework of the American regime.

As Aleksandr Solzhenitsyn pointed out at Harvard University in 1978, the modern Western states advanced the notion of liberty. There were those suspicious of freedom — particularly in light of the forces unleashed by the French Revolution in the name of "liberty, fraternity, and equality." Freedom and democracy were subsequently viewed, as noted in the writings of Joseph deMaestri, as being almost antithetical to the faith of Christ.

The major questions for our consideration here are two fold:

First, does the absence of a moral authority figure in the United States produce tensions between the Church and State?

Second, does the social teaching of the Church conflict with the framework of the American regime?

The Problem Is One of Understanding Original Intent, Human Nature, and the Natural Law

The first question must be answered in the affirmative. Consult, for example, Belloc:

> Up to the present day the position of the Catholic in the United States has insecurely fitted in with this modern conception of tolerance, through the fact that the dogmas taken for granted by the State, and enforced in practice, were mainly Catholic dogmas; and that the action of the State, where its dogmas differed from Catholic dogma, was mainly negative and permissive.
>
> *But such a state of affairs cannot be permanent;* and to prove that it cannot be permanent I will give two examples.
>
> It may well come about, at any moment, that the State shall pass a law compelling those who have the guardianship of human beings incapable beyond a certain degree, to see to the removal of those human beings. The State may take it for granted as a universal doctrine to be held and enforced upon all citizens, that the preservation of imbecile or imperfect life, much more its continuance from one generation to another by the propagation of children, is destructive of society; and it may order that these unfortunate beings be placed in what is called, in our modern scientific jargon, the legal chamber.
>
> Now for a Catholic to act in this fashion is, by Catholic definition, *murder;* and what is more, any action supporting, or even permitting this thing, is also from the Catholic point of view, murder. If A. is a Catholic receiving an order to put out of life the imbecile B., he not only commits murder if he obeys, but he commits murder if he hands over the imbecile B. to the State official C., whom he knows will so act. More, he will be committing murder if he does not do everything in his power to *prevent* the official C. from carrying out the law.

Obviously, Belloc's prescient prophecy is most apropos of our present situation (as it relates to both abortion *and* euthanasia). The absence of a moral authority source does lead to tensions between Church and State.

As it is the role of the Church to lead all men to Salvation, to refute falsehood, and to channel Christ's grace into the souls of every human being, the Church will be seen as illegitimately filling a void that the Founding Fathers supposedly meant for secular institutions (the three branches of government) and/or popular will to fill. To view the Church as an illegitimate actor in *any* society — but particularly in a pluralistic state — is the logical consequence of the modernist acceptance of egalitarianism as the basis of civil government.

There is the popularly-held belief that egalitarianism extends to the realm of ideas. To assert that one set of ideas contains absolute truth is, according to this mindset, to "impose" upon society concepts not accepted by the majority. Concepts not sanctioned by the majority are unjust and unfair. Individuals will be permitted to *hold* certain ideas — but even the merest promotion of those ideas in public is said to be a violation of the separation of Church and State!

Such beliefs fly in the face of the history of Western civilization. Such beliefs demonstrate an ignorance for the fact that the teaching of the Decalogue — those laws enscribed on the hearts of all men — has been the basis of Western culture for the past five thousand years. While it is true that the Decalogue has been eroded in the West and superceded in the East, no one can in good conscience assert that the American Republic was based on a *denial* of objective truths as the basis of just public policy. Yet, the absence of a moral authority figure leads to such ignorant and dangerously irresponsible conclusions as the ones listed above.

Civic virtue — the cornerstone of the Republic — is too slender a thread upon which to sew together the fabric of society. Its threads were quickly disintegrating in the face of material and geographic expansion shortly after the formation of the new federal Republic. De Tocqueville predicted grave consequences for the nation as a result of greed and selfism. The influence of the French Revolution, the spread of Jacksonian democracy, and the eventual victory of social science would all conspire to make self-denial, selflessness, and civic virtue seem antiquated values of another era. Statesmanship was viewed with scorn by politicians who understood all too well that careerism — the offshoot of Puritan beliefs in divine favor bestowed upon successful individuals — was the new beat of the New World.

The absence of a source of moral authority within the United States leads many well-intentioned individuals to look for a substitute. Individuals want to be told what is right and wrong, permissable and impermissable. Thus, the Supreme Court of the United States became — particularly after Earl Warren and his merry band of judicial barbarians began to plunder any real meaning out of the Constitution — the arbiter of right and wrong. It is, of course, true that the Founding Fathers did not intend such terrible abuses of their institutions. But it is also true that there are, given the framework of the regime, no guarantees against such abuses save for a civicly militant citizenry who understood the purposes of life and the limitations of social structures.

The second question — does the Church's social teaching conflict with the framework of the American regime? — must be answered in the negative. Well, a negative with a qualification: the social teaching of the Church does not conflict with the framework of the American regime as that framework was intended by the Founding Fathers.

The goal of the Constitution — to pursue the new republicanism and balance the tension between liberty and order — is a noble one. Moreover, there is not one goal of the United States Constitution as it was written which is in conflict with Catholic doctrine. Examine the Preamble to the American Constitution:

> We, the People of the United States, in order to form a more perfect union, establish justice, insure domestic tranquility, provide for the common defense, promote the general welfare, and secure the blessings

of liberty for ourselves and our posterity do ordain and establish this Constitution for the United States of America.

The conflicts which have arisen between the social teaching of the Church and the laws of the State are the result of the negligence of Catholics to take seriously the principle tenets of their faith. In fact, Catholics in the United States have generally taken great pride in gaining acceptance to prestigious schools, "fitting in" with others, and accepting the American goal of material success as the epitome of human existence. There was no need for Catholics to consider the possibility of a conflict between their Church's social teachings and the State because, for the better part of two centuries, State laws reflected — more or less — those teachings to a fault.

Human respect, however, has its price. When human respect — the desire to be respected, approved, and accepted by others — becomes the guiding principle of life, deference will be given to that which makes life more expedient. The "law" is the law and it must be obeyed. Who are Catholics, of all people, to insist that the precepts of their religion be the basis of public policy? We must defer to the majority in the expectation that the majority has the best intentions of the country in mind.

And, too, the intellectual justification for Catholics failing to stand up in defense of the natural law and the just moral order was given impetus by John Kennedy. It was the then Senator Kennedy, appealing for votes at a convention of the Southern Baptists in Houston, Texas in 1960, who said that he would defer to the Constitution in the event of a conflict with his faith. It was John Kennedy — backed, we must note, by the late Richard Cardinal Cushing of Boston — who posited an *artificial* conflict between the Constitution and Roman Catholicism. For, properly interpreted (and we may yet get that proper interpretation as a result of personnel changes on the Supreme Court), there can be no conflict between a Constitution based in the natural law and a Church which stands as the guardian of the natural law.

Kennedy, though, made the statement almost in passing — as though it were already an accepted part of Catholic thought in the United States. Many Catholics, eager to have one of their "own" in the White House, readily agreed. But Kennedy was to be outdone by other Catholics — not excluding one who sits at present on the United States Supreme Court and has done everything in his power to undermine the just moral order.

The ranks of our United States Congress, Federal Court system, Executive Mansions in the Fifty States, State Legislatures, City Halls, City Councils, Boards of Aldermen, County Executives, County Legislatures, Town Supervisors and endless numbers of civil servants are replete with Roman Catholics who wax eloquently about their need to uphold the law or popular will or both. The murder of innocent human beings must be tolerated as the respect we have for divergent viewpoints. Perhaps it is closer to the truth to state that the toleration of murder, sodomy, immorality, greed, materialism, and the like makes possible career advancement, respect, and success.

One who has crystallized all of these arguments in recent years is the Governor of New York, Mario Matthew Cuomo. It is Mario Cuomo who has given what he, at least, believes to be well thought-out arguments about how, in effect, Catholics must privatize their beliefs from public policy. A man blessed with eloquence — the type of eloquence that could *change* hearts and minds to an acceptance of the natural law — uses his eloquence in the service of the destruction of the just moral order. How many women — how many women — have had an abortion because Mario Cuomo has said it is their right?

In the end, you see, we are to blame. And we have been to blame from the very beginning. We preach a gospel of suffering and the Cross. We profess to understand what Simeon foretold of the infant Jesus when proclaiming Him to be the Sign of Contradiction at the Presentation in the Temple. Yet, in this country, we have historically — with some exceptions — sought accomodation and acceptance from the majority. Catholics, though small in number, could have considered it their solemn obligation to participate in public life in defense of the just moral order at the dawn of the Republic *because* civic virtue was such a slender thread to rely upon. But, by and large, they shrunk from the responsibility out of difficulty, prejudice, or expediency. The immigrants from Ireland, Italy, and Southern Europe gradually came to learn that it was acceptable to worship at Mass on Sunday — but acceptance in society was equally as important. Thus, the swelling of the ranks of the big city political machines with immigrant Catholics had less to do with the political strength of Catholics than the desire of new immigrants to become an accepted part of the system. And now, of course, those individuals who insist upon standing up for the truth of Christ are considered authoritarian, narrow-minded, and ignorant bigots who are closed to pluralism, dialogue, and authentic democracy.

This perception of Catholics who take seriously their vows at Baptism and Confirmation is one that is fueled by those articulate public office-holders who themselves profess Roman Catholicism as their faith. It is they who posit an artificial tension between our faith and the framework of the American regime. It is they who wax eloquently about the need to serve the poor on religious principles, while claiming that abortion is solely a religious matter. It is they who seek to confuse the American public about the nature of their faith by privatizing Christianity. It is they who seek to sanitize education from all semblance of Judeo-Christian values in the name of the Family of Man. It is they who seek to promote themselves as the possessors of knowledge, wisdom, and sophistication as opposed to the ignorance of individuals tenaciously holding onto a vision inappropriate for man as he heads toward the Twenty-first Century.

We have no one else to blame but ourselves. We, members of the Catholic faith, have the opportunity in this society to insist upon the truth. We have the obligation to bring all people to partake of the Body and Blood, Soul and Divinity of Jesus Christ at the Unbloody Representation of Calvary in the Mass.

We have failed because we do not pray enough. Those of us assembled at this Convention — more accurately, most of *you* assembled at this Convention — are acknowledged as scholars. I am sure that many of you pray daily. But we must pray more. We must understand that all of our knowledge is meaningless unless we abandon ourselves in prayer. We must pray for our country, for ourselves, for our fellow Catholics, our separated brethren, unbelievers, and those who are outrightly hostile to the faith. It is only through holiness that we can break the tensions which now exist between Church and State. Twelve men changed the world by the grace of God. So can we.

And for those of you in the field where I have spent the past fourteen years of my life, college education, please — if you do not already do so — give your students to drink of the truth of Christ as your discipline and courses permit. It is relatively easy to incorporate the truth of Christ into political science courses as one cannot understand human behavior in society without understanding the mystery of sin and grace. I urge all of you who are doing so at present to continue to fight the good fight; the harvest is vast — and the students are willing and eager to respond. For their sakes, let us be shameless apostles and care not for the repercussions.

In this Year devoted to Mary — and with the visit of the Holy Father so recently concluded, let us mirror the Pope's tender devotion to the woman who made possible the Redemption of the human race by her fiat at the Annunciation. Let us be, with Her, humble cooperators of the will of God, enlivened by the Holy Spirit, in order to remake all things in Christ.

Let us reflect upon the words of the Holy Father from his Apostolic Exhortation of 1984:

> Whenever the Church speaks of *situations* of sin, or when she condemns as *social sins* certain situations or the collective behavior of certain social groups, big or small, or even of whole nations and blocs of nations, she knows and she proclaims that such cases of *social sin* are the result of the accumulation and concentration of many *personal sins.* It is a case of the very personal sins of those who cause or support evil or who exploit it; of those who are in a position to avoid, eliminate or at least limit certain social evils but who fail to do so out of laziness, fear or the conspiracy of silence, through secret complicity or indifference; of those who take refuge in the supposed impossibility of changing the world, and also of those who sidestep the effort and sacrifice required, producing specious reasons of a higher order. The real responsibility, then, lies with individuals.
>
> A situation — or likewise an institution, a structure, society itself — is not in itself the subject of moral acts. Hence a situation cannot in itself be good or bad.
>
> At the heart of every *situation of sin* are always to be found sinful people. So true is this that even when such a situation can be changed in its structural and institutional aspects by the force of law, or — as unfortunately more often happens — by the law of force, the change in fact proves to be incomplete of short duration, ultimately vain and ineffective — not to say counter productive — if the people directly or indirectly responsible for that situation are not converted.

The Constitution of American Public Discourse and the Privatization of Religion

by

Gerard V. Bradley

The title is my thesis: religion — especially religiously-grounded morality — is being evicted from public debate over how to order our common life. That is what I mean by "privatization." The intolerant land-lord is our two hundred year old Constitution, or at least judicial inter-pretation of it since 1947. I offer an illustration, one which came to my attention when drafting these remarks. On August 24, 1987 the *New York Times* ran an article headlined "Birth Control Ad: The Fight For TV Time."[1] The controversial advertisement says: "Four out of five young women who don't use birth control get pregnant before they want to. Birth control — from saying 'no' to taking the pill. You're too smart not to use it." All six commercial stations in New York City refused to broad-cast it. This represents a curiosity. The same networks which bombard us with fornication and adultery blanche when asked to run even an ecumenical reminder of the natural result of sexual adventurism, a caveat inviting chastity as well as artificial contraception. I suspect, though, that their demurrers make depressing sense. TV moguls are not schizo-phrenic Puritans, much as that might explain their waffling. They simply shrink from controversy. Adultery — or the public depiction of it at any rate — no longer rankles viewers while birth control evidently does. The *Times* reported that the stations' opposition "reinforced the battle lines in a persistent controversy: Is the use of television to promote birth control in the public interest, or does it intrude upon religious and moral values?" That passage is susceptible of varying interpretations, none of them heartening. The most obvious is the "strife-avoidance" one: "intruding upon religious and moral values" means people will write in to complain, even threaten to boycott advertisers. But that has to be fleshed out to reveal its deep "privatizing" tendencies, for there is more than mere cowardice at work here. Implicit in this "no offense" approach to civic debate — and I think it a very common way of thinking — is the notion that public discourse cleansed by irenic impulses of religious and moral values is somehow still meaningful, even good or correct.

A more intriguing related account begins with emphasis on the dichotomous formulation, the use of the disjunctive "or." *Either* the ads are in "the public interest" *or* they "intrude upon religious and moral values." But not both. The lurking normative principle is that matters of religious morality are not relevant to the "public interest." If birth control ads implicate religious and moral values they ought not be on the airwaves. Why? Because the public interest is ascertainable — both descriptively and prescriptively — without reference to the religious and moral values of the people. Birth control is a public health issue and public discussion of it is skewed when "personal moral values" intrude.

This also is a good elaboration of "privatization": religious morality is not publicly relevant, and can influence law only when disguised as something called secular morality. That's where our courts have taken constitutional law.[2] I say "something called secular morality" for a reason. The reason is that I want to prescind from debating whether such an animal exists, and if so, whether it is present in measurable amounts in our United States. I must interject though that the framers of our Constitution certainly would answer "No" to both queries. There is, in fact, no more commonplace principle of political economy among Americans up until the late nineteenth century than that morality is essential to social order and that religion is essential to morality. No wonder the universal expectation of the founders was that religion — usually rendered as "Christianity" and meaning Protestantism — would be fostered, encouraged and supported by government, and that religious morality be the substance of both public debate and policy.[3]

The American people have come a long way from this, and the Supreme Court would take them even farther, all the way to the total elimination of religious morality from public life and discourse. The *Times* article faithfully though perhaps unreflectively mirrors the law's guiding principles. The airwaves carrying TV signals are, in fact, public property. Television is the predominant source of information for modern Americans, and the medium through which candidates for political office sell themselves to voters. In sum, the airwaves are the modern counterpart of the New England town meeting: common property upon which the public debate about our common life is conducted.

My exploration of the privatization phenomenon is split in two. First, there is the evidence of privatization; later, the reasons for it. The most important item for scrutiny is the most basic: that there is a constitutional law of something commodiously denoted "church and state" at all. The Constitution nowhere refers to "church and state" or to the now legendary "wall of separation" between them. In fact, the ubiquitous wall metaphor stems from an 1802 Thomas Jefferson letter to a group of Connecticut Baptists.[4] Its life was for long a time thereafter uneventful. The Supreme Court made casual reference to a "wall of separation" in an 1876 polygamy case,[5] a decision rooted in anything but, for it really incorporated Christian morality into the Constitution. The 1947 *Everson*[6] case resuscitated the image, and it has been a mainstay of the law and commentary since. Both academic and popular observers gauge Supreme Court trends by the structural integrity of the "wall." We have articles on the "crumbling," "serpentine," "variable," or "impregnable" wall. These are presumably intended as serious communications of substance.

However, separation of church and state — walled, barricaded or otherwise — is not a solution to any problem. It verbalizes the dualism present wherever the monisms of theonomy and a "secular" totalitarian state are rejected. It symbolizes the permanent tension in Western civilization between the demands of successful pragmatic existence and the consciousness of divine reality arising in men's souls. "State" and "church" are the polar pulls in the field of tension. The Christian tradition provides many cognate symbolizations: the "sacred" and "profane," Augustine's two cities and the medieval two "sword" imagery, connoting the spiritual and temporal powers. The Gospel, I submit, concentrates the tension in an unsurpassable way. Jesus' Sermon on the Mount is as uncompromising as it is unsuited to successful mundane existence. The whole New Testament says little more about Christian political praxis as the tautological Caesar's coin discourse attests. We know now that part of the lacuna owes to the first Christians' expectation of an imminent parousia. Hence, for this and because Jesus' kingdom was not of this world, there is perhaps no greater challenge for believers than to fill out the Christian prescription(s) for societies organized for action in history.

The Middle Ages wrestled with the problem of two orders — priestly and princely — and wondered which was "superior." Eventually, they decided that each is superior: the priest in spiritual affairs, the prince in temporal matters. This recognition is hailed as the "separation" of "church and state." And it is, of a sort. Yet the historical problem was hardly solved. There may be two orders, but they are not separate because they are two aspects of one and the same thing or occurrence. Mircia Eliade wrote that *every* human experience is capable of being lived on a different, transmundane level. So one outgrowth of the medieval settlement was agreement that popes could not literally depose kings. But, by excommunicating a king, the pope effectively deposed him just the same. My favorite contemporary illustration of Eliade's point is the Supreme Court decision two years ago in a church-state case involving Social Security numbers.[7] The state might think itself securely ensconced in its own temporal sphere when writing out survivors' or old age checks. But the plaintiff said her spirit was diminished by having a number assigned to her. The moral is that any governmental action is liable to cross the imaginary wall between church and state. The "wall of separation" is thus hopelessly indeterminate. Judges, who venture into the field of tension, do so without compass or map. But it still provides a valuable service to the privatizing project. It grants judges access to the entire field of tension, of expansively defining the Constitution's ken. Almost every irruption of public religiosity engenders a lawsuit, and almost always the Constitution is implicated. Catholic outbreaks are peculiarly liable to result in litigation. President Reagan's decision to send an ambassador to the Vatican spurred a challenge by a diverse array of clergyman.[8] The Pope's recent visit led to litigation too. Specifics included a suit against the City of Miami for spending public dollars on the papal visit, and one against the Postal Service for issuing a commemorative stamp for the occasion.[9] The Church's visible opposition to abortion stirred up a still unresolved attack upon its tax-exempt status.[10] The Hyde Amendment, which cut off federal funds for abortion, was challenged as an Establishment of Roman Catholicism.[11]

Then there was Marjorie Maguire's suit against Marquette,[12] and the one promised by Charles Curran against Catholic University. The practical result of all this lawyering is that constitutional law is coextensive with the church-state problematic. This means that judges are our ministers' plenipotentiary for "church-state", defined by the choice of that phrase for the entire front between religion and law.

What of the Constitution itself? Well, there are only three relevant passages. One bans religious tests for federal office. You have probably never heard of it because there has never been a judicial opinion authoritatively construing it. It's no help. That leaves the First Amendment: "Congress shall make no laws respecting an establishment of religion or prohibiting the free exercise thereof." By judicial elaboration, this amendment binds the states as well. I grant that the untutored eye might read free exercise expansively, but the necessary acquaintance with historical context shows it to be a more limited creature. In any case, there is no legitimate reading of the "free exercise" clause which renders it a cap on public religiousity. Free exercise provides centrifugal force and is suggestive of visible faith exciting the public square. The courts know this, which is why *it* has been eclipsed by the Establishment Clause.

One might think it too would be little help. For instance, recently retired Justice Powell remarked a few years back that "at this point in the 20th century we are quite far removed from the dangers that prompted the framers to include the Establishment Clause in the Bill of Rights."[13] So we are. And an informed translation of the term "nonestablishment" is "no partiality or discrimination among sects or beliefs." Put affirmatively, the Clause should be read to condemn only government favoritism or preferences towards a particular religious group or belief. At this point in our pluralistic experience, such a concern is among the least of our problems. The Supreme Court has invalidated many establishment government practices, but rarely because of sect discrimination. This anachronistic quality did not escape Justice Byron White. He candidly admitted that historical recovery revealed the Clause irrelevant to modern problems. But when White dropped the other shoe it made an unexpected noise. One would expect White to consign the Establishment Clause — along with the test ban — to a constitutional museum. Each addressed issues vital and controversial at the founding. But the issues have faded. So has the test clause. But not the Establishment Clause. White startingly concluded that courts have gone on to "carve out" their preferred policy on various church-state issues.[14] Or, as Justice Robert Jackson candidly admitted, the judges' own prepossessions are the substance of the law.[15]

The two lines of analysis so far developed add up to this: the Constitution is decreasingly relevant to an increasing constitutional job description. Courts have positioned themselves to manage the entire church-state complex and they write the managerial handbook upon tabula rosa. The result is judicial superintendence of religion and law, without external constraints upon the law's substance.

But is there any "law" at all? Ostensibly, yes. There is a three-part test that government behavior must satisfy to survive the Establishment Clause scrutiny: the law or practice must have a secular legislative purpose, a primary effect which neither advances nor inhibits religion and must not entail excessive entanglement between religion and government.[16]

There are several senses in which these apparently objective inquiries obscure a "privatizing" reality and I submit that all there really is to the law is a privatizing principle. To begin, the language of the test is, upon closer reflection, as indeterminate as the wall metaphor. There are so many qualifiers of degree ("primary," "excessive") and vague question-begging terms ("secular," "purpose," "entanglements") that these doctrinal formulae are little more than objective-sounding sieves through which deeper principles pass unmediated to the practical problem at hand (say, tuition tax credits or a creche on public property).

No law has ever been struck down because it "inhibited" religion, so the second prong is less than it seems. More, the remaining prongs collapse into a single principle, which is privatization, starting with the third "no-entanglements" test. Over the past two years the Supreme Court translated "no entanglements" into its new fetish "symbolic union of church and state."[17] Symbolic union occurs wherever a court spies too much coziness between government and religion. The paradigm case is the widely litigated "creche in the public square." Most recently, a nativity scene in Chicago's City Hall was held an unconstitutional "symbolic union."[18] Other common examples involve bureaucratic entanglements, like those attending any state involvement with parochial schools. Two years ago, for instance, the Supreme Court struck down New York City's implementation of the federal mandate to give remedial help to *all* school children — including those attending religious schools. Sending public school personnel into religious schools — the logical response — forged an impermissible "symbolic union."[19] Given the pervasive presence of government — federal, state, local — in our common life, "no symbolic union" practically means "no trace of religion in the public square." That is privatization.

The vice of "symbolic union" is commonly identified as government "endorsement" of religion. For instance, the federal court in Chicago opined that the City "endorsed" Christianity by positioning a creche in the city hall.[20] Now this is partly a semantic game played by privatizers. Prohibited "endorsement" in this sense is indistinguishable from permissible (occasionally, required) "accommodation" of religious belief. This is evidenced by a very recent example. Because Jews bury the dead within 24 hours, they need to get burial permits in a hurry. Consequently, New York City now gives burial authorizations by phone, precisely to cope with the demands of Jewish faith. Does this symbolically "endorse" Judaism or just "accommodate" it? Or does it do both? If so, where is the resolution of the case? In all, with rhetorical aid from empty themes like "neutrality," "symbolic union" so conduces to the fastidious erasure of angelic traces from "public" business that a "naked public square" is almost unavoidable.

Jumping over to the "secular purpose" inquiry. The Supreme Court issued about thirty-five Establishment Clause opinions between 1947 and 1985. In most of them laws were invalidated, but only two laws lost due to the absence of "secular purpose." One required posting the Ten Commandments in public schoolrooms,[21] the other was a true Scopes law — not to be confused with the recent Creation Science case — where Arkansas flatly prohibited the teaching of evolution.[22] Even school prayer did not stumble over that prong but instead fell before the "no advancement" test.

The number just doubled to four. In 1985 the Court struck down a "moment-of-silence for meditation or prayer" because it lacked a "secular purpose."[23] Then, it invalidated Louisiana's Balanced Treatment Act, which required that "creation science" be taught whenever evolution was for it also lacked a "secular purpose."[24] Note that Louisiana neither forbade nor required anyone to teach evolution or creation science. The law said simply that when either was selected for instruction, the other be given equal coverage.

These cases proclaim a distinctive invigoration of the long dormant secular purpose prong. The Louisiana legislature, for instance, stubbornly identified its purpose as a secular one. It sought to insure students' academic freedom by balancing information available in classrooms dominated (in most instances) by teachers who teach evolution as fact. And if evolution is taught as "fact" then the state pronounces literal interpretations of Genesis like those held by many Louisiana students "false." This eclipse of free exercise interest did not impress the Court.

Now recall that the usual recitation of the three part test required "the law [to] have a secular legislative purpose." In *Edwards v. Aquillard* the Court pronounced that "the legislature must have adopted the law with a secular purpose."[25] The switch of subjects from law to lawmakers is momentous for it permitted the Court to translate "purpose" into "motive." And the *Edwards* Court needed the help. It *never* concluded that Creation Science was a sham, that it was really Genesis dressed up in scientific jargon. And it couldn't have, for it is not. Whatever its other vices, "creation science" purports to be no more than the sum of scientific — not scriptural — evidence for creation ex nihilo. Apparently there is such evidence though not enough to persuade most scientists. The creation scientists usefully point out the similarly conjectural nature of evolutionist theory, and Thomas Kuhn's analysis of scientific inquiry[26] must give pause to anyone but the most "scientized" among us.

The Justices did not hesitate to call the legislature's proclaimed "purpose" a "sham", thereby demonstrating that, while they may not know a scientific lie when they see it, they do know politicians. Against the overwhelming evidence marshalled by Scalia in dissent, the Court said that the "pre-eminent purpose" was clearly to advance the "religious viewpoint" of creation and to "endors[e]" religion in violation of the Establishment Clause. Now that is *not* a characterization of creationism but rather of the reasons at least one legislator had for favoring equal time for it. They are very different things. The latest status report on the *Everson* no-aid formula reads as follows: legislation may not advance religion (that's prong two), may not *seem* to advance it by doing anything construable — even by "impressionable youngsters" — as "endorsement" of religion (that's "symbolic union"), and lawmakers may not wish to accommodate the religious sensibilities of even a captive impressionable audience (that's *Edwards).*

Edwards continued a development initiated two years ago in *Wallace v. Jaffree,* the "moment of silent meditation or prayer" in Alabama public schools case. That case was generally reported as one invalidating moments-of-silence in public schools. That's incorrect, and one evidence of that is the upcoming decision in another moment-of-silence, this one in New Jersey.[27] The Alabama case turned on the "secular purpose" test, and the law failed because of some evidence — and it was no more than that — that legislators acted from the desire to get as much religion into the classroom as the Constitution would allow. That damned the law. What the cases share is the Conclusion that religious motives — read, religious morality or belief — prompted (in part) the enactment. Of this development Georgetown's Mark Tushnet quite accurately observed: "The secular purpose requirement thus means that if enough people take religion seriously, they cannot enact their program but if they favor the same program for other reasons, they can enact it. It seems fair to say this rule does not accept the view that religion should play an important part in public life."[28]

Is there anything new and different in the "no advancement" effect prong? No, there is not, and there are several reasons. One is that the surrounding phases of the three-part text are actually (as just mentioned) differentiations of a "no advancement" core. The core was established in the first, the seminal, and by far the most analytically important case of the modern era, *Everson v. Board of Education.* The issue presented in that 1947 case was the constitutionality of state funded bus rides to and from school for children in private schools, then largely Catholic grade schoolers. The Court sustained the expenditure but for profoundly incorrect reasons. The correct analysis of the Establishment Clause challenge would have asked simply whether any preference or discrimination among sects or beliefs was displayed. For that is what "no establishment" meant to the colonists, to the Framers, to the legal tradition, and to most Americans before *Everson.*[29] Since the transporation subsidies were equally available, the subsidies passed muster.

The Supreme Court had other ideas. They invented an Establishment Clause all their own, an invention adequate to the task of inserting judges into the entire church-state problematic. To the *Everson* Court nonestablishment meant (among many other things) no governmental support, encouragement or fostering — financial or otherwise — of religion, even on an entirely nondiscriminatory basis. In a baffling — at least to the dissenting Justices — application of this "no-aid" rule, the Court approved the appropriation. The consequence of this ban on evenhanded sustenance cannot be overstated, can be grasped analogously. It is the difference between a boisterous choir of religious voices vying in the public square with equal government treatment, and silence.

The point is that the compact no-aid rule has blossomed into the three-part test. Put differently, the other parts are merely aspects of no-aid. For instance, "symbolic union" — the earmark of entanglements — is bad because it constitutes government "endorsement" and thus — assertedly — promotion of religion. The purpose prong, in its *Jaffree-Edwards* incarnation, twists "no public aid to religion" into "no religious contributions to political discourse." In Justice Scalia's dissenting observations, religio-political activism was the Courts' unmistakable target.[30] And religio-political activism is the flip side of privatization.

Here is where the privatizing drive is made manifest. The term "secular morality" is at least (at most?) a heuristic one, pointing it toward the normative principles and concepts whose public utterance and legal incorporation the Court sustains, and away from the condemned "religious morality." "Religious morality" is that which the Court keeps off the public square, for it is clear that "morality" generally is not so constrained. The 1986 gay sodomy case made this clear.[31] Community morality is a permissible basis for law but religious morality is not. Similarly, religious speech is handicapped — if not excluded — from public forums while *all* other speech — from the sublime to the ridiculous to the vulgar — is constitutionally welcome. Here are some examples. A moment of meditation is almost surely constitutional but one for prayer is doubtful. Student religious groups must struggle for "equal access" to school facilities — and usually fail — while all others are granted their due. More importantly, a federal district court — in a decision certain to be reviewed by the Supreme Court — invalidated the Adolescent Family Life Act as an establishment of religion![32] The "problem" was that government funding of family counselling by religiously-affiliated agencies impermissably promoted religion. My bet is that President Reagan's intention to ban funds for abortion counselling and referral will be held violative of the recipient's free speech rights. The critical point is that religious speech is suspect while all other is constitutionally protected. That too is privatization.

If all the "doctrines" reduce to the privatization project, why should this be a surprise? The Supreme Court has made clear all along that its self-assigned task was no less than to make religion safe for democratic politics. The kicker is that the technique chosen is removal of religion from politics. The scope and direction of their efforts — the privatizing drive across the entire front between religion and law — are amply explained by this "divisiveness" rationale. Typical of the Courts' rationales is this passage from the 1971 *Lemon* case:

> Ordinarily political debate and division, however vigorous or even partisan, are normal and healthy manifestations of our democratic system of government, but political division along religious lines was one of the principal evils against which the First Amendment was intended to protect....The potential divisiveness of such conflict is a threat to the normal political process....The history of many countries attests to the hazards of religion's intruding into the political arena or of political power intruding into the legitimate and free exercise of religious belief.[33]

Divisiveness is a part of an answer to the question: why privatization? But it is a superficial part. First, it is difficult to believe the Justices think that but for their pacific efforts, the United States might erupt into a bleeding cauldron of sectarian hatred. At least the Court has never provided any evidence for such assertions, just the assertions.

So, what explains the drive? Well, there is here the normal ration of ignorance and bigotry. The onset of modern judicial activism came in the 1947 *Everson* case and it, like so many other cases, involved state aid to Catholic schools. I, for one, am convinced that simple anti-Catholicism was at work in *Everson* and has infected the law ever since. Justice William Douglas, for instance, said things in early opinions that could have — and probably did — appear in the *Edinburgh Review* three hundred years ago. Now Christian fundamentalists seem to particularly irritate the Court, and so some cases — one example involved *Bob Jones University*[34] a few years back — are at least partially explainable as "spank the fundamentalists" cases. There is too a pervasive undercurrent or reductionism — of religious faith to psychology or emotion, and into the idiom of modern subjectivism. In sum, religion is mere superstructure, if not a total fraud. As for the law professors who write about church-state, Kent Greenwalt (who is on the inside) writes: "Many [of them] like other intellectuals display ... a disguised contempt for belief in any reality beyond that discoverable by scientific inquiry and ordinary human experience. [They] regard religious convictions as foolish superstition."[35] More symptomatic of the precise problem is the observation of another law professor who is an exception to Greenwalt's rule. Fred Gedicks remarks that "[e]ven among legal educators who are religious, there often is a reluctance to conceive of their religious convictions as relevant to the subjects they teach."[36] My own experience in the legal academy confirms both these commentaries.

These observations allow us to answer the question, why "privatization?" And the answer is a common feature in much of the most original recent work in constitutional theory, a feature I call the "national communitarian urge." The "urge" is for principles of commonweal, a unifying conception of American public life, some overarching account of the "public good" so that we can begin to articulate the outlines of a truly national community, or, as Mario Cuomo says, "the American family." In Harvard Professor Frank Michelman's apt expression (coincidentally a key component of Catholic social thought), this is "solidaristic" constitutional law.

Privatization of religion — the evacuation of religious morality and insights into common life from the public square — is perceived as the precondition to establishing a "national community." The reason is a simple one: religious belief in our pluralistic society is what particularizes persons and peoples. When those beliefs enter the public realm they, by definition, forestall the unity of principle and vocabulary that national community presupposes. More, since religion — at least the monotheistic variety on the American scene — is inevitably (and sometimes aggressively) public, communitarian privatizers take no prisoners.

The short — and I believe adequate — response to judges embarked on this course is that they have no constitutional warrant for it. Ours is simply not a communitarian Constitution. And I think they know that, which is why they invent constitutional doctrine. Still it behooves even the unsympathetic critic — and I am surely one — to take on the communitarians at their strongest point. There *is* a deep and honorable aspiration at work. It at least resembles that missing link in our common life identified by the authors of the sociological portrait, **Habits of the Heart.** And the impatience, even the disgust, of those weary of interest group politics, the clashing and clanging of self-interested lobbies in the public square, where political might — and not right — makes for law, is understandable.

My critique of communitarian constitutional law is really simple: *it* cannot work. I believe that the closest we will ever come to a national community in this country is one with religious substance. So long as monotheism rooted in Judaeo-Christian tradition predominates among our fellows, that much is assured.

A final comment. "So long as" is the operative phrase in the preceding prediction. Close scrutiny of the communitarian project — a project beyond this paper's scope — will reveal it to be communitarian in rhetoric, not substance. It rather appears that this jargon is but the noise of another great clash of interests, a clash very roughly between the "New Class" described by Peter Berger[37] and the real people. The appropriate symbolism is not a "naked public square," for the attempt rather is to undress a square constructed by religious people — one containing a creche — and to reclothe it with the symbol of another, spiritually dead worldview. That view stands no chance of achieving hegemony in a fair electoral fight with the faith of the masses — however much that faith seems a hollow image of what it once was. But with courts administering the realm, the issue becomes one of who can convert the King and his princes. How that will turn out I just don't know.

FOOTNOTES

[1] *New York Times,* Aug. 24, 1987 p. 16, col. 2.

[2] See G. Bradley, "Dogmatomachy: A Privatization Theory of the Religion Clause Cases," 30 *Saint Louis L.J.* 275 (1986).

[3] See generally, G. Bradley, **Church-State Relationships in America** (1987).

[4] See *Lynch v. Donnelly,* 465 U.S. 668, 673 n.1. (1984).

[5] *Reynolds v. United States,* 98 U.S. 145, 164 (1879).

[6] 330 U.S. 1 (1947).

[7] *Bowen v. Roy,* 106 S.Ct. 2147 (1986).

[8] *Americans United v. Reagan,* 786 F.2d 194 (3rd Cir. 1986).

[9] See *National Law Journal*, Sept. 14, 1987, p. 3, col. 1.

[10] *Abortion Rights Mobilization v. Reagan,* 603 F.Supp 970 (S.D. N.Y. 1985).

[11] *Harris v. McRae,* 448 U.S. 297 (1980).

[12] See *Crisis,* May, 1986.

[13] *Wollman v. Waller,* 433 U.S. 229, 263 (1977) (separate opinion of Justice Powell).

[14] *Committee for Public Education v. Nyquist,* 413 U.S. 756, 820 (1973) (White, J., dissenting).

[15] *McCollum v. Bd of Education,* 333 U.S. at 203, 238 (1948) (Jackson, J., concurring).

[16] The test has been deployed in virtually every Supreme Court case since 1947. On its development and usage, see Bradley, *supra* note 2, *passim.*

[17] For a thorough analysis of this development, see W. Marshall, "We Know It When We See It: The Supreme Court and Establishment," 59 *So. Cal. L. Rev.* 495 (1986).

[18] *American Jewish Congress v. Chicago,* 56 U.S.LW. 2127 (Sept. 8, 1987).

[19] *Aquilar v. Felton,* 105 S.Ct. 3232 (1985).

[20] *Supra* note 18.

[21] *Stone v. Graham,* 449 U.S. 39 (1980).

[22] *Epperson v. Arkansas,* 393 U.S. 97 (1968).

[23] *Wallace v. Jaffree,* 105 S.Ct. 2479 (1985).

[24] *Edwards v. Aquillard,* 107 S.Ct. 2573 (1987).

[25] **Id.** at 2577.

[26] T. Kuhn, **The Structure of Scientific Revolutions,** (2d edition 1970).

[27] *Karcher v. May,* No 85-1551, decided below as *May v. Cooperman,* 780 F.2d 240 (3rd Cir. 1985).

[28] M. Tushnet, "The Constitution of Religion," 18 *Conn. L. Rev.* 701, 725 (1986).

[29] See Bradley, *supra* note 3.

[30] 107 S.Ct. at 2594 (Scalia, J., dissenting).

[31] *Bowers v. Hardwick,* 106 S.Ct. 2841, 2846 (1986).

[32] *Kendrick v. Bowen,* 657 F. Supp 1547 (D.C. Dist. Ct. 1987).

[33] *Leman v. Kurtzman,* 403 U.S. 602, 622, 623 (1971).

[34] *Bob Jones Univ. v. United States,* 461 U.S. 574 (1983).

[35] K. Greenwalt, "Religious Conviction and Lawmaking," 84 *Mich. L. Rev.* 352, 356 (1985).

[36] F. Gedicks, R. Hendrix, "Democracy, Autonomy, and Values: Some Thoughts on Religion and Law in Modern America," 60 *So. Cal. L. Rev.* 1579, 1609 n. 138 (1987).

[37] See, e.g., 17 *This World* 6 (Spring 1987).

Commentary

by

Gary D. Glenn

Bradley's principal thesis is in my judgment incontrovertible though not widely understood: "religion — especially religiously grounded morality — is being evicted from public debate over how to order our common life." His paper adumbrates this thesis and considers several explanations why the Supreme Court has led us in this direction. In addition to his legal and social explanations, I would like to add a more political explanation. Privatization of religion is necessitated by the secular world view of those elites which control the Court and which supply the intellectual frameworks and assumptions which guide the Court, i.e., the academic elites (including the leading law schools), legal elites, journalistic elites (especially of the leading big city print media), and the "new intellectual class" which predominantly has its home in the leading universities but circulates into and out of Washington public bureaucracies, private think tanks and lobby groups.

Let me also argue more explicitly than Bradley, but not in opposition to anything he says, that the seed of the decisive departure towards evicting religion from public life in constitutional law occurred when the Supreme Court began to interpret the First Amendment religion clauses to require not merely governmental neutrality among religions but neutrality between religion and nonreligion. This was in the *Everson* case (1947). The key theoretical point is that neutrality among religions requires only *religious pluralism* in public life; but neutrality between religion and nonreligion requires *secularism* in public life. Consequently, the expansion of the religion clauses to require the latter eventually requires the banishing of religion from public life.

Let me expand and clarify this argument. There are at least two possible meanings of "governmental neutrality" in this context. One is nonsupport or nonencouragement of either religion or nonreligion by government. I take it this is the meaning favored by "strict separationism." The second is support or encouragement for all religions on some kind of equal basis. I take it this is the meaning favored by "nonpreferentialism." If we adopt the latter meaning, neutrality need not mean secularism in public life. If we adopt the former, public life secularism seems inevitable. For the effective practical consequence of the former meaning is that we must ban from public institutions religious prayers, readings, education, traditions, practices, and symbols. At least these have been the practical consequences the Court has drawn when it has tried to base its decisions on neutrality between religion and nonreligion.

I would argue that neither meaning of neutrality works as intended if we understand neutrality to mean "not taking sides." The "strict separationist" meaning has the effect of permitting only secularism in public life and hence tacitly conveys the impression that religion is less publicly relevant and less worthy of public support and encouragement than nonreligion. The "nonpreferentialist" meaning has the effect of tacitly conveying the impression that religion is worthy of public support and encouragement, thereby taking sides against the secular view.

In view of the apparent impossibility of government "not taking sides" between religion and nonreligion in public life and notwithstanding sincere protestations to the contrary, we seem to have no choice but to give one or the other tacit public sanction and encouragement. That is what the Court seems to have understood and to have done by and large over the last two generations by giving such sanction and encouragement to secularism in public life.

I have undoubtedly been insufficiently precise in formulating my argument. A more adequate formulation would distinguish between that religion which understands itself as essentially private and hence having no public role and that which regards itself as having a public role. The former would not see public life secularism as siding against religion whereas the latter would. I do not have time now to develop this point. I mention it to acknowledge the limitations of my remarks and also to introduce a second reflection on Bradley's paper.

Part of the reason which has driven the Court, erratically but over the long run clearly, towards public life secularism is increasing confusion over the constitutional meaning of "religion." In *Torcaso v. Watkins* (1960) the Court stated for the first time that religion did not require belief in God, that is, it removed the traditional theistic requirement for "religion" to be considered "religion." It went so far as to describe "secular humanism" as a "religion." This obscuring of the distinction between religion and nonreligion reached its zenith in the draft cases of the 1960s and 1970s when the Court held that even frank nonbelievers, whose purely rational ethical views served the same or a similar function in their lives that religion did in the lives of believers, were entitled to the same draft exemption as religious conscientious objectors. Thus the Court reached the conclusion that the constitutional meaning of "religion" now included nonreligion which would seem to deprive religion of any distinctive constitutional status worthy of special protection. Moreover, if "religion" now means the same as its opposite, "religion" ceases to be a term of distinction and thus is in the process of disappearing. This process proceeds apace with the Court's decision in *Bob Jones University* (1985) justifying removal of tax exempt status for a religious institution which practiced racial discrimination. Part of the reasoning was that the statute granting tax exemption granted it conditioned upon the institution's charitable purposes being consistent with public policy. Although the statute distinguished between charitable and religious organizations, the Court assimilated them, holding that the same condition ("consistent with public policy") applied to religious organizations. I believe it is a fair reading of this case to say that religious organizations are no longer constitutionally distinguishable from charitable institutions, that is, that both are granted tax exemptions because they serve public purposes. The traditional view was rather that religion was a right which existed independent of any public purposes which it might serve.

PART THREE:
The Church, Culture and Media

The Elements of Catholicism as a Developing Counter-Culture in America, Approaching the Year 2000

by
Msgr. Eugene V. Clark

A genre of historical writing is dedicated to undoing what we are doing. It criticizes the premature identification of movements. On the other hand, one of history's uses is to give us insight into our own affairs and for that we need words. We are subject to amused correction in the next century. But let us try, as best we can, to discern where the Catholic community in the United States is headed. It is a projection, not a prediction.

It is the conceit of this paper to foresee Catholicism as a possible counter-culture in America.

Let us hypothesize that American culture in its social, moral, literate and political dimensions will continue on its present graph line toward uncritical, aggressive secularism. In that case, many believing American Catholics will find the present symbiosis with market place American culture distinctly less congenial and more threatening than it was in mid century. At that time it was commonplace for Catholics to rejoice in most American thinking and practice. That is not likely in the year 2000.

Catholicism has no choice but to be a *minority* culture since the dominant and established American culture is even now manifestly and powerfully oriented to successful life in this world and this world only — an uneasy but straightforward secularism. It has moved from the innocent faith of eighteenth century Enlightenment to a resolute pragmatism in personal and community affairs, restricting its loyalties to those persons and entities that reinforce pragmatism; and it — the establishment — accepts the growing inhumane margins of post-decalogue American practice as "the way it always is," dismissing a Christian's pursuit of virtue and eternity as a solipsistic children's game.

Christianity's minority role in America is beyond dispute to anyone who reads current literature, scholarship and journalism, and who listens to electronic broadcast and private conversation.

When, at 7:00 P.M., the American breadwinner returns to a clipped lawn and lovely home in the suburbs and greets everyone in the foyer including small children with "Christ, what a day I had!", he or she no longer can recall why anyone might object to the expression. He or she belongs to a secular culture.

There will be more and more who do not know who Christ is, beyond Christmas allusions, since we must assume the powerful media denigration of creedal Christianity and the already weary scandal of Catholic high school and college teaching must surely reduce the number of believers. (Of course, if the Lord intervenes, He may change all that and further enlarge the inaccuracy of this paper).

Let us not fail to see the significance of the media orgy of ridicule aimed at papal views for the three weeks before the Pope came to the United States in Septemeber. Despite the media's manipulation of interviewees, a truth emerged. The message for us was not how secularists dislike the Catholic Church and its morals. We knew that. The message is the breath-taking ignorance and secularism of a very large number of nominal Catholics in this country. This fact may — sooner or later — dictate a serious change in the Church's apostolate.

In 2000, Catholics will surely be a minority; counter-culture, only maybe. There is a great difference between the two. In this speculation of ours, the phrase "counter-culture" suggests a cultural resistance and a visible choice. Between non-believers and Christians of 19th century France and England, each side might have called itself a counter-culture; today, Christianity hardly merits the term in either country. In Italy, Catholicism is a counter-culture at least among the young. Behind the Iron Curtain, Catholicism is a counter-culture in every way.

An edgy dimension to these considerations is that for a counter-culture to have vitality it must have a core of true believers. Only believers will be ready for the predictable sacrifices which will range from social rejection to bitter persecution. But who neatly certifies a believer institutionally? We know how messy that question can be. As far back as the age of the first persecutions when some demanded rebaptism for defectors, the Church suffered painful crises in its attempt to identify true believers. Doctrine was more easily defined (not very) than practitioners identified. Catholics suffered serious centrifugal losses during the 17th and 18th century quarrels over grace. Jansenists often occupied the front pews. And we know the anger evoked at the mention of Modernism which had not reached its conclusion in the 1920's but is still cresting in the 1980's. Today Modernists are accepted as Catholic leaders in many areas, despite the Church's proscription of the doctrine. For this reason, any announcement that Catholics are circling their wagons as an orthodox counter-culture may drive many cowboys to sign on with the Indians.

A counter-culture, therefore, is not necessarily a sharply defined proposition. It can be intellectually and socially befogged for many. In France, varieties of Catholicism continue to be remote from one another while they shrink to low single-digit proportions of the French population. In Holland, the official church, practically speaking, became secular-Protestant. A Catholic counter-culture in the United States may not develop and, in the year 2000, we may all be cowering in our condominiums.

Whether Catholicism in America will become a counter-culture or will be swamped like French Catholicism (and, interestingly, French Judaism) is beyond our guessing.

Let us be of good cheer and hope that the vitality and the charism of the American Church, so powerful in mid century America, will not be entirely snuffed out and will, for a number of reasons, stand opposed in the year 2000 to the still dominant secularist establishment in the nation. In what areas will the motions take place and what will some of the problems be?

We can discern, I believe, areas of polarity between the American liberal secular establishment and minority creedal Catholicism, flash-points of contradiction and the *loci* of individual choice. If American Catholicism has the staying power to become a counter-culture, it may occur in areas where fissure is already visible.

Let us consider them in order not of importance, but of popular visibility and, therefore, most likely to evoke popular reactions:

I. Public Health and Disease.

It is possible that homosexuals will stop sodomizing one another and it is possible that the Federal Government, after spending a few billion dollars will find a remedy so that homosexuals may go on sodomizing one another. Neither is likely; nor is it likely that the strains of herpes, syphillis, AIDS, and all the rest will become weaker, and that all intravenous drug users will line up every morning to get clean needles. The coinciding facts of physiology, pathology and disease follow a larger law than convenience, and may well establish a new branch of apologetics and moral reflection. Practice of the moral code will offer a double reward — health here and the rewards of obedience in the next life. Catholics who cross that line will no longer be thought wicked; they will be thought lunatics.

Liberals in matters of sexual morality will speak as dreamers. Moral Christians will avoid their company and a liaison with a person of liberal views in this area will be a kind of social suicide.

II. The Protection and Formation of Children as Devout Christians.

Secular liberalism never developed a philosophic mechanism whereby children can be protected in their formative years by curtailing the freedoms of certain adults like pornographers, homosexuals, heterosexual orgiasts, lying entertainers, prostitutes and drug sellers. In the failure of social restraint, the canonized freedom of bad guys and the inadequate defense for children have become an accepted liberal balance in society. Creedal Catholics are horrified and deeply angry about the received failure to offer children protection. A grim example: gay rights' laws now commend those who praise homosexuality in schools to redress earlier prejudice. To creedal Catholics, this is not a theoretical question; it touches their young children directly and will become increasingly intolerable.

To this we add the insistent question of catechetical instruction of children along creedal and supernatural lines or along the attitudinal lines that so altered the face of believed Catholicism from the late 1960's to our time.

III. Devotion to the Ideal of a Secure, Life-long Marriage.

The psychological and emotional horrors of divorce will be increasingly clear. Catholics will look nostalgically to earlier Catholic mores of marital stability. There will be a magnetic pull to it.

On principle, liberals will say binding marriage in every circumstance is intolerable and barbaric. Surely the two groups will face in sharply different directions. This longing for family stability will be a powerful element in Catholicism as a counter-culture.

IV. Formation of a Catholic Feminism.

I will not elaborate on this subject because Dr. Little will have insightful things to say about it in this volume. But it will surely be part of the life, background and focus of Catholic women in the year 2000.

V. Reaction Against the Morbid Exhibition of Every Sexual Motion, the Rude Distribution of Condoms and the Subsequent Destruction of Romantic Privacy.

The establishment may have made it axiomatic by that time, that early-sex-with-contraception is as acceptable as fast food. The institutional but rarely stated purpose of contraception for children will continue to be the suppression of population and welfare support. Health will be the stated purpose despite statistics to the contrary. This general mind set and practice will alienate, increasingly, creedal Catholics and perhaps give the Catholic style of life and schools a new popularity.

VI. Reaction Against Materialism.

Liberal culture is, in our era and place, radically materialist and draws on the *possession* of things and people, for personal comfort, self-esteem and psychological security. It is so well known that Americans traveling abroad instinctively defend themselves from an unspoken charge of materialism. The cultural experience of creedal Catholics, not to mention their normal instincts, suggests that materialism robs people of inspiration, romance, vitality and reliable norms for higher living, all of which are signs of functional belief in the supernatural. Catholic belief in the next world is both theoretical and very personal, and it is a primary reason why believing Catholics will be increasingly uncomfortable trying to share their lives and goals with establishment people.

VII. Reaction Against Abortion.

Surely abortion will remain a reminder of a great moral division between Americans. Since neither the courts nor Congress want the public credit for undoing the right to abortion, the dispute will either be exactly where it is today or it will have been sent back to the states for decades of controversy. While Americans continue to slaughter the unborn, Catholics and Fundamentalist Christians will stand out sharply defined against this morally revolutionary practice.

These are some of the fissures likely to turn to chasms in America and help set up the opportunity for consistent Catholicism to act as a counter-culture in the United States.

But what will be the likely configurations of the Catholic community itself? Like all futurism, our speculation is based on current trends.

Creedal Catholics who fear the influence of exclusively secular norms in their lives and liberal Catholics who are sure they can and should incorporate secular goals into their Catholicism will talk less and less to one another. Even today many fail to realize how incompatible — even incomprehensible — in vision and language the two groups are. The annoyance factor will be very high. Each will assume the *real* Church is in its corner. And "Church" will mean entirely different things. Historians will calmly recognize the situation; but Catholic romantics will be appalled. A glorious community will be sundered.

The Bishops, we may assume, will continue to administer their institutions, encourage all good works and address questions of justice, ethics and public policy in the larger society and around the world. It is unlikely that they will sharply define Catholicism in this country. Neither side will receive comfort. The Bishops will themselves be uncomfortable with each side: the liberals will draw them into practical materialism and a vagueness open to heresy; the creedal Catholics will request that they drum the materialists and virtual heretics out of the Church. Some Bishops may take sides. But the result will likely be a feudalization of the Catholic community on the level of parish and institution. Battles will be fought in individual parishes and one side will win. If you travel, one Sunday you may attend mass with a priest vested before an altar; he will preach on remembered doctrine, morals or Scripture and the choir may sing in Latin. People may kneel for communion. The following Sunday, 10 miles away, you may find a priest in no vestments, served by altar girls; a layman will preach, lay ministers will dominate; the music will be contemporary rock. If the Episcopalians will forgive us, we will have high, low and broad churches. This assumes that the Holy

See and the Bishops will not intervene forcefully. It is a possibility that they will. But we are here only projecting from the practice of 1987.

Catholic schools may divide even more sharply and may be owned, like country clubs, by the users since many bishops and pastors may not want continuing fiscal responsibility. Indeed, the clergy may be thought by parents to be unreliable as directors, given their short terms of office and the regular replacement by clerics of unpredictable views.

It is also an outside possibility that these schools may flourish through an educational-economic-political development. If public schools get worse — a reasonable prediction — parents and teachers may turn to private schools, and a voucher plan for parents may be enacted into law. Private schools may then rapidly replace a large percentage of parochial schools as well as public schools.

Unless they are touched by grace, some creedal Catholics may slip into a new severity of personal outlook partly because they will concentrate on the effects of sin and therein distinguish themselves angrily from liberals. They may develop a new strictness of life to block out vulgarity in language, entertainment, places of recreation, the people they visit and, of course, in the church institutions they patronize. Liberals will call that a new Jansenism, a spiritual arrogance, and will be reinforced in their own choice of relaxed alternatives.

Perhaps the meanest dimension of the civil war will be verbalized in broad brush accusations by liberals against Creedalists and Papalists as *petite eglise* types, neo puritans and inquisitors; very likely the Creedalists will use more precise language to indict liberals.

This stand-off will wreck a million conversations and hundreds of parishes. The fact that Creedal Catholics will formulate specific reasons why they can no longer accept Catholic secularism, does not mean that secularists will respond intellectually to their theses. Secularists are as emotional and fantasy-oriented as anyone else. They will respond in normal American style. They will say it is too bad that Catholic fanatics have dulled their minds against freedom, education, community involvement, ecumenism, universal brotherhood and concern for whales.

Creedal Catholics will surely enlarge a few specific absolutes, e.g., the mandate to fight abortion, which may become a litmus paper test for conservatives and the primary area in which liberal secularist Catholics will desparately seek to discover a *via media.*

Sex education, not fully resolved theologically or practically, will not only be a source of angry accusation between the two groups but will cause unsettling disputes within each group, particularly the conservatives.

By the year 2000 most Catholic colleges and universities will be openly liberal and secularist, formally separated from the Church in many cases. They may try to be, in the canonized phrases, respectful of their Catholic origins and cultural orientation. Like a federal agency they will try to rise in Olympian fashion above American Catholic feudalization to recruit students of any and all views and to prevent their student body from being overwhelmed by non citizens. Many of these colleges will not make it because of Catholic divisions and conservative boycotts and will be absorbed by state or secular institutions.

Creedal Catholics will be uncomfortable using many Catholic schools. Upper middle-class Catholics may create and fund their own lay-directed elementary schools. They will find it impossible to create more than a few college level institutions and those that survive will likely be filled to capacity. For the majority of creedal Catholic students, two institutions appear to be useful and natural growths in the near term: (1) independent faculties of theology and philosophy for students determined to find magisterial teaching outside their own colleges and universities, and (2) Sorbonne-like residences for Catholics attending universities. Both these institutions are relatively inexpensive and could reach levels of some quality for their consumers. Such institutions will be less a speculation than the only possible roads open to creedal Catholics when the one time Catholic universities will be indistinguishable from secular institutions. Of course, creedal Catholics may choose to do none of these things. They may also diminish in numbers and visibility.

Vocations to the religious life are as unpredictable as the birth rate.

It is conceivable that as children in public schools have condoms forced on them and as television and popular music plum new depths of sexual explicitness, celibacy among the clergy may become a valued witness to what Christianity represents in its ascetical dimension. This is just a possibility. On the other hand, if the bishops salute but do not enforce the traditional celibate disciplines against sodomy and dating, there may be a divided priesthood. One group of vow-conscious, non-dating heterosexually-oriented celibates will serve creedal Catholics and a homosexually-tilted priesthood will serve and be patronized by a liberal Catholic laity. This clerical polarity is not likely to last but, in the short term, it will be decided largely by the lax or strict administration of the Bishops and the seminary faculties they appoint.

If present trends continue, there will be very few teaching nuns left by the year 2000. It is possible that some religious communities will fall into great disrepute by battles over community property. However, stricter communities and those dedicated to hands-on-care of desparate people are now flourishing and may give the institutional life of the Church a new zest by the year 2000. The care of the elderly and of AIDS patients may be areas of such splendid work that some religious communities will grow rapidly on that account.

Associations of the laity, dedicated and focused on the needs of the Catholic community, may mushroom into high profile positions in both creedal and liberal Catholic communities, with the odds of survival being better in the creedal community. Groups like *Opus Dei* will show what organization and spiritual discipline can accomplish.

Around these main groups, the Catholic community in the United States may suffer and be entertained by a zoo of people claiming to be Catholics. There will be Catholics for abortion, contraception, man-boy love, lesbian religious, married-divorced-and-remarried Catholics, and mystics for a third magisterium. Priests will offer mass for them, laymen will baptize them and activists will dance down the main aisle for them. The Church in America may not have a mechanism to discourage anyone effectively.

Who will survive as Catholics and what their numbers will be are questions quite beyond us.

What is reasonable to predict is that liberal Catholicism, advocating moral relativism, indeterminate secularism and selected belief and practice, will not be a counter-culture. It cannot be. It will be a half-way house, a bridge, a *via media* that will have a difficult time securing respect from either American secularists or the integrist creedal Catholics.

On the other hand, creedal Catholicism, in so far as it recognizes Apostolic authority, the supernatural connection and absolute moral norms, will be a *potential* counter-culture. It will have to tread carefully. It will be a real counter-culture — of whatever success — if it maintains its *elan* and does not disappear into a sharply parochial mentality; if it loathes the sexual excesses of the secularists but does not create a "Catholic puritanism" of equal excess; if it does not attach itself to individuals or institutions and see in them a unique salvation for the Church. Let us pray it will not.

As a postscript, we should consider personal culture in the traditional sense of the word: the Catholic enjoyment of creation in its finest flowering. "Culture" in this elevated sense requires careful definition today since many students are unaware of its meaning. None of us say this meanly or snobbishly. Moreover, we mention it in a Catholic context where, if we may say so, it has its strongest roots. We could possibly, in 2000, be almost the sole American custodians of a rich personal tradition.

For the purpose of our thesis let us define high culture as a cultivation of mind and a deepening of humane satisfactions. As Catholics, we mean the following:

— A theological recognition that some gifts of God reflect both reliable earthly pleasure *and* eternal verity;

— A personal appreciation of simple truth, shared human enjoyment, bonding human virtue, and the beauty of persons and their achievements;

— A prejudice for personal generosity and openness of mind; gratitude for all good feeling; a conscious enjoyment of sensuality as God's gift and a corresponding abhorrence of excess in sensuality which clouds God's purposes and spoils our rewarding cooperation with the Donor of all good things.

Those Americans who believe that a relationship with God (religion) is the enemy of enjoyment in life, are left with few guide lines for refined satisfaction beyond what pleases or distracts.

For these people, nature and the arts are and will become more and more thin enjoyments. The art of gracious and attractive human engagement — spiritually strengthened friendship and manners born of esteem for others — is already *terra incognita* for many in America. The recognition of such gifts as spiritual, and of cultivated minds and instincts as virtuous, is largely the fruit of Catholic civilization. Those gifts were expected to flower in the lives of Catholic scholars and students, in their families and descendants. Alas, a large number have joined the weary positivists and sensualists who, as the phrase goes, "want it all" and will wind up in paralyzing boredom. Like the early Benedictines and the seventh and eighth century Irish, or even poor Charlemagne trying to get the clergy to wash, it may be, in the year 2000, that only contemporary Catholicism may offer Americans reasons to sustain the disciplines that underpin refinement of mind, guided sensuality and reliable courtesy.

Before you introduce you children to Mozart and Raphael; before you tell them to stand when older people enter the room; before you share your thoughts about a sunrise in the country; before you tell your adolescent that the love of a human being is more spiritual than gland-ular, accept a recommendation: Pray. You'll need it. And when you fail to win your point the first few times, remember that you richly deserve your favorite beverage and a half hour with Handel. You are trying to preserve at once Western Civilization and your sanity. You deserve the best to keep your spirits up.

Those of you who will be 50 in the year 2000 will have a work to do. The rest of us will be reading the *Oservatore Romano* in Spanish as we sit in our verandas cheering you on.

To Be or Not To Be . . . Female

by
Joyce A. Little

Since sharing seems today to be one of those things universally recommended, I would like to begin by sharing with you one of my pet peeves. (And I must also confess that I seem to have garnered out of my 'lived experience' as an American Catholic an alarming number of this particular type of pet in recent years.)

The one I have in mind has to do with those politicians (of every shade on the political spectrum) who, when confronted with any uncongenial suggestion that something in the way we are living today has gone awry, hasten to assure us that we need not worry, because the American people are intelligent and can be trusted to do the right thing. I don't know who first stumbled upon this wonderful rhetorical device, but he must have recognized almost at a glance that it ranks, in terms of human inventiveness, right up there with fire and the wheel.

This avowed trust in the American people kills several birds with one stone. In the first place, it allows us, the people, to bask in the warm rays of our own virtue. Secondly, it allows the politician to present himself as one who recognizes and appreciates our virtue. Thirdly, it manages to suggest that we Americans are a cut above other nations, whose people cannot always be trusted to get things right. And, fourthly and most importantly, it tries and often manages to cut off discussion at the outset, by suggesting that anyone who thinks there is a problem clearly does not trust the American people.

I bring up this particular pet peeve, because, annoying as this notion that Americans are somehow exempt from the fallenness of things might be in the political realm, it is downright pernicious when it raises its head within the Church, as we see happening today. I cite only one quite recent example of it. Just a month ago, NBC, in anticipation of John Paul II's second Papal visit to the United States, aired a program entitled "God Is Not Elected," hosted by Maria Schriver.[1] In the opening segment from San Francisco, Fr. George Fitzgerald of Old St. Mary's Cathedral, addressing the differences which American lay Catholics have with the Papacy today, said: "I think that part of the reason why you experience the conflict in the American church is you have a very articulate, educated laity, and they're simply saying, 'We want to have an active part and an active role in making some determinations about being Catholic.' "

All of this sounds at the least quite benign and at the most quite positive . As an articulate and educated lay person, ought I not bask in the warmth of my own virtue and take great heart that, in this "age of the laity," I am finally coming into my own?

Before rushing to embrace Fr. Fitzgerald's happy appraisal of the

American Catholic laity, we ought perhaps first look at some of the articulate and educated laity showcased on this particular program. First, there was Edwina. Characterized as a devout Catholic because she attends Mass thrice weekly and refused to marry her boyfriend, a divorced man, unless he obtained an annulment from the Church, Edwina admitted she engages in pre-marital sex with her boyfriend and believes herself not culpable and no less a Catholic for doing so. How did she articulate her educated faith? "I know the Vatican is against abortion, I now know the Vatican is against artificial insemination, I know the Vatican is against birth control, but that's about the extent of my knowledge of what the Vatican says or doesn't say."

Then there was Kevin, a sexually active homosexual, a member of Dignity and a welcome participant in the mass at Old St. Mary's. He said: "Pronouncements from Rome don't always reflect the lived experience of people in the United States." (Clearly no one has educated Kevin on the Fall and how it tends to affect our "lived experience," even in America.) Since Kevin is presumably one of those articulate and educated parishioners about whom Fr. Fitzgerald waxed so enthusiastically, we may safely assume that Kevin did not have himself in mind when he told us that "a lot more listening needs to happen."

My own personal favorite on the program, however, was Lennie, an Italian Catholic in Los Angeles. Asked how she feels about the Church's teachings, she articulated her educated faith as follows: "There are some doctrines, especially that the Pope has come out in the last year or two [sic], that I don't feel good about. The issues ... brought up recently on homosexuality, birth control, artificial insemination — he's taken many steps backwards [sic] and has alienated a lot of very important, educated Catholic people."

I doubt that anyone, even the Pope, could fully appreciate my own lived experience as I listened to her. Here sat I, with my doctorate in theology from a reputable American university, and somehow it had escaped my notice that the Pope has spent the last couple of years fabricating doctrines. And why, I asked myself, had my dissertation director at that reputable university, a Jesuit whose knowledge of the faith I much respected, never even so much as intimate to me that Popes are not supposed to alienate important, educated Catholics? (I too had read **The Pope and the Jesuits**, and I trusted implicitly that, whatever else might be said for or against them, the Jesuits could be counted on to pass along information of this kind). In fact, my situation was even worse than that. I had actually been laboring for several years under the impression that this Pope at least is himself an important and educated Catholic.

Of course, it is easy to poke fun at the alleged education of many American Catholics today, and indeed we must sometimes laugh at it if only to avoid crying. But we must admit that a great many Catholics today no longer have even a Baltimore Catechism knowledge of their faith and, even more tragically, no longer have even that sense of the faith which can often be relied upon to keep us from going astray when all else fails.

And we must also face the fact that these lay Catholics are not entirely culpable for their ignorance. Why is it that Edwina, attending Mass three times a week, knows almost nothing about what the Vatican has to say? Lay Catholics are familiar with the problem. Most of us have our stock of horror stories regarding the imaginative and sometimes even bizarre accounts of the faith to which we have been subjected in recent years. It is no longer even particularly surprising to learn, as we did from Edwina, that the priest counseling her and her boyfriend for marriage has no problem with their practicing birth control, on the grounds that the Pope doesn't play the game and therefore shouldn't make the rules.

TV Guide a few months ago ran a cartoon in which one woman says to another, as both are watching TV, "I am shocked by the things which no longer shock me." I know exactly what that woman means. Only rarely anymore do I hear anything which genuinely shocks me, and that fact has begun to disturb me greatly. It no longer surprises me at all, for example, when my students say, as one did recently, that, if it be true that God calls everyone to holiness, she is happy that most people don't enthusiastically embrace the call, because the world would be awfully uninteresting if they did. But it did quite literally shock me to hear Fr. George Fitzgerald say, from the pulpit of Old St. Mary's and on NBC: "If the Church were only to exist for the good, how terribly boring life would be." Let us be grateful that we do not have to hear his homily on heaven. But let us also not be surprised that he happily welcomes into his parish active homosexuals and heterosexuals routinely practicing artificial contraception and that, when he looks out over his congregation, he sees many people whom he personally knows to have undergone abortions. One gathers that his parishioners rarely bore him. If it be true that lay Catholics frequently get the priests they deserve, it is apparently also true that sometimes, at least, a pastor gets the parishioners he deserves.

We the people of God have a right to be educated in our faith, and we are therefore well within our rights to ask why it is that, when we turn to our priests and bishops for the bread we so desparately require, we are so often handed a stone. While many of our clergy manage frequently to avoid answering our question, we fortunately do have good reason to believe that someday, sooner or later, they will have that same question addressed to them by Someone whom they cannot avoid.

In the meantime, however, we lay people have our own question to answer. It has, in fact, been quite forcefully articulated in a recent novel, **The Thanatos Syndrome**, by Walker Percy.[2] In that novel, we meet Father Smith, a self-admitted failed priest who is, among other things, an alcoholic. But precisely because he can admit his failure, he is an honest man and an honest priest. His parishioners can expect no false flattery from him, no easy assurances that the Pope doesn't appreciate their education and can't understand their lived experience. Having faced his own sinfulness and guilt, he is indelicate enough to suggest that his parishioners ought to do the same. He's not at all interested in expanding the number of his flock, in welcoming into the parish more members. Oddly enough and if the truth were known, he seems to think that many already there have somehow inadvertently wandered into the wrong place, and he gives the impression that they ought to think a bit more about whether or not they really want to be there. We are not surprised when told that he manages to offend everyone.[3]

At the end of the novel, we find ourselves at a Mass celebrating the opening of a hospice for the sick and dying whom our society no longer cares about and indeed has be euthanatizing at a pretty steady rate at a nearby place called Fedville. The chapel is crowded and the television crews are on hand to cover the big event. Fr. Smith walks in to celebrate the Mass.

Does Fr. Smith smile into the camera and thank everyone for coming? Does he applaud those who are present for being loving and caring people? Does he congratulate them for their sensitivity and compassion? Happily, Fr. Smith is not a recent product of our seminaries and therefore knows how to put the time he has to much better use. He tells them he recognizes their tenderheartedness, but suggests it might be indistinguishable from that tenderheartedness which motivates others to support euthanasia. He tells them he recognizes they experience no guilt in their lives, but, modern psychology notwithstanding, he seems oddly unhappy about their lack of guilt. He claims he cannot see a sinner among them, but that fact clearly brings him no joy. Father Smith says he knows very well what he is doing there in that chapel, though it is clear that most, if not all, of his audience has lost its grip on what he is doing there.

Father Smith doesn't particularly care whether his parishioners know what he is doing among them or not. But there is one thing he does think they ought to know, one question he does think they ought to be able to answer. He points out that the folks over at Fedville, the doctors and the nurses employed to abort and euthanatize human beings, know what they are doing there. And then he looks out over those gathered in the chapel. "I wonder," he says, "if you know what you are doing here!"[4]

The reader has an advantage over the audience in the chapel, for the reader is privy to Father Smith's earlier conversation with and confession to the narrator. When asked by the narrator why he had become a priest, Father Smith answers, "In the end, one must choose — given the chance." "Choose what?" the narrator asks. "Life or death. What else?"[5] Father Smith, indeed, does know what he is doing in the Catholic Church, but he is not convinced that many of his parishioners can say the same.

While Walker Percy, as a convert to Catholicism, may wonder at just how many lay Catholics in general know what they are doing in this Church, I as a female theologian have to wonder at just how many female Catholics in particular know what they are doing here. This question is a pressing one, for, just as those folks over at Fedville knew what they were doing, so today's feminists, and especially those who remain nominally Catholic, know what they are doing. And what they are doing is, if possible, even more unpleasant than the goings-on over at Fedville.

Indeed, Fedville represents only one of many unpleasant projects today's feminists are happy to support. If Walker Percy is correct in saying that to choose to be Catholic is to choose life, and I think he is, it is also and equally true, I believe, that, for women in particular today, to choose to be Catholic is to choose to be female.[6]

Until very recently, it would have sounded strange to say that a woman must choose to be female. After all, women are by nature female and therefore would appear to have no choice at all in the matter. But today we are watching, thanks largely to the feminist movement in general and feminist theology in particular, an enormous irony being played out before our eyes. Women, in the name of women's liberation, are deliberately rejecting those values most explicitly grounded in femaleness. Women, in the name of their own empowerment, are systematically discarding the very strengths which are embodied by the female. And, in so doing, they necessarily find themselves in conflict with the Catholic Church, which virtually alone among today's secular and religious institutions, insists that the real values of the female be recognized and lived.

No one has pinpointed more accurately the character of the controversy between the Catholic Church and radical feminism than Rosemary Radford Ruether when she observed:

> One might say that if the Vatican lost its credibility for "infallibility" in matters of morals with the birth-control controversy, it lost its credibility for "infallibility" in matters of faith with the declaration on the admission of women to the priesthood.[7]

Artificial birth control, on the one hand, and a male priesthood, on the other, do indeed define the framework within which the Church would insist that we understand human sexuality, the first by addressing the religious significance of what we do with our sexuality, the second by addressing the religious significance of who we are by virtue of that sexuality.

It is by now well understood that the first of these Church teachings, the ban on artificial contraception, conflicts with the feminist view that women must be freed, as it were, from their biology. Feminist arguments for abortion, of course, proceed very much along these same lines. One feminist, locating herself in a tradition going back to Simone de Beauvoir, tells us, "I am endangered by motherhood. In evacuation from motherhood, I claim my life, body, world, as an end in itself."[8]

What feminists reject here is the identification which Western thought has consistently made between femaleness and materiality. Mother Nature and Mother Earth are but popular expressions of this long-standing identification. Linguistically the identification is equally clear. Karl Stern notes: "Woman, in her being, is deeply committed to *bios,* to nature itself. The words for *mother* and *matter,* for *mater* and *materia* are etymologically related."[9]

Were there no Catholic Church to guide us at this point, the feminist rejection of this identification would be virtually irrefutable. Their case goes something like this. Western thought extending back to Plato and Aristotle has made two assumptions about reality — first, that spirit is superior to matter, and second, that males are to be identified with spirit while females are to be identified with matter. In Plato, this meant that the seductive or destructive characteristics which he attributed to matter are to be attributed to women. In Aristotle, this meant that the inferior characteristics which he attributed to matter (particularly its passivity) are to be attributed to women. Hence women have had to contend with male views of the female which turn women into either seductive temptresses who try (quite often successfully) to bring the male down or passive instruments at the service of male activity. One obvious solution presents itself. Women must be freed from these clearly oppressive identifications with materiality. Women must be freed from their biology.

There is a second solution, but it is not at all obvious, and indeed one could argue that, in the absence of the Christian revelation, it might never have occurred to anyone. This second solution is simply the reverse of the first. Instead of rejecting the identification of femaleness with materiality, this solution says we ought to embrace it. But, also and of crucial importance, instead of accepting the notion that spirit is superior to matter, this solution tells us we ought to rethink it or, more accurately, perhaps we ought to think about it for the first time, for, so obvious has it seemed to us that spirit is superior to matter that we have never seriously questioned that assumption at all.

In point of fact, no sense can be made out of the Church's ban on artificial contraception unless we suppose that the human body, human sexuality, human materiality is far more important than we are accustomed to thinking it is. Although Paul VI was the author of "Humanae Vitae," it is John Paul II who has set for himself the task of exploring the implications of this teaching. And it is John Paul II who has characterized the results of that exploration as a "theology of the body." The Pope is opening before us, as perhaps no one else in the history of our faith has done, a view of creation and salvation in which the striking and singular importance of the human body and human sexuality can at last be appreciated as it never has been before. Indeed, we are beginning to realize that *what we do* with our bodies is in the final analysis indissociable from *who we are* and that who we are is itself indissociable from our maleness and femaleness. And that brings us to Ruether's second problem with Church teaching, the male priesthood.

It is commonplace today among feminists and others to hear it argued that, as long as women cannot be priests, women will feel like second class citizens in the Church. Indeed, one could easily conclude, listening to media accounts of this controversy, that women who seek equal access to the priesthood are comparable to blacks seeking equal access to better paying jobs. In fact, however, the actual issue is quite different. Once again, Ruether goes to the heart of the matter:

> Feminist liberation communities necessarily must dismantle clericalism, which is an understanding of leadership as rule that reduces others to subjects to be governed. Clericalism, by definition, disempowers the people and turns them into "laity" dependent on the clergy. The basic assumption of clericalism is that the people have no direct access to the divine. The clergy alone have authorized theological training; they alone are authorized to preach, to teach, to administer the Church. They alone possess sacramental power.[10]

The notion that we have "no direct access to the divine" is indeed indissociable from the notion of priesthood, but it is also indissociable from the entire Judaeo-Christian tradition. According to that tradition, our access to God is always mediated, whether by the materiality of creation, or by the Law and prophets of the Old Testament, or by the Incarnate Word, or by the written word of Scripture, or by the public, visible Church, Magisterium and councils, or by the public, visible sacraments instituted by Christ. Indeed, it is quite literally true to say that in Catholicism there is no purely spiritual realm, for even the Trinitarian God Whom we worship is, by virtue of the Incarnation, Resurrection and Ascension of the Son, eternally united to human nature and human materiality. To remove these elements of mediation from Catholicism is to destroy Catholicism. The feminist critique of the male priesthood, because that critique involves the rejection of material principles of mediation, constitutes the single most all-embracing rejection of Catholicism we face today.

Even the Protestant Reformers, despite their rejection of the Church and many of her sacraments, never went so far as to suppose that we have a totally unmediated relationship with God. For them, the Bible, if nothing else, continued to be regarded as an authentic and utterly essential mediation of God's word without which we cannot know Him as He is. But the feminist 'hermeneutics of suspicion,' as Elizabeth Schussler Fiorenza among others has characterized it, would take even that away from us, relegating Scripture to the dustbin of patriarchal texts inspired by a culturally-conditioned male chauvinism.

American Catholics today are subject to two powerful streams of thought, one theological and one philosophical, which operate to undermine our sense of the faith. The first of these, the theological one, is the Protestant Reformation, with its partial, though substantial, rejection of Catholic sacramentality. Walter Ong notes: "The real, deeply felt, but little understood difficulties of separatists were and are not with [the authority of Fatherhood], but with the mitigated, mediated authority, the symbol of which must be feminine..."[11] These difficulties led the Reformers to reject (1) Church teachings as regards the importance of the Virgin Mary, (2) the Church as female, that is to say, as sacramental and mediational, and (3) human sexuality as sacramental, i.e., marriage as a sacrament. Ong points out: "Almost every characteristic tenet of separatist bodies can be charted in terms of the impulse to insulate religion from the femininely polarized aspects of reality."[12]

Modern Western philosophy, as Karl Stern's **The Flight from Woman** amply illustrates, constitutes a similar rejection of the female. The foundation of this flight is Descartes' methodological doubt, from which contemporary philosophy has been unable to free itself and which feminist theology has made its own under the rubric of hermeneutical suspicion. The Cartesian doubt was and continues to be a flight from materiality.

> For to all of us, the core and meaning of reality was at one time, before all cogitation, the certainty of carnal presence. Descartes, the adult and philosopher, postulates to "doubt sensible things because they have deceived us"... The certainty of the flesh which is the foundation of all

Such doubt renders meaningless the Incarnation and all that proceeds from it. Stern points out, and this should come as no surprise to us today: "This wave of the Cartesian tide has left its stain everywhere, even on Christianity — as we witness in certain trends of present-day theology."[14]

American history is, as Herbert Richardson points out, "an effort to 'spiritualize' all of reality."[15]   Richardson, himself a Protestant, applauds this effort. Indeed, his study on American sexuality, **Nun, Witch, Playmate: The Americanization of Sex**, in which he makes the above observation, is an attempt to demonstrate that human consciousness has throughout history moved from an original carnal and biological notion of human sexuality to a progressively spiritualized notion.

This spiritualized view, of course, insists that we see ourselves as "persons" in abstraction from our maleness and femaleness, and relies heavily upon abortion and artificial methods of birth control as the means by which heterosexual relationships achieve their spiritualization. Homosexual relationships, of course, no longer constitute a moral problem, inasmuch as our concern is with persons, not with males and females *per se.* Indeed, one might even argue that homosexual relationships lend themselves more readily to this spiritualizing process, since they require no mediating contraceptive devices to achieve it.

This is the atmosphere in which we live today. And if it has any lesson to teach Catholic women, it is that the feminists are quite wrong in supposing male chauvinism to be our primary enemy. Male chauvinism, in fact, never was the enemy, but only a symptom of the real villain in the piece. For the real villain is today, as it always has been, the uncriticized assumption that only spiritual realities matter (pun intended). No other idea is or ever has been as powerfully entrenched in human thought as is this one. It will not be dislodged easily.

The Catholic Church today stands embattled as she has never been embattled before, because the Catholic Church alone among all religions, systems of thought and institutions in the modern world, has the faith, the reason, the will and the resources to wage and win the war against this false spiritualization of the humanity which the Trinitarian God created in His image male and female, whose salvation the Son undertook by becoming flesh, who continues to be present among us in both his Eucharistic Body and his Mystical Body, whose union with that Mystical Body is the "one flesh" union of groom and bride anticipated in Genesis, and whose resurrection and ascension, together with His Mother's assumption, anticipates and realizes the desire of all creation for salvation in a new heaven and a new earth.

Women even more than men have a stake in this war and its outcome, because women, even more than men, have a stake in the material, the biological and the carnal and all of the values with which God endowed them before standing back and calling His creation, His very material creation, good.

By the year 2000, it should be obvious to most, if not all, women in the Church that, in the final analysis, we cannot free ourselves from the biological without simultaneously ridding ourselves of the sacramental. It should by then be obvious that to choose to be Catholic is to choose to be female, because only the Catholic Church, by affirming the value of the material and the sacramental, is in a position to affirm the value of all that is most explicitly and properly identified with the female. Indeed, the way things seem to be shaping up now, to be Catholic may well be the only way open to us to be female as we enter the third millenium of our faith.

NOTES

[1] *God Is Not Elected.* Host: Maria Schriver. NBC News Special. KPRC, Houston. 8/25/87.

[2] Walker Percy, **The Thanatos Syndrome** (New York: Farrar, Straus & Giroux, 1987).

[3] **Ibid.**, p. 357.

[4] **Ibid.**, p. 358.

[5] **Ibid.**, p. 257.

[6] Indeed, one might well argue that, for women in the Church, the choice for life and the choice to be female are simply two sides of the same coin, given the fact that Eve is the "mother of all living" (Gen. 3:20) and Mary, as the Mother of God, is mother of all who enter into the new life made available to us in Christ her Son.

[7] Rosemary Ruether, "The Roman Catholic Story," in Rosemary Ruether and Eleanor McLaughlin (eds), **Women of Spirit** (New York: Simon & Schuster, 1979), p. 380.

[8] Jeffner Allen, "Motherhood: The Annihilation of Women," in Marilyn Pearsall (ed), **Women and Values** (Belmont, CA: Wadworth Publishing Company, 1986), p. 92.

[9] Karl Stern, **The Flight from Woman** (New York: Farrar, Straus & Giroux, The Noonday Press, 1965), p. 23.

[10] Rosemary Radford Ruether, **Sexism and God-Talk** (Boston: Beacon Press, 1983), pp. 206-207.

[11] Walter J. Ong, **In the Human Grain** (New York: The Macmillan Company; London: Collier-Macmillan Ltd., 1967), p. 190.

[12] **Ibid.**, p. 192.

[13] Stern, **The Flight from Woman**, p. 100.

[14] **Ibid.**, p. 104.

[15] Herbert Richardson, **Nun, Witch, Playmate: The Americanization of Sex** (New York/ Evanston/San Francisco/London: Harper & Row, 1971), p. x.

PART FOUR:
The Church, Science and the Arts

The Church's Message to Artists and Scientists
by
B. M. Ashley, O.P.

Recently I revisited the remarkable Rothko Chapel in Houston, a part of the complex centered on the recently opened Menil Museum. When this chapel was first opened by its distinguished Catholic donors John and Dominique de Menil, I happened to be there when the paintings by Mark Rothko were actually being uncrated and installed. I also celebrated what I believe was the first Catholic liturgy in that ecumenical chapel. Seeing it some sixteen years later I was deeply moved to find that (whether it was the effect of changed lighting or some change in the paint itself or in myself) these almost entirely black panels had begun to glow with a hidden radiance to which I was before blind.

For me that chapel expresses the spiritual question of our age, no longer modern but "post-modern." Rothko was an artist of deep spiritual sensibility who soon after he completed this work died a violent death, probably but not certainly at his own hands, trapped in the toils of the frauds and exploitations of the art market — in any case a victim of our times which rewards some artists extravagantly in money yet isolates them in a spiritual void. A Jew uprooted from heritage, Rothko was inspired in this final work by a visit to the remarkable Byzantine Christian chapel of Torticello on a Venetian islet.[1] He wanted to do some thing analogous for our times, on the theme, some say, of the Passion of Christ, ranging from Salvation to Damnation.[2]

The result is utterly puzzling to many visitors. In a simple octagonal brick building hang fourteen large rectangular panels which appear at first sight to be monochrome black: four single panels on the diagonals of the octagon, one on the entrance wall, and three triptychs on the east, west, and north walls. Gradually, one sees that on some panels the black is set against a very dim red, and that a red or violet wash suffuses the black. As the light changes others atmospheric tones glow in the void.[3]

What is its "meaning?" Although many painters resent such questions, Rothko is quoted as saying, "I'm not interested in relations of color or form ... I'm not an abstractionist," and as declaring that he wanted to express "basic human emotions — tragedy, ecstasy, doom ... The people who weep before my pictures are having the same religious experience I had when I painted them. And if you, as you say, are moved by their color relationships, then you miss the point."[4]

Rothko was faced with the fact that "modernism" was an expression of what we can reasonably call "secular humanism," the religion of Man created by the Enlightenment in opposition to a Christianity which seemed to be destroying itself by fratricidal wars. Yet this anti-Christian humanism had a positive content that we find in the neo-classical, realistic, and impressionistic art of the nineteenth century in its glorification of a purely human, empirical, anti-metaphysical world and in the so-called revolutionary expressionist and abstractionist cult of pure creativity. But post-modernism can no longer trust in the human future and is left with an empty aspiration for transcendence. Harold Rosenberg said: "Thus having cancelled or submerged tradition, in modern [read "post-modern"] art the new has reached the point of cancelling itself."[5] Similarly, Michelangelo Antoniani said to Rothko: "We have much in common. I film nothing and you paint nothing."[6]

Because all the images of the past, including the images of modernity, seem to have undergone a total *kenosis* of meaning, an artist like Rothko, deeply religious by temperament, knew that in our pluralistic post-modern times an ecumenical chapel could only be a place for meditation in a silence which would be receptive of every word, human or divine, because it had no message to convey, but only the question.

II

Vatican II spoke for the Christian Church of this post-modern silence as follows:

> Although we must be careful to distinguish earthly progress clearly from the increase of the kingdom of Christ, such progress is of vital concern to the kingdom of God, insofar as it can contribute to a better ordering of human society. When we have spread on earth the fruits of our nature and our enterprise — human dignity, brotherly communion, and freedom — according to the command of the Lord and in his Spirit, we will find them once again, cleansed this time from the stain of sin, illuminated and transfigured, when Christ presents to his Father an eternal and universal kingdom "of truth and life, a kingdom of holiness and grace, a kingdom of justice, love and peace." Here on earth the kingdom is present in mystery; when the Lord comes it will enter into its perfection (**Gaudium et Spes**, n.39).

Vatican II set for Catholic scholars the hard job of trying to discern what in our modern culture is the result of human cooperation with the Creator and therefore to be cultivated for the future, and what is the result of human sin and therefore to be pruned if the future is to be fruitful. This job cannot be executed in a spirit of mere conservatism, as if the *status quo* were simply God's work; nor in a spirit of mere progressivism, as if real progress is guaranteed by following the trends of the time; but only in the spirit of a good physician who looks not only for the symptoms of a patient's disease but also for his "vital signs" that promise a possible recovery if supported by the healing art. I want to speak to you chiefly of what seem to me "vital signs" in the arts and sciences of our time. Hence I must first attempt to diagnose its illness.

What do literary and art critics mean when they speak of "post-modernism?" By "modernism" they mean the movement of radical experimentation that began at the end of the Victorian-Edwardian era with World War I, typified in literature by James Joyce and Ezra Pound, in the plastic arts by Picasso and Henry Moore, in architecture by Frank Lloyd Wright and Ludwig Mies van der Rohe, in music by Stravinski and Schoenberg. It declared itself free of all historic forms and styles and accepted the pluralism and individualism of the twentieth century.

Yet post-modernism, which began with World War II, expresses disillusionment with this whole enterprise. It tends to see these experiments, brilliant as they were, as ultimately dead-ends. Consequently, post-modernism accepts the conclusion of Martin Heidegger that the great human effort to control the world by human science and technology has worked itself out as it was fated to do, and that we must now recover the "Being" we have forgotten, that is, the sense of the transcendent All of which we are a part, by a radical new way of thinking, perhaps by the mysticism of the East.

In the sciences in our century there has been a different development which we might at first suppose is a story of continuous progress. Certainly from the fundamental discoveries of Einstein at the beginning of this century there has been a steady and unprecedented advance in all the natural and life sciences and in their technological application. We seem close to a unified field theory of all basic natural forces and a grasp of molecular biology which will explain all life and its evolution. Cosmology has opened up an astonishing new vision of the universe, perhaps of many parallel universes, each expanding like bubbles from a Big-Bang into nothing, or disappearing down black-holes.[7] Meanwhile our technological control of the world advances ever more rapidly. Yet even in the sciences there is a sceptical post-modernistic mood for two reasons. The most obvious reason is that we have become aware our technology may destroy our environment and ourselves unless it is politically and morally controlled. A deeper reason is that the more our scientific theories are perfected the more they seem to show us a world without any purpose or human meaning, a world that can be described mathematically, but whose reality and value slips away from all elucidation. Consequently, scientists, like artists, continue to go about their business, but with the haunting anxiety that all their efforts merely enhance the cosmic absurdity.

What light does theology cast on this historical situation?[8] If we view history in terms of the relation of culture to Christ, we see that our intellectual dilemma did not begin with the modernism of our twentieth century, but with the Enlightenment in the eighteenth. The religious wars between Christians disillusioned most of the intelligentsia of Europe and the Americas with Christianity. At the same time modern science and its technology, which Christians had begun to develop in the seventeenth century, appeared to these disillusioned intellectuals to provide an alternative to Christianity. There could be, in Kant and Hume's terms, a religion of reason (i.e., science) and morality without revelation, i.e. without Christianity. This new religion of humanity rather than God, went through a deistic phase and then an agnostic one, which finally produced Marxist atheism. As Christianity was faced with Islam in the seventh century, Christianity has been faced with secular humanism since the eighteenth — a force which now dominates all Western culture.

The term "secular humanism" is being given a bad odor by the fundamentalists, who in fact are much more influenced by it than they imagine, as witness their glorification of our deistic Founding Fathers. However, they are not mistaken in thinking it is the rival of Christianity in our times.[9]

From the outset humanism was internally polarized. The scientific ideal, as its philosophers understood science, required science to be value free. From where then could come a system of human values without which human life is impossible? The answer was found in Romanticism, the other pole to Scientism. Romanticism says that human values are essentially esthetic, a matter of sensibility, feeling, taste, and, therefore, without objective standards. Values are created by human beings, and often come down to, as it was said by G. E. Moore, the guru of the Bloomsbury crowd who typifies modernism, "esthetic value and friendship."[10] The doctrine of "human rights" as put forward by most writers today, free of any basis in natural law, amounts simply to "a sense of decency" and crumbles in the face of issues like abortion.

Thus the root of the moral problem of our culture is the notion of science as "value free." Certainly if this simply means "objective," i.e., free from prejudice, the notion has validity. All thinking ought to be objective. But "value free" here means an interpretation of science which requires the elimination of all teleology from nature. If nature is not teleological, there can be no natural moral law, no human purpose or value in nature, including our own human nature which our reason and will must respect.

Moreover, art also must cease to be an "imitation" of nature in the Aristotelian sense, because nature is in the eye of the beholder. It is not a discovery by the artist, but a pure creation, a projection of the artist's own expressive power. Thus the development of modern art toward abstractionism, and of literature toward a realism that is simple reportage of human absurdity, and of formal experiments which make the means more important than the end become perfectly intelligible. The only subject of art becomes art itself. Its meaning is deconstructed so as to be exposed as arbitrary.

I have said theology casts light on our post-modern dilemma, but let me also note that theology itself seems to be suffering from the same dilemma. Many theologians today believe their proper task is to revise classical theology by taking "the turn to the subject" with modern philosophy so that the objective truths of the Gospel become "hermeneutically transformed" into "religious experience" transcendent to empirical reality.[11] Thus theology is being romanticized, estheticized and further separated from the world with which science deals and which technology manipulates.

But has not the marvelous progress of modern science and technology proved that this "value free" objectivity to be the only way to get ahead in science, whatever the cost? And has not the remarkable emancipation of artistic and literary creativity in our century, including the burst of original thought in theology, demonstrated the same for the subjective pole of our culture?

III

What then is sound in modern culture? My answer would be that it is science and the technological power it gives us, but only if science is freed of the false philosophical interpretation given it by humanism, chiefly by Immanuel Kant. **Gaudium et Spes** was the first conciliar document to recognize (although Pius XII had already done so in a less solemn way) that science is the work of the Holy Spirit, not of the devil. God calls us to understand and marvel at his creation, and to use this knowledge to guard and cultivate our garden earth. The great mistake of Christians of the eighteenth century was to permit the humanists and then the Marxists to take science away from the Church which had laid its basis in the Middle Ages and fostered its modern development in the seventeenth century.

But this science, like every human endeavour in our fallen world, must be redeemed. By redeeming science we redeem creation. We must restore teleology to scientific explanation and thus recover the sense of "nature," i.e., that God has made things to act not simply mechanically (although they use mechanisms) but for intrinsic built-in goals. This does not introduce into science some occult cause, because teleology is not an efficient cause. It merely means to quit ignoring the observable fact that natural causes work in a directed way. Teleology got excluded from science first by mathematicism and then by Kantian philosophy. This exclusion played into the hands of humanism which from the time of deism came to a view of the world as a blank check leaving man totally free to write in his own values.

Once we have rethought the scientific picture of the world and have shown that nature has a purpose; that the world is not ultimately self-explanatory and therefore requires a Creator; and that we as humans are the culmination of the evolutionary process but not ourselves completely explicable by evolution, the whole ground is cut out from under humanism. Then human culture, including its arts, will be revitalized, because it can draw from the infinite meaningfulness of nature and can be open to the mystery of God, serving as a liturgy in His praise and no longer as a dumb idol.

With this restoration of the central idea of nature and a nature open to God, we can begin to reassimilate all the elements of Christianity that humanism and Marxism have taken from us. Vatican II has taught us that no Christian strategy is so mistaken as to attribute everything outside the Christian fold to the devil. It is true, as St. John says (1 Jn. 2:16), that all that is in the world and is not of Christ is of the evil one; but the "world" has never been deserted by God, the Holy Spirit has always been at work in it, to redeem it. Consequently, Vatican II taught that the best way to approach other religions is not by pointing out their errors in order to enhance Christian claims, but to point out what is of God in them. We must do the same with humanism and Marxism. If we make clear enough what is good in them, it will become evident this good has only been corrupted by what is evil and can regain its pristine splendor only within the light of the Gospel.

We need to acknowledge that the reason other religions have emerged is because believers in the true religion have failed its own principles. To punish and correct us, God has shared the gifts we have abused with those of other faiths, so as to shame us. Therefore, we should see the rise of humanism and Marxism as punishments on the Church for its failure fully to appreciate human dignity and the gifts of science and technology given us by God. Therefore, as we were humiliated by Islam's great missionary spirit, which Christians neglected because of their internal squabbles; and as Catholics were humiliated by the Protestant zeal for the Scriptures which we also neglected; so now we are being punished by seeing what humanism has done with science and for human rights, which we failed to do. Our conversion must inspire us to recapture these treasures for Christ.

The first step, I have been arguing, is a better philosophy of science. Many of our best philosophers since Marechal, such as Lonergan and the Transcendental Thomists have accepted the Cartesian and Kantian turn to the subject as the necessary starting point of understanding the modern world in a critical way, and have tried to show that there were roots of this in St. Thomas. Our leading theologians such as Rahner and Schillebeeckx have accepted this.[12] They were not mistaken in seeing that Kant is the key figure, but I believe they made the grave mistake of simply accepting his interpretation of science which empties it of all ontological meaning. Until we have corrected that misstep we will continue to run into a blank wall in our efforts at a true theological *aggiornamento.*

In this respect Teilhard de Chardin and the followers of Alfred North Whitehead have been closer to the right road, but in both cases they made the serious and gratuitous mistake of introducing teleology into science by way of panpsychism.

Once we have set science back on the teleological track where it first took off and the cosmos has ceased to appear empty of meaning, as a *second* step we can safely acknowledge many of the insights made by Romantic, idealistic philosophy. It is true that Thomism gave very little attention to human historicity and subjectivity. We have become aware by the dialectic between value-free scientism and the romantic exploration of subjectivity how conditioned every human vision of reality is by the culture, experience, pre-understandings, and special interests of the knower. Consequently, we no longer believe as Aquinas that most people who disagree with our faith are in bad faith.[13] It becomes possible for orthodox Catholics to accept doctrinal development, the modern notion of Biblical inspiration, and epistemological pluralism, without losing a firm grounding in transcultural and trans-plural objectivity. Thus the way to true dialogue about our most profound convictions is no longer blocked by our failure to acknowledge the limits of our perspective. It is as if through Vatican II we have heard the Lord's voice saying: "I have left an open door before you which no one can close." (Rv. 3:8)

As a third step, the field of the arts can once again be closely related to the sciences and to ethics. They need no longer be expressions of merely private worlds. This does not imply that the artist will be restricted to a photographic realism which would only express that exaggerated objectivity to which science has condemned itself. Instead, artists will find their inspiration in the inner dynamic natures of creatures as these resonate empathetically with human experience, and they will express these by all the variety of formal techniques employed by modern art. Yet because they will no longer see the natural world as alien to humanity but as revelatory of God's purposes for the whole cosmic community, they will once again be able to find a public language understood by more than an elite. Architecture will be revitalized by its contact with natural forms and the environment. Literature too will no longer be limited to descriptive realism, but will be free to uncover universal ethical values, not by preaching, but by insight into the meaning inherent even in the tragedies and absurdities of human life.

Yet Vatican II warns us that the earthly kingdom which we build contains the Kingdom of Christ only "in mystery' and, until he comes to transform it, it will always remain ambiguous. Consequently, science always will be capable of atheistic misinterpretation, technology of polluting abuse, art of idolatry, literature of lying and pimping. These risks, however, cannot hold back the Catholic from entering into the world and contributing to its life. We need to ask why Catholics have so often lacked creativity in the sciences and the arts, or when they have achieved it have done so only at a sacrifice of the purity of their faith.

I think we must acknowledge that fidelity to the Gospel will continue to raise certain obstacles for gifted Catholics who strive to fully realize their scientific and artistic potentialities. As the world creatively rushes toward destruction, Christians remain somewhat peripheral to its main currents. If they were to plunge fully into the stream, they would be lost. Catholic writers, for example, cannot be a part of that sinful world which makes such vivid material for a secularist writer. The result is that Christian creations are often tame and tasteless, lacking the serpentine subtlety and bite of worldly authors. But we should not be ashamed to let the world do what it can, since it has no future.

I would therefore hope that Catholic scholars who wish to be faithful to Christ by fidelity to his Church will not waste their time in nostalgia for the past, nor in bitter denunciations of the errors of the present, but will turn their energies to carrying out the work of Vatican II in a positve way. They will occupy themselves with an analysis of our culture to find in it what is good and true and then will bend every effort to assimilate this to the perennial light of the Gospel which can transform it. This requires a critique both of our culture and of the traditional cultural forms of Christianity, a critique which will enable the Gospel to stand out in its full radiance.

I would particularly point out that the great tensions which are now felt by many between the Vatican Congregations and scholars is not so much the result of a resistance of the Congregation to theological or cultural advance as it is the misunderstanding by scholars of the respective roles of shepherd and scribe. There is a serious ambiguity in some theologians' self-understanding. On the one hand, they claim for themselves the right to be creative, i.e., to criticize old solutions and propose new ones, which is a part of the modern academic notion of what scholarship is all about, and, on the other, they retain the old-fashioned notion that theologians share the ecclesial magisterium of the hierarchy and can therefore serve as a safe guide for the faith and praxis of the laity.[14] That obsolete conception was based on the premise that all theologians are missioned by the Church and are under direct control of the hierarchy. We cannot have it both ways. We must establish clearly in the Church the understanding that the contribution of theologians to the Christian community (unless they accept a mission from the Church and with it an obligation to conform to official teaching) is not direct pastoral leadership but scholarship in the modern sense of exploration without claim to be a direct guide to faith or conscience.

I am optimistic such a more clear cut delineation of the respective roles of bishop and theologian will be worked out. What is more fundamental, however, is that theologians and Catholic scholars in general come to see that in the coming century the task will not be to modernize the faith, which already prophesies the final outcome of history, but to assimilate to the faith all the scattered riches of the Spirit, including those of science and art, both for the clear manifestation of what is implicit in the faith and for the transformation of the culture. In a pluralistic global society this means a spirit of genuine ecumenism in its broadest conception.

John XXIII mocked "the prophets of gloom and doom" when he called for Vatican II. Many today wonder whether they may have been right and the saintly pope wrong. I am convinced, however, that his was the authentic Christian spirit of hope. The upheavals in the Church produced by the Council simply reveal that the Church was not as healthy as it seemed. Every act of God is life-giving, but it also involves a judgment of those who resist it or misread it. Our task is to seek to understand the message of the Council in its deepest and authentic significance and then to help the Church and the world to understand that meaning and how it can be radically implemented in the opportunities of our times. We should not waste our energies in nostalgia, condemnation, or discouragment, but should employ them in doing well what we believe others are doing badly. What is more useful: a good critique of a bad book or a good book on the same subject?

NOTES

[1] For a biography see Leo Seldes, **The Legacy of Mark Rothko** (New York: Rinehart and Winston, 1978); for artistic appreciation Diane Waldman, **Mark Rothko, 1903-1970: A Retrospective** (New York: Harry N. Abrams, Inc. in collaboration with The Solomon R. Guggenheim Foundation, 1978).

[2] Waldman, p. 68; Seldes, p. 63 f.

[3] For an esthetic analysis of the paintings see Sheldon Nodelman, **Marden, Novros, Rothko: Painting in the Age of Actuality** (Seattle: University of Washington Press for the Institute for the Arts, Rice University, Houston, 1978). Also Dore Ashton, **About Rothko** (New York: Oxford, 1983), pp. 168-185.

[4] Waldman, p. 58. Rothko especially loved the works of Fra Angelico, p. 59.

[5] Quoted in the introduction by Dore Ashton to Bonnie Clearwater, **Mark Rothko Works on Paper** (New York: Hudson Hills Press, 1984), p. 59.

[6] Seldes, p. 64.

[7] See Heinz R. Pagels, **The Cosmic Code: Quantum Physics as the Language of Nature** (New York: Simon and Schuster, 1982) and the remarkable Gifford Lectures of Sir John C. Eccles, **The Human Mystery** (New York: Springer International, 1979) for the current scientific picture.

[8] What follows presents a historical hypothesis argued at more length in my **Theologies of the Body: Humanist and Christian** (Braintree, MA: Pope John Center, 1985).

[9] Martin Marty has argued that what the Fundamentalists call "secular humanism" is really nothing more than the *pluralism* of American society which must remain neutral to religious differences. I think this neglects the basic *uniformity* of the ethical outlook which dominates our education and the public media and from which it is socially risky to dissent publicly.

[10] Moore's ethical views have been very influential. Yet they were for him very tentative. See the discussion by Frederick Copleston, **A History of Philosophy** (New York: Doubleday-Image Books, 1967) vo. 8, Pt. II, pp. 168-174.

[11] The Kantian element in Transcendental Thomism is the effort to find an *a priori* element in knowledge, but this negates Aquinas' thorough anti-Platonism, the very basis of his originality as a theologian.

[12] David Tracy, **Blessed Rage for Order** (New York: Seabury, 1975) and **The Analogical Imagination** (New York: Crossroads, 1981) and Francis Schuessler Fiorenza, **Foundational Theology** (New York: Crossroad, 1984) survey these trends in theology.

[13] Aquinas, S. T., II-II, q.11, a.3, defends the death penalty for obstinate heretics, although elsewhere he says that the soldiers who crucified Christ were probably innocent of sin because they supposed they were executing a criminal.

[14] Reference is frequently made to Yves Congar's study of the use of the term *magisterium* in which he showed that in the medieval period it included university theologians, but it should be noted that these professors were subject to episcopal and papal censure, and their custom of condemning positions as heretical (e.g., the condemnations of Luther) is hardly one to be revived in our day.

Four Developments in Modern Physics That Subvert Scientific Materialism

by

Stephen M. Barr

I. INTRODUCTION

For more than three centuries the advance of scientific knowledge has had a prejudicial effect on religious belief. I believe that this situation is changing, or *can* change if the opportunities that present themselves are seized and exploited. The dominant philosophical world view among most physical scientists (in my experience) is "scientific materialism." What I mean by that term is a system of belief characterized by three denials: a denial of purpose or design in nature; a denial of the centrality of man in nature; and a denial that non-physical realities can exist (such as God or the human spirit). In other words, this philosophy is both materialistic and mechanistic. There exists also a strong positivist bias. The proposition that God exists is regarded as impossible to prove or disprove and hence "operationally" meaningless. Religious belief is thought to have no rational ground and hence understood in fideistic terms. Usually these views come together with various prejudices about religion and its historical role, and about the Church in particular, which is seen as obscurantist, intolerant, and superstitious. This whole complex of hostile attitudes cannot be overcome easily. (Indeed it is too much to expect that it will ever be overcome for more than a minority of scientists.) However, the theme of this conference is the 21st century, and I am hopeful that by that time a lot of intellectual (if not sociological) ground can be recaptured.

Why am I hopeful? The reason is that modern physics itself has uncovered various aspects of nature that are in their implications subversive of scientific materialism. I will attempt to explain the substance and significance of four of these developments in this talk.

The body of this talk is, I hope, self-contained. However, I have left the greater part of the detailed explanations and argumentation to a series of appendices.

II. THE BIG BANG THEORY

It is now believed by scientists on the basis of numerous pieces of strong and convincing evidence that the universe began about 10 to 15 billion years ago. There is no question that the big bang theory strongly discomfited many atheists. This was manifested in various ways. In some quarters there was a prolonged and somewhat irrational attachment to a theory called the steady state theory, according to which the universe was infinitely old, even when the experimental and theoretical indications were heavily on the side of the big bang theory (though before conclusive verification of it). After the fact of a big bang was essentially confirmed, the idea became popular that this explosion was but the expansive phase of an endlessly "bouncing" universe — again one of infinite age. This notion became popular in spite of the facts that *no* evidence, either theoretical or experimental, existed to support it, and that there were several strong arguments against it. In the first place, such a bouncing universe would require a "closed" rather than an open universe, while the (admittedly preliminary) observational evidence suggests an open universe. (Though in recent years purely theoretical arguments have made a closed universe more likely.) Secondly, no plausible mechanism for such bouncing has been advanced. And, thirdly, even if the universe were bouncing, it is probable that entropy would increase from one bounce to the next. This would imply a finite number of past bounces (probably) and hence a universe of finite age. It is clear from this persistent and obviously strong "theoretical prejudice" that many atheistic scientists feel that a temporal beginning to the universe somehow threatens their cherished beliefs. Why is this?

Let me make very clear at the outset that it is naive to suppose that the question of the existence of a Creator logically hinges upon whether the age of the universe is finite or infinite. The proofs of God's existence would be no less compelling were the age of the universe infinite, as St. Thomas understood quite clearly.[1] And, conversely, if God's existence could be rationally denied in the case of an infinitely old universe, so could it be with equal consistency in the case of a universe of finite age. Nonetheless, the materialists are right to be discomfited.

The point is that philosophical positions are rarely maintained for strictly logical reasons, but also from a sense of the way things are, the way the world works, what is true to life, or what is fitting. Almost a poetic sense is involved. For example, it was easier to believe that man was central to a divine plan when it was also believed that he dwelled at the geometrical center of the world. Now that man is banished to the periphery of the solar system, i.e., the periphery of a galaxy lost in the inconceivable vastness of the universe, it is easy to fall into thinking that he is insignificant in the cosmic scheme. Logically this does not follow, but psychologically it often does.

Just so, the fact that the universe made a dramatic, sudden and explosive "appearance" out of nothing about 15 billion years ago adds nothing to the logical force of the arguments for a Creator. But to the psychological force, it adds a great deal.

In my view the deep significance of the big bang theory is that it strikes at the very root of the scientific materialist's notion of causality and explanation. In essence, what this notion amounts to is the idea that the only meaningful and valid kind of explanation is in terms of physical processes. In particular a set of circumstances is to be explained as the result of a prior set of circumstances evolving according to the laws of physics. In this sense, the "cause" of a situation or event always lies in the past. This has profound implications for arguments for the existence of God as "First Cause" or as "Designer" of the universe. Indeed we believe that this very contracted notion of causality lies at the root of scientific materialism. We explain why this is so in Part I of Appendix A. In Part II of that Appendix, we discuss the relationship between causality and time in the light of the insights of modern physics on the past-future distinction — the so-called "arrow of time." Here I only wish to say that the big bang theory is disconcerting for the scientific materialist since the big bang cannot be explained in terms of its past as it has no past, and, at least classically (i.e., before quantum effects are taken into account), the big bang is a space-time "singularity" to which the laws of physics do not apply. As long as the universe was believed to be infinitely old the scientific materialist could explain anything in particular — though not everything in general. But if there is a beginning to the universe and hence to time, his chain of efficient causality abruptly ends. The materialist comes to the inexplicable initial conditions in terms of which he tried to explain everything else. Of course, even in an infinitely old universe, he does not really have an explanation for the way the world is. This incompleteness in the materialist's scheme of explanation is somewhat subtle and requires some imagination to grasp in the case of the infinitely old universe. But in the universe of finite age it becomes embarrassingly obvious.

III. THE QUEST FOR BEAUTY AND UNITY IN THE LAWS OF NATURE AND THE ARGUMENT FROM DESIGN

The argument from design for the existence of God is ancient. It can be found at least implicitly in both the Old and New Testaments. A very beautiful statement of it was given as follows by the Latin Apologist Minucius Felix writing ca. 235 AD:

> If upon entering some home you saw that everything there was well-tended, neat, and decorative, you would believe that some master was in charge of it, and that he himself was much superior to those good things. So too in the home of this world, when you see providence, order and law in the heavens and on earth, believe there is a Lord and Author of the universe, more beautiful than the stars themselves and the various parts of the whole world.[2]

We have already referred to in passing one of the stumbling blocks of the materialist in accepting this kind of argument, namely his inability to conceive of a cause external to the physical universe. But the progress of science has thrown up other obstacles as well. The first is raised most sharply by evolution and the mechanism of natural selection. Natural selection shows how, in principle at least, a combination of law and chance can cause complicated structures to emerge. Indeed most scientists believe that all of the amazing variety and intricacy of biological forms can be explained in this way.

The general question is whether structure and order can spontaneously emerge from mere chaos and disorder. The example of evolution — and simpler examples such as the growth of crystals — seem to say yes. However, such an answer is superficial. It is not difficult to see that all such supposed instances of the spontaneous emergence of structure and order actually presuppose that it exists at a deeper level. In particular I would argue (see Appendix D) that *all explanations of structure and order at the level of phenomena presuppose it at the level of law.*

A second issue has to do with the various kinds of order and structure. Some are more suggestive of design than others. To illustrate, suppose we detect signals from some distant part of the galaxy. What would we look for in them to decide if they originated from an intelligent source or were merely manifestations of some inanimate physical processes? A totally chaotic or random signal would not suggest intelligence, but neither would certain kinds of regular patterns. Simple periodic pulses have been observed — they come from pulsars — and have been convincingly explained as being generated by rapidly spinning neutron stars, which act much like natural lighthouse beacons. But suppose a signal were detected which was at once very complex and yet highly structured — something like, say, a Bach fugue? Or suppose it could be deciphered and turned out to be a message — perhaps a formalized mathematical proof? Surely all would draw the obvious conclusion that intelligence had been found.

Ultimately, then, the argument from design leads one to ask: Do the laws of nature themselves exhibit structure? And is that structure of the kind that suggests intelligence? If what we argued above is valid, then the first answer must inevitably be yes. Since scientific explanations always derive structure at one level from structure at a deeper level, then obviously the very deepest level of physical law must exhibit structure of some kind. Physicists have made great progress in uncovering the deepest levels of physical law. In fact, many of them believe that they are very near to a unified mathematical theory of all physical phenomena. And what characterizes these theories? A structure that is at once extremely rich and complex and yet exceedingly unified, symmetric, harmonious and beautiful. It is order, but not trivial order. It is complexity, but not chaos. That is just the sort of thing we do ordinarily associate with intelligent design. As physics has developed in the last century the role of symmetry in nature has been increasingly appreciated by researchers until, indeed, the search for better theories has become dominated almost entirely by considerations of symmetry, simplicity and beauty.

IV. THE ANTHROPIC COINCIDENCES AND MAN'S PLACE IN THE COSMOS

One of the consequences of the advance of scientific knowledge that has been most prejudicial to religious belief has been the ascendancy of the notion that man is peripheral and insignificant in the cosmos. The Copernican revolution deposed man from the center of the solar system. The discoveries of modern astronomy have shown that the sun itself is a rather ordinary star among the 100 billion in the Milky Way and, indeed, is on the periphery of that galaxy. Furthermore, over 100 billion galaxies are known to exist (and if the universe is open there may be an infinitude of them). Astronomy has also become aware of the vastness of both the age and size of the universe compared to human scales of time and distance. In biology the Darwinian revolution has had a similar humbling effect. Science in uncovering the hidden workings of nature has revealed an order which seems governed not by a wise and caring "Providence" but by a combination of impersonal laws and blind chance. The universe appears vast, cold and indifferent to human strivings and sufferings. As the Nobel laureate Steven Weinberg wrote in his popular book **The First Three Minutes**:

> It is almost irresistable for humans to believe that we have some special relation to the universe, that human life is not just a farcical outcome of a chain of accidents ... but that we were somehow built in from the beginning .... It is very hard to realize that [the entire earth] is just a tiny part of an overwhelmingly hostile universe. .... The more the universe seems comprehensible, the more it also seems pointless.[3]

Man has looked into the structure of the physical world "seeking for a sign" of a Providence that cares or a Purpose somehow related to human purposes. But no Sign has been given to him but the sign of the prophet Jonah. However, this situation too has changed.

In recent decades physicists and cosmologists have become increasingly interested in what have become known as "anthropic coincidences."[4] These coincidences have been uncovered by asking how, if the *laws* of nature (not the phenomena) had been slightly different, the world would have been changed. If this fundamental constant or that qualitative feature of nature's laws were slightly modified, would intelligent life have been possible and would evolution have been able to occur? The answer seems to be no. There are numerous examples where the actual structure of physical law as uncovered by scientific investigation and the requirements of a universe where life, especially intelligent life, can evolve seem to coincide. That is why these are called anthropic "coincidences." (See Appendix C for examples of such anthropic coincidences.) The key point is that it does at least *seem*, in the words of Weinberg, that "we were somehow built in from the beginning."

What attitudes can one take toward these coincidences? First, one can try to explain them scientifically. All such attempts involve one or another form of what is called the "anthropic principle." We believe that while some may be explicable in this way, such explanations can never fully succeed. (This is discussed in Appendix D, Section II, C.) Secondly, one may argue that the laws of physics must be as they are in every particular for reasons of self-consistency or because some underlying unifying principle requires it. In that case one cannot do the "gedanken experiment" of adjusting the laws of nature in this or that detail. There is some sense in this objection since, within the framework of particular schemes of "unification," there is often no freedom to contemplate small changes in the theory, which is completely constrained. However, one can contemplate theories that are based on different schemes of unification or that are not "unified" at all. Unless one is prepared to argue (as some are — see Appendix D, Section II, B) that the laws of nature are absolutely necessary and unique, the anthropic coincidences cannot be disposed of thus. Thirdly, one may simply shrug them off as being indeed nothing but coincidences. This possibility is always open. Evidence for anything can always be dismissed as circumstantial by those indisposed to believe it. Finally, one can regard these coincidences as being simply what they appear to be: evidences of design.

The mistake most natural theologians made in the past was to look in the wrong place, i.e., at the level of phenomena rather than at the level of law. Why, in retrospect, would one necessarily have expected that man, if he were central to the order of the cosmos at the level of purpose or value, would also be central to it geometrically? What does it really matter where he is, or how big or small, or whether he is round or square? If we want to know whether we were "built in" from the beginning, we should look at how the universe *is* built — at its *laws*. Looking at those laws — as we are in a better position to do than those living in the past — we find that the dethronement of man was an act of revolutionary folly, an act far removed from the letter, the spirit and the purpose of the Law.

As we noted, one of the dramatic facts of science that has helped to destroy the notion that man is important in the design of nature is his smallness in comparison to the cosmos. However, even this can be understood in a different, "anthropic" way. According to general relativity, the great size of the universe is necessary for its great longevity. A universe whose maximum extent were, say, the diameter of the solar system would last but a few hours before it collapsed upon itself gravitationally. But if the evolution of stars and planets and eventually life was to occur (processes requiring billions of years), a universe whose maximum extent is at least billions of light years is required. Pascal wrote: "... the eternal silence of these infinite spaces frightens me."[5] We see that, if looked at aright, even those infinite spaces and that eternal silence may point to man!

V. THE IMPLICATIONS OF QUANTUM THEORY

It would be impossible even with much more time and space to do justice to this subject. I will try to give only a summary account, with more details in Appendix E. The philosophical issues that arise from quantum mechanics flow from two aspects of it. First, it is inherently probabilistic. The basic mathematical description of physical systems is in terms of something called the "wavefunction." Wavefunctions tell us probabilities. Secondly, in the traditional understanding of quantum mechanics [as opposed to the so-called Many Worlds Interpretation, see Appendix E], when an "observer" makes a measurement on a "system," the corresponding wavefunction undergoes a sudden and discontinuous change or "collapse" which cannot be analyzed physically within the framework of quantum theory.

Many people who understand and accept the traditional understanding of quantum theory and have thought it through have come to certain conclusions. These may appear to be highly controversial. But they can only be avoided by abandoning quantum mechanics (which indeed might someday become necessary) or embracing the Many Worlds Interpretation of quantum mechanics, which is just as controversial. What are these conclusions? First, the "observer" plays a central role in quantum mechanics. In the traditional understanding there is a radical dichotomy between the "observer" and the "system"; they have a completely different status in the theory. This dichotomy corresponds (in philosophical terms) to the dichotomy between the subject and object of knowledge. Secondly, the wavefunction must be regarded as representing not the system itself but the observer's state of knowledge of it, because the theory is essentially probabilistic. Probabilities are used when there is incomplete knowledge. Thus, knowledge, and someone who knows (the "observer") must enter the theory at a fundamental level. Moreover, it is when a measurement is completed — when the observer knows the result — that the wavefunction collapses. This makes perfect sense if the wavefunction represents his state of knowledge; for when his state of knowledge changes then logically so must the wavefunction. There are other viewpoints but they lead to absurdities (such as solipsism) or paradoxes (such as the "Wigner's friend paradox"). Thirdly, the process (if we can call it that) by which the wavefunction collapses — and hence by which the observer's knowledge increases — is not subject to physical description within the framework of quantum theory.

If one accepts the foregoing, a picture quite inconsistent with simple materialism emerges. Materialism is monistic; quantum mechanics is not. Materialism reduces *all* mental operations to physical processes. There is no question that much of what we call thinking can be completely understood in physical or cybernetic terms. A human brain certainly performs many operations (such as processing, storage and retrieval of information; motor control; computation; as well as other functions, including many associated with cognition) that are purely mechanical in the sense of reducible to the operations of a physical system. However, quantum mechanics, as understood by some at least, will not allow us to say that the act of knowing is completely mechanical. Ultimately, the "I" who is the subject of "I know" is not purely physical. And if that is so, there is no reason to deny the same of the "I" in "I will."

VI. CONCLUSION

I have tried to describe four developments in physics that subvert the world-view I have called scientific materialism. Some people believe that one cannot or should not draw philosophical or theological conclusions from science, that these disciplines deal with different subject matters. But historically, people *have* drawn philosophical conclusions from scientific facts, conclusions hostile to religion in general, and to Christianity in particular. In many cases these conclusions are based on outdated science. The old materialist prejudices are simply not justified anymore (if they ever were) by the state of scientific knowledge. Yet they live on.

I believe that this century will be seen as climacteric in the relation between religion and science. Science itself has furnished us with new weapons with which to combat the shallow prejudices of an earlier era.

The time for rearguard actions is past and the time for a counter offensive is at hand. This is one of the most important tasks for the scholars and intellectuals of the Church in the 21st century and in the years remaining in this century. The perspective on the nature of modern science must be appropriated and used as the basis for constructing a more sophisticated and reinvigorated natural theology.

The wheel is coming full circle. Science was born in the Christian West of a belief that the world has an intelligible structure because it is the work of an intelligent Being; a belief that the world which reflects the glory of its Creator is a place of order, beauty and law. Materialism has had its apparent victories. But the enterprise which is science has not and will not in the end betray the sources of its original inspiration.

REFERENCES

[1] St. Thomas Aquinas, **Summa Contra Gentiles**, (Univ. of Notre Dame Press, ed 1975), Bk II, Ch. 38.

[2] Minucius Felix, **Octavius**; English translation in **The Faith of the Early Fathers**, William A. Jurgens, Vol. I, p. 109. (The Liturgical Press: Collegevil e, Minnesota).

[3] Steven Weinberg, **The First Three Minutes**, (William Collins, Glasgow, 1977), p. 148.

[4] See for examples and discussions "The anthropic principle and the structure of the physical world," B. J. Carr, and M. J. Rees, *Nature*, Vol. 278, p. 605 (1979); John D. Barrow and Frank J. Tipler, **The Cosmological Anthropic Principle**, (Oxford Univ. Press, 1986); and P. C. W. Davies, **The Accidental Universe**, (Cambridge Univ. Press, 1980).

[5] Blaise Pascal, **Pensees**, no. 206.

APPENDIX A

TIME AND CAUSALITY

I. The Scientific Materialist's Notion of Causality

One of the classical proofs of the existence of God is the so-called "cosmological argument." According to this argument the universe must have a cause. This argument has little or no force for the scientific materialist because he does not know what a cause is. His notion of causality is so restrictive that the possibility of a first cause is ruled out *a priori,* and, indeed, becomes totally incomprehensible.

To assign a cause for a thing is to explain it, and, corresponding to the variety of ways we have of explaining things, one can speak of a variety of types of causes. Indeed, the medieval schoolmen (following Aristotle) spoke of "efficient," "final," "material," "formal" and even "meritorious" causes. Some of these kinds of causes can even lie in the future of their effects. For example, a student might say he is studying *because* there is an exam tomorrow. Or someone might say that water flows downhill to reach the sea. These kinds of "final" causes are clearly connected with the notion of "purpose."

Since Newton's time, physics has had no essential use for final causes. Historians of science tell us that with the overthrow of Aristotelian physics teleology has been progressively banished from science. The Newtonian physicist could claim that, given complete information about the state of the world at a time (t_1) and knowledge of the laws of physics, he could *in principle* exactly calculate, or predict, the state of the world at a later time (t_2). To make this prediction he need not know anything about what happens *after* t_2. The past completely determines the future. Thus for the physicist the complete and sufficient "explanation" or cause of the present state of things lies in the past state of things, together with the laws of physics. For this reason, it seems an evident principle to most physicists that *a "cause" must precede its "effects" in time.* Indeed, this *is* true of what I would call physical causes. It does not follow, as the scientific materialist believes, that physical causes are the only type of causes, or that this principle need apply to causality in general.

The devastating consequences that this notion of causality must have on religious belief should be clear. There can be no cosmological argument for God's existence. If God is to be the cause of the universe, according to this view, He must precede the universe *in time*. If the universe is infinitely old, this is obviously impossible. What is less obvious but equally true is that even if the universe has a finite age (as appears to be the case), God cannot precede it in time. This can be demonstrated in two ways. In the first place, as modern cosmology and general relativity teach, it makes no sense to refer to a time before the initial moment of the universe — a point brilliantly grasped already in the 5th century by St. Augustine. Secondly, God cannot be located in time any more than in space, since temporal relationships like spatial ones obtain only among things or events in the created world [see Appendix B].

Not only the cosmological argument suffers, but the argument from design and the whole idea of purpose in nature. For the idea of purpose is connected with final causes. Yet final causality is taboo to the scientific materialist.

Central to scientific materialism is this restricted notion of causality. It is my contention, however, that modern physics undermines this faulty notion in two ways. The first way has to do with the notion of the past-future distinction, or, as it is sometimes called, "the arrow of time." This is not completely understood by physics at the present day; however, enough *is* understood to see through certain naive fallacies. In my view, a careful consideration of the physical origin of the arrow of time reveals that the notion of *causal priority* underlies the notion of *temporal priority*, rather than the other way around. This is not in any way to deny the physicist's "principle of causality" as applied to physical cause and effect. But it is to assert that temporal priority forms no part of the definition or *general* notion of cause, but rather derives from it.

II. The "Arrow of Time" and What We Can Learn From It

We have argued that a critical postulate of the scientific materialist's philosophy is that *a cause must always precede its effect in time.* This is not regarded as merely an empirical statement but as an absolute metaphysical principle which would apply to any kind of cause and in any kind of world. It is, then, essential to the idea of cause, and can be used as a criterion for recognizing causes.

For this viewpoint to be correct, *it must always be possible to decide whether A comes "before" B in time, that is, to distinguish "past" and "future" in some absolute sense, without prior reference to causal relationships,* or else we would be involved in a circular definition. We shall see whether this is true.

To distinguish past and future appears to be very easy. Most people think of time as something that has an inherent movement in one direction like a river. Events float along on this river and we can see whether they are upstream or downstream without paying any attention to what they are or how they influence each other. However, to a physicist, these notions are naive. It is true that one can set up time coordinates and locate events in time without much reference to what they are. But the difference between "past" and "future" is not so easy in theory (as distinct from practice). Time itself, from the physicist's point of view, does not "flow" or move. Events, rather, have an ordering in time. The psychological feeling of a motion of time comes from the causal and informational structure of physical processes: we can only get information about or remember the past; we can only affect the future. This, in turn, is the result of the fact that the physical processes by which information is transmitted and stored, decisions formulated, and actions carried out involve something called "thermodynamic irreversibility." The main point is that time in and of itself has no "flow." The space-time manifold itself seems to be quite symmetric between past and future. And the laws of physics appear to be essentially symmetric under "time reversal symmetry." Why then can we not reverse certain processes? Why does water never flow uphill? Why do spilt milk and broken glasses never reassemble themselves? This has to do with the fact that certain *processes* have intrinsic orientations. The apparent "flow" of time has to do with the relative orientations in time of our mental processes and the processes we observe, rather than some intrinsic velocity of time itself. And the orientations of processes are ultimately *causal* orientations. We remember only the past because only events in the past or "information" from those events can cause impressions in our organs of sense and memory. Our activity is future directed because we can only cause events in the future. It is the causal structure of our world that underlies the notion of past and future not the other way around. Cause and effect relationships have to be recognizable if the past and future are to be distinguished. The notion of cause is a part of the definition of past and future.

We explain the confusing in terms of the clear and simple, the apparently unrelated or disordered in terms of the intelligible pattern. This aspect, which causes have that leads us to regard them as explaining their effects, has nothing inherently to do with time. For want of a better word I will call it "coherence" or "orderliness." This concept has an analogue in physics that can be made precise. It is called entropy, or rather "low entropy." Entropy (or "disorder") increases as we go from the physical efficient cause to its effects. This precise physical concept of entropy is only applicable when we are analyzing a physical process *as* a physical process. There are processes which may occur in and through physical mechanisms which we would never analyze in terms of the motions of atoms and fields, as, for example, economic, political or sociological processes. That is why, in identifying causes in a more general context than the purely physical, I would argue that some less easily defined and quantified notion, which has its analogue in physical entropy, is involved. We can consider the same processes from different points of view and give different *kinds* of explanations of the same things.

In our universe, entropy — on the average — is increasing everywhere, and at every time and in all physical systems *in the same direction in time.* This is what gives rise to what is very misleadingly called "the arrow of time." This is why we never see milk unspill, watches unsmash, water flow uphill, or people grow younger. This is why the causal arrows of our cognitive processes are lined up in the same direction as those of the physical processes we observe, and therefore why time seems to "flow." But *why* this is is a profound mystery of physics at present. It seems that in some sense the universe had *very* low entropy initially. This is not at all understood. Thus the future directedness of physical processes in our universe is not somehow a metaphysical necessity; but it may easily appear so because we naturally take it for granted. It has become part of our intuition.

We conclude from all this that causal priority is a more fundamental notion than temporal priority, and really underlies it. It may be helpful to give an example where temporal priority is clearly not involved in the notion of cause. In even the materialist's favorite kind of explanation physical law is invoked. The apple fell on Newton's head *because* he was sitting under it *and because* of the law of gravity. But the law of gravity is not something that can be located in time. It is immanent in the structure of the process. It is indeed a cause of the apple's falling, what would be called in Scholastic philosophy a "formal cause;" and it obviously does not have to precede in time that of which it is the cause.

Cause, then, is "bound up" with time but only for those causes that operate through physical processes. (Even then, causes only precede effects in time if they are efficient causes.) But the notion of God as Cause does not involve the idea that He creates the universe through a physical process. Rather He is to be thought of as an infinite Mind whose creative act occurs not in time but timelessly and eternally.

APPENDIX B

The Augustinian and Scholastic View of Creation and Time

The conception most believers have of the act of Creation is that it was an event in time. Their conception of God's "eternity" is that it is infinite duration in time. God existed for an infinite time "before" the creation of the universe and will continue to exist for an infinite time "after" it comes to an end. From the viewpoint of modern physics, such a conception makes little or no sense. Time, like space, is something physical. Indeed, it cannot be thought of as something apart from space. Spacetime is a set of relations between events in the physical world. It is influenced physically by those events. Spacetime can be curved, can oscillate, and can even carry energy in these oscillations. At the big bang, time began. It is meaningless to discuss time "before" the first moment of the universe, because the first moment of the universe was the first moment of time.

Not only modern physics but also theology has told us many of these things since the time of St. Augustine, who realized that time is an aspect of the created world: "There can be no time without creation."[6] Indeed, he realized that time is itself created: "Or what times could there be, . . . not made by you [God]?"[7] Remarkably he even grasped that there was no time "before" the universe: "You made that very time and no time could pass by before you made those times. But if there was no time before heaven and earth, why do they ask what you did 'then?' There was no 'then,' where there was no time."[8]

Nor can the idea of a God existing for infinite time be maintained theologically. Since space and time are a feature of the universe they do not pertain to God. He cannot be localized in time anymore than in space. He is extended neither in time nor space. Indeed God, as the medieval scholastics emphasized, is utterly "simple," without parts, or extent.[9] There are no real distinctions in God. One cannot distinguish properly one part of God from another, or one act of God from another. One cannot even distinguish God Himself from His acts; there is only one Act of God to which He is Himself identical.[10] God is pure Act.[11] This Act is an eternal act of love, knowledge, will, understanding, and creation. So God is an utterly simple One in Whom there is no change[12] and, therefore, in Whom there is no time.[13] He lives in "the sublimity of an ever-present eternity."[14] Now one *can* say that God causes the many events of the universe to unfold in time, but the causation does not unfold in time, and the cause is not many but one. Just as many things can be grasped in a single act of understanding[15] so many things are created by a single act.[16]

The creative "Word" which God spoke in Genesis is not therefore to be understood as a Word spoken in time, it is a Word which proceeds from Him eternally, timelessly, even though its effects may enjoy among themselves temporal (and spatial) relationships.

God, then, as the Cause of all things, precedes them, indeed, in a causal sense but not in a temporal sense. As St. Augustine said: "It is not in time that you precede time."[17] Moreover, God as Cause does not need to precede the world in time since He does not create the world through some physical process. Rather this creative act is the eternal Act of an infinite Mind. This notion of God may be difficult to grasp, especially for those who are used to conceive of mind in purely materialistic terms. I recommend to those for whom all philosophical writings that predate modern physics are opaque Bernard J. F. Lonergan's **Insight, A Study of Human Understanding**.[18]

APPENDIX C

ANTHROPIC COINCIDENCES

The existence of an "anthropic coincidence" is usually established by a certain kind of contra-factual argument. One contemplates what the universe would be like if some single quantitative or qualitative feature of the laws of nature were different than it is.

An objection to this kind of argument is that if the laws of nature form a unified system it may be inconsistent to contemplate one feature being different without the whole structure being different. Indeed some physicists anticipate that the true "unified theory" will turn out to have no "free parameters" and to have a structure completely determined by some basic principles or symmetries. In this case no arbitrariness would remain in the laws of nature. Of course, this objection only has force if one can argue that the unified system of laws that govern the physical universe is somehow logically necessary and absolutely unique. But this cannot be the case. There are an infinity of selfconsistent theories any one of which could be the law of a possible universe. Admittedly, "most" of these would lead to somewhat boring or trivial universes. But, unless one is willing to involve some variation of "the Anthropic Principle" (see Appendix D), that is beside the point. The laws of nature are *not* somehow logically necessary. That is why physics is an experimental science rather than a branch of mathematics.

A second objection is that one may overlook some less obvious consequences of an altered physical law that may somehow compensate for the negative consequences (for evolution) that one considered. Or it may be that a plurality of very different paths of biological evolution are possible, and that were the laws of nature different another, totally unsuspected path would open up at the same time that the actual path followed on our own planet was closed off. It is hard to absolutely rule out such possibilities, but they would require a certain kind of conspiracy in favor of life that is rather far-fetched. While the anthropic coincidence arguments may be lacking somewhat in demonstrative force they certainly suggest that the probability that life — especially sentient life — can evolve depends very sensitively on the precise details of the laws of nature. If this is so, the existence of life is as much an evidence for design as ever it was if one transposes the argument from the level of phenomena to the level of law.

We will now present a few examples of anthropic coincidences. For more on the subject see the works cited in reference 4 of the main text.

(1) Water

All life on earth is based on water. It seems unlikely that any other compound could replace water in this role. (Ammonia has sometimes been suggested.) This is because water has a set of very special — almost unique — properties.

> Water is actually one of the strangest substances known to science. This may seem a rather odd thing to say about a substance as familiar but it is surely true. Its specific heat, its surface tension, and most of its other physical properties have values anomalously higher or lower than those of any other known material. The fact that its solid phase is less dense than its liquid phase (ice floats) is virtually a unique property. ... these strange properties make water a uniquely useful liquid and the basis for living things. Indeed, it is difficult to conceive a form of life which can spontaneously evolve from non-self-replicating collections of atoms to the complexity of living cells and yet is not based in an essential way on water.[19]

(2) Nucleon Masses

Neutrons (n) are slightly heavier than protons (p). Were it the other way around most protons would have decayed into neutrons in the early period of the universe. There would be little hydrogen (except deuterium) today and hence hydrogen-burning stars like the sun would not exist. Even more disastrous, there would be essentially no water.

(3) The Nuclear Force

Probably, the strength of the nuclear force that holds nuclei together has to be very close to its actual value for life to have been able to evolve.[20] If slightly weaker, deuterium would not exist and the build up of the heavier elements in stars inhibited. If slightly stronger, protons would have fused into ^{2}He and no ordinary hydrogen to speak of would exist.

(4) Nucleosynthesis

The heavy elements required for life were synthesized mostly in stars. There is a barrier to the synthesis of elements heavier than Be due to the famous mass gaps at mass 5 and 8. The gap at 8 is bridged only due to a very delicate process known as the "three alpha process." However, the three alpha process would not proceed at a high enough rate were it not greatly enhanced by the existence of a "resonance" in the ^{12}C spectrum at just the right energy. Were it not for this very strategically placed stepping stone, again, life would not exist.[21]

(5) The Large and Small Numbers

Certain important ratios of constants of nature have astonishingly small numerical values. An important example is the ratio of the "cosmological constant" to the Planck energy density. This is known to vanish to at least 120 decimal places. Were it larger than that the universe would have collapsed shortly after the big bang. That the universe has persisted for over 10 billion years is sometimes called the "oldness problem"[22] and is connected to the "cosmological constant problem."[23]

Another important ratio is that of the proton mass to the Planck mass (or unification scale). The exceeding smallness of this ratio is sometimes called the "gauge hierarchy problem."[24] In grand unified theories ("GUTs") this ratio has to be less than about 10 (to the −14th) if protons and neutrons are to have lasted from the time they were formed in the big bang to the present day. But aside from this, the size and and lifetimes of stars depend on this ratio. Every change of a factor of ten in this ratio would change the lifetime of stars like the sun by a factor of one hundreth.

In any event it is clear that very small and very large numbers are required if life is to evolve. Evolution takes a long time: the ratio of astrophysical to chemical time scales has to be enormous. One needs many particles: a human body contains about 10^{29} of them. One probably needs many stars and planets to have even one "successful" planet in evolutionary terms. The kinds of numbers that enter into the equations of most mathematically elegant theories tend to be (like 2, e, pi, etc.) "of order one."

(6) The Dimensions of Space and Time

Even the dimensionality of space and time have "anthropic significance."[25] Moreover, it is not somehow a matter of logical necessity that there are one time and three space dimensions. (Indeed theories with more space dimensions are currently fashionable.) If the number of space dimensions were less than three one could not have complicated circuitry: "wires" would cross. Probably complex brains would be impossible. With more than three space dimensions (and leaving the general form of the laws of gravity and electromagnetism unaffected) certain disasters would occur. Atoms would be unstable, with electrons falling into the nucleus. Planetary orbits would be unstable due to perturbations, and temperatures on planetary surfaces would vary drastically over time.

The number of time dimensions is even more critical. Were there none or more than one, obviously, the whole causal structure of the world would be radically different. It is hard to imagine what biology could be like at all.

(7) The Arrow of Time

This has been discussed at length in Appendix A. This too can be regarded as the greatest of all fine tuning problems.[26] It would appear that the total entropy of the (observable) universe started out something like 10^{120} times smaller than it could have been. The "orderliness" of the big bang was incredibly high!

(8) The Fine Structure Constant

The fine structure constant, alpha, determines the strength of the electromagnetic force. It is believed to be small due to the great ratio between the "weak" and "Planck" scales (the so-called "gauge hierarchy"). In some sense, then, this is already understood in terms of grand unification. But what if alpha had been close to one instead of approximately equal to 1/137? All but very small nuclei would be unstable due to spontaneous fission. Only a few stable elements would exist and the possibilities for chemistry and biology would be severely limited. Again, almost certainly, no life would be possible.

(9) Qualitative Features of the Laws of Nature

Up to this point we have been talking quantitatively. But what about the gross qualitative features of the laws of nature? How can we account for the fact that there is an electromagnetic interaction and hence light and atoms.[27] Why is nature quantum mechanical instead of classical? In a classical world matter would be unstable and have continuously variable properties. There would be no periodic table, and chemistry as we know it would be impossible. What about the particles like quarks and leptons of which we are made? The so-called standard model would be equally consistent without them. The list could be indefinitely extended.

APPENDIX D

THE ARGUMENT FROM DESIGN

I. An Objection to the Argument

The main "scientific" objection to the argument from design is that order can emerge spontaneously from chaos through the operation of physical laws. For example, if a glass of water is left outside on a day when the temperature is below 0° C, it will freeze. The water molecules, which were very chaotic in their movements, will settle down to a highly ordered crystalline structure. Dramatic examples exist in nature of configurations that look like the work of human engineers but are purely the result of natural forces. The theory of evolution by natural selection dealt one of the greatest blows to the argument from design. For natural selection is certainly a mechanism which can explain the evolution of complex biological forms from simpler ones. All of these examples show that indeed "blind" forces *can* lead to the emergence of highly ordered structures.

The response to this objection is simple. The "blind" forces *themselves* exhibit structure and symmetry! Consider the freezing of water or the formation of any kind of crystal. First, it is important to point out that the regularity of crystalline structures would not emerge were space itself not symmetric. Space is, at least on small scales, "rotationally invariant" and "translationally invariant" (that is each point is equivalent to any other). Secondly, it is crucial that all water molecules have identical properties. These two underlying symmetries, as well as others that are responsible for the orderly structures of crystals, can in turn be traced further back to symmetries in the fundamental laws of nature. In particular, they can be traced to the "lorentz" and "general coordinate" invariance of the laws of gravity (and indeed of the other laws) and the quantum principle of the indistinguishability of particles (which itself flows from the principles of quantum field theory). To take another example, why is the earth's orbit nearly circular, and why are planets and stars nearly spherical? Again, these shapes emerge through blind physical processes. But these particular shapes would not have arisen except for the rotational invariance of the laws that govern those processes.

To turn to the major example, biological evolution may indeed happen according to "blind" physical laws, but not all physical laws would lead to evolution. This is something we discussed at length under the rubric of "anthropic coincidences." How many of all the conceivable systems of physical law would admit the possibility of self-reproducing structures like DNA? Surely, very few. Moreover, evolution is driven by a competition for scarce resources. What would a "resource" be except in the overall context of the First and Second Laws of Thermodynamics?

("Resources" are usually *energy* resources, which brings in the First Law: energy conservation. The need to replenish resources would seem to be connected to the Second Law.) But the First and Second Laws are not absolute metaphysical principles but aspects of the particular laws that govern our universe.

To summarize, structure, whether it is of objects (like crystals or DNA) or processes (like evolution) or organisms, requires and presupposes structure at the level of laws. Sometimes, admittedly, it is possible to explain the structure of the laws in some dynamical way. For example, in "Kaluza Klein" theories, one tries to explain the "gauge symmetries" of the laws from the shapes of extra space dimensions. However, these shapes are themselves a consequence of the symmetries of an underlying theory. One *cannot* escape from order.

II. Three Ways to Escape Design

There are various ideas that are probably motivated, at least in part, by a desire to escape the argument from design. All involve an attempt to eliminate in some way the *arbitrariness* of the world we see or of its laws. (For "arbitrariness" suggests, as the etymology of the word implies, "will"). I will describe these under the headings "Triviality and Chaos," "Uniqueness," and "The Statistical Ensemble and the Anthropic Principle."

(A) Triviality and Chaos

We have argued that structure can only emerge "spontaneously" from prior structure, and that the very rich phenomena of our world must and do come from a very "non-trivial" structure in the basic laws of nature. Some physicists[28] have tried to derive the known laws of nature from a chaotic or random starting point. However, no one has succeeded in deriving laws from complete chaos. Obviously they cannot because to "derive" anything requires a *rule of derivation,* and then the starting point is not chaos but a rule. Though these ideas may have some limited success and utility in avoiding the fine-tuning of initial conditions, they are doomed from the start.

More interesting is the possibility that very rich structure at the level of phenomena can come from very simple structure, even almost trivial structure, at the level of laws. That is, the world is to be reduced — not to chaos — but to triviality.

There is a fascinating mathematical game invented by the mathematician J. H. Conway[29] called the "game of life." It is an instance of a class of mathematical structures called "cellular automata" which have been much studied in recent years. What makes the life-game interesting to some people is that a system obeying a very simple set of rules can exhibit very complicated behavior, including processes reminiscent of reproduction. Indeed, it can be shown that the life-game cellular automaton can act like a "universal computer." Such games do teach us one thing, viz., that simple rules acting on a large number of objects can generate complex results. However, such games are far from showing that structure can be derived from what is truly trivial.

We actually know something about the basic "rules" of nature, and they are certainly *not* trivial. A final refuge of the trivializers could be that the laws of physics as we now know them might themselves be merely "phenomenological laws" that emerge from an even deeper level where the laws are much more trivial. Even if this were true, it would remain the case that these supposedly trivial ur-laws would have to be remarkably special. (If they were truly trivial and not very special, we would not have to wait for the long and laborious process of scientific investigation to reach its goal. We could just hit on them by guesswork with very little trouble and show that they lead to a world like our own. I think this is patently absurd.) But if such laws were very special, then we are back to design.

(B) Uniqueness

A more popular notion among physicists is that the laws of physics are in some sense unique.[30] In fact some thinking has gone beyond this to the idea that the *universe* is the only uniquely possible one. This larger claim would involve showing three things: that the laws are the uniquely possible ones; that the "initial conditions" or, more generally, the boundary conditions are uniquely fixed; and that these laws and initial conditions uniquely determine everything, i.e., that physics is deterministic. Let us deal with the last two points first:

1. Initial Conditions. There is an interesting paper by the Relativist J. Hartle on the subject of initial conditions.[31] He discussed four possible "attitudes" toward them:

Attitude 1: "That's the way it is." In other words, many initial conditions are possible. The actual ones are arbitrary to be taken as given and not to be explained by physics.

Attitude 2: "The boundary conditions which determine the universe are not initial conditions but present conditions and in particular the fact that we exist. This idea is related to the set of ideas called the anthropic principle." This either involves the notion of a design which had man in view or, as Hartle says, some version of the "anthropic principle."

Attitude 3: "Initial conditions are not needed; dynamics does it all." What is meant here is that the dynamics are such that, whatever the initial conditions, the outcome is qualitatively the same. That is, cosmology is insensitive to initial conditions. Normally, this is not so. In fact, in standard cosmology the initial conditions must be very special to lead to the type of world we see. A very promising idea for eliminating much of this sensitivity to or unnatural "fine-tuning" of initial conditions goes by the name of "inflation" or "inflationary cosmology." However, only certain kinds of theory lead to acceptable inflation. In fact, no fully satisfactory model exists. So that the price of eliminating the specialness of the initial conditions may be the specialness of the theory.

Attitude 4: "There is a law of physics specifying the initial conditions." This is the only real way to eliminate entirely the arbitrariness of initial conditions. The same remark applies here: only special theories would have this feature. So far this is only a hope.

2. Indeterminacy. To eliminate the indeterminacy of quantum mechanics one must either modify quantum mechanics, which is very difficult, or one must adopt the so-called "Many Worlds Interpretation" of quantum mechanics (see Appendix E). This is one reason for the popularity in some quarters of the Many Worlds Interpretation.

3. Uniqueness of Laws. Even if the arbitrariness of the initial conditions and of quantum indeterminacy can be eliminated, one remains with the central issue of the laws themselves. There are some definite reasons why the notion of unique laws has been advanced. In the first place, as the known laws of physics have become more "unified," certain features that seemed arbitrary were found to be dictated by the requirements of unification. For example, if "grand unification" is correct, the strengths of the strong, weak, and electromagnetic interactions, otherwise arbitrary, must have a definite relationship to each other. Moreover, it is now appreciated that certain theories have *no* free adjustable parameters because they are so constrained by a unifying symmetry, and yet have a rich structure. One example is QCD, the theory of strong interactions (if we neglect quark masses); another is the class of superstring theories, now popular as a candidate for a complete theory of physics. A second reason is that if we make certain realistic requirements of a theory it is sometimes found that there are few ways of satisfying them.

Is it possible that somehow the laws of physics are the uniquely possible ones and thus somehow necessary? The answer is obviously *no*. One can write down many perfectly self-consistent sets of laws that could be the laws of physics for some possible universe. Most of these universes would be devoid of life and utterly boring. To take an extreme case, I could imagine a universe with one "degree of freedom" governed by, say, the pendulum equation! Uniqueness only begins to make sense when one requires the theory to satisfy certain conditions. For example, if we specify that it must be a unitary, renormalizable, quantum field theory including gravity, the possibilities become very limited. But these requirements are necessarily *themselves* of an arbitrary nature. Without requirements, there is an infinity of possibilities. Similarly, the possible requirements that could be imposed are infinite. One requirement that some have discussed is that life — specifically intelligent life — could evolve. Either this leads us back to design or it leads to some version of the "anthropic principle." But uniqueness as a separate possiblity cannot work.

(C) Statistical Ensembles and the "Anthropic Principle"

This idea is best explained by an analogy. Suppose (as is probably the case) that the conditions on the surface of the earth are just right to support life (temperature, chemical abundances, surface gravity, etc.). If the earth were the only planet in the universe, this would appear as a coincidence — an "anthropic coincidence" — and perhaps an evidence of design. But suppose (as is the case) that there is a vast and perhaps infinite number of planets on which the conditions vary over a whole range of possibilities. Then given any particular conditions (such as those required to support life), there is bound to be at least one planet that fulfills them. The "coincidence" evaporates.

One might hope to explain at least the "anthropic coincidences" we discussed in this way. This type of explanation is referred to as the "anthropic principle," which comes in various forms.[32] More ambitiously, one might hope to eliminate all "arbitrariness." This would require that the universe we observe is but one of a vast statistical population or "ensemble" of actually existing "universes." This might come about in one of two ways: either (a) the laws of this universe are such as to give rise to a large or infinite number of different sectors, mutually unobservable, where very different conditions or phenomena occur; or (b) one has an ensemble of universes which have nothing to do with each other.

The first kind of ensemble actually arises in two types of theory we already discussed. In the "Many Worlds Interpretation" of quantum mechanics, the universe has many "branches" that are constantly subdividing as all quantum "probabilities" are realized. In certain versions of "inflationary cosmology," the universe contains many regions which are so far apart that they are outside of each others' "horizons." Such ensembles could be used to explain some "initial conditions problems" and even certain of the anthropic coincidences. However, as such ensembles of "branches" or "regions" of the universe only arise in certain special types of theory, that cannot fully eliminate "arbitrariness," the "anthropic coincidences," or the argument from design. Again, it is at the level of *law* that arbitrariness must be eliminated.

To really be able to destroy the argument from design and explain the anthropic coincidences, the ensemble must be of the second kind and include many different universes *with different laws.* Indeed it must include *all possible universes with any self-consistent laws or even without laws,* for any limitation on the membership of the ensemble is inherently arbitrary. The "statistical ensemble" attack on design only works in this extreme case, which essentially amounts *to eliminating the distinction between the possible and the actual or real,* since all possibilities are realized. In that case to "exist" is just to be "self-consistent" and the cosmological argument is destroyed as well. Unfortunately or fortunately, this whole approach is self-destructive. For, if *all* possibilities are represented in the ensemble and we use the statistical reasoning which characterizes these arguments, we would have to conclude that there is essentially a zero probability that the laws of physics will continue to be obeyed tomorrow or 5 seconds from now! Indeed, there are universes in the ensemble where they will be, but for each one of those there is an infinity where they will not! And, indeed, for each universe which exhibits the regularity we call law, there are an infinity that do not or where that regularity is sporadic. The whole framework of explaining things by laws disintegrates since anything can (and does) happen. A further difficulty is that when dealing with an uncountable infinity of possibilities, as we are, to talk about "probability" requires what is called a "measure" of probability. One has to decide what is equiprobable. But there are an infinity of completely arbitrary ways of doing this. Only in the framework of some all embracing theory that describes the whole ensemble and provides a "measure" for it, as in the first type of ensemble, can we really talk about probabilities. But then we are back in the soup. How are the special features of that theory to be accounted for?

APPENDIX E

THE IMPLICATIONS OF QUANTUM THEORY

This is a much controverted[33] and confused subject. I will present here my own view, which can be supported both by solid arguments and by the authority of weighty figures in the field. First, I will clear up some terminological confusion.

People often talk about various "interpretations" of quantum mecanics (Q.M.). There are really only two: the traditional interpretation (T.I.) and the "Many Worlds Interpretation" (M.W.I.) The formalism of Q.M. is mathematically unambiguous, there is only *one theory* of Q.M., universally agreed upon. And, until 1957, when the M.W.I. was proposed by Everett, one could say that there was also only one "interpretation" of Q.M. (Peierls,[34] who regards the M.W.I. as a semantic confusion, still says that there is only one "interpretation." Hence, he regards the word "interpretation" as mischievous and misleading). Sometimes one hears people talk about the so-called "Copenhagen interpretation" of Q.M. It is a term with no agreed upon meaning. Some people mean a set of beliefs held by Niels Bohr, including all sorts of subjectivistic metaphysical baggage. Others mean no more than the T.I. In any case, it is a term best avoided. Wigner, since he presumably did not want to use this misleading term to describe the T.I., chose to call it in his writings the "orthodox interpretation."[35] Before 1957, I think this would have been appropriate. Now that it has a competitor in the M.W.I., I have chosen a more neutral term. Of course, Q.M. may be incomplete. Our discussions are all based upon the (dangerous) assumption that the principles of Q.M. are true, since they have stood for the last sixty years.

In Q.M. one talks about "the system," "the observer," and "the wavefunction" (w.f.) of the system. As Wigner says (following von Neumann), the wavefunction of the system changes "in two ways."[36] Between measurements made on the system, the w.f. evolves *in an absolutely deterministic way* according to the laws of Q.M., namely the so-called "time-dependent Schrodinger equation." The element of chance enters when "the observer" makes a measurement or observation of the system. The w.f. (usually) does not predict definitely the result of this observation, rather the w.f. contains various "components" corresponding to the various possible outcomes. The magnitudes (squared) of these components allows the observer to predict the relative probabilities of these outcomes. After the measurement is completed, however, the outcome is certain. Only one component of the w.f. represents the true state of affairs, although *which* one could not have been predicted even in principle beforehand. The w.f. thus "collapses" as it is said. How it collapses is random and not determined by any equation or law. The component corresponding to the actual result is set to one, and the others are set to zero. Most of the controversy and all of the significant questions raised by Q.M. revolve around the issues of *what* the w.f. represents, *when* and *how* it collapses, and *who* is "the observer" whose observation collapses it.

There is a famous "paradox" that brings these issues into focus called the "Schrodinger's cat paradox." What it essentially involves is a "system" which includes a cat (albeit it doesn't have to be a cat). An experiment is devised whose possible outcome includes situations in which the cat has been killed by the experiment and in which the cat has been spared. Until the observer comes along and makes his observation of the result, the w.f. according to Q.M. must have components corresponding to both of those possibilities. Only at the moment of the observation does the w.f. collapse, unpredictably, to a live cat or a dead cat. [This is even more paradoxical than at first appears, since in most cases in Q.M. components of the w.f. representing apparently exclusive possibilities can "interfere" with each other.]

If we adopt an obvious and natural viewpoint, namely, that *the wavefunction is a description of the system,* we will get into trouble. (By the system here, I mean the system as it exists in reality apart from anyone's knowledge of it.) In the Schrodinger's cat experiment since prior to the observation the components representing a live cat and a dead cat were equally a part of the w.f., they must equally have been a part of reality. The cat would appear to be in a state of suspended animation! This is disconcerting because a living being is involved, it is less so for, say, an electron. [That such paradoxical things actually happen for electrons can be demonstrated experimentally, since one can actually set up situations where the aforementioned interference occurs.] A more telling version[37] of this paradox goes by the name "the Wigner's friend paradox." Instead of a cat, a human (Wigner's friend) is involved, and not his life or death but his state of knowledge is at issue. The punchline comes when Wigner makes his observation by means of asking his friend a yes or no question about what he has seen and receiving a reply. According to Q.M., *if* Wigner can describe the contents of the mind of his friend using a w.f., then, until Wigner receives his answer, the state of mind of his friend is not decided. It also is in a state of suspended animation.

There are two ways to avoid these troubles. The first is the M.W.I. According to this, the w.f. *never* collapses even when an observation is made. The components of the w.f. representing the various conditions of the cat (alive or dead) all correspond to equally real "branches" of the world's history. Before the observation, the observer knows the same things in each branch, but afterwards his knowledge is different in the different branches. In some, he "knows" the cat is alive, in others he "knows" the cat is dead! In fact, the world is continually splitting up into branches with every quantum transition, and we each have an infinity of life histories and fates, all equally real. Of course such a viewpoint is not open to an orthodox Christian. [The M.W.I. is also impossible to subject to any empirical test since the "branches" are "non-interfering."] We will briefly return to the M.W.I. later.

The second way out of trouble is to abandon the "obvious and natural viewpoint" underlined above, namely, that the wavefunction describes the system itself. Rather one must say that *it describes the observer's state of knowledge of the system.* This is not at all to deny the reality of the system; it is not to say anything about the system! It is only to make a statement about what the wavefunction is. If we cling to the idea that the w.f. describes the system itself — the reality of the situation — then one must say that Wigner's friend's mind in reality had no definite thoughts until Wigner got an answer to his question. That is, Wigner's consciousness is given a special status higher than that of his friend. One is led inexorably to some variety of solipsism or subjectivism. Moreover, if the w.f. is interpreted as being the objective state of the system, one runs into the problem of *which* observer is "the observer" who collapses *"the* wavefunction."

On the view of the w.f. as the observer's *knowledge* of the system, many difficulties evaporate. It is not the cat (or Wigner's friend's mind) that is in "suspended animation" but the observer's judgment that is suspended. Corresponding to each "observer" of a system there is a w.f. That is, a w.f. is not just associated with an object, a system, but with a particular subject, an observer. Who then is "the observer" who collapses "the wavefunction?" Obviously, it is the observer whose state of knowledge is represented by that wavefunction! How then is the collapse of the w.f. to be understood? If the w.f. represents a state of knowledge, then when that state of knowledge changes (as it does when an observation is made), the w.f. must naturally also change as suddenly. This is common sense.

There are four questions that are usually thought to be embarrassing to the T.I. (1) What is the dividing line between the system and the observer? (2) When in the complex process of performing a measurement does the w.f. actually collapse? (3) Who is "the observer?" Must it be a human? and (4) How does the w.f. collapse?

The answer to the first question is that there is some arbitrariness in drawing the line. The observer could, if he were interested in describing physically the measurement process itself, define the system to include not only the thing being measured but also the measurement apparatus and even the observer's own interaction with these devices, his sensory organs, nervous system, etc. The observer can never be totally swallowed up by the system, however, and completely included in the physical description. Unless he remains distinct from the system, there will never be an observation, the w.f. will never collapse, and the description will be completely deterministic (as in the M.W.I.) rather than probabilistic. Thus there is an irremovable boundary between system and observer.

This corresponds to Western philosophy's metaphysics where the subject and object of knowledge are sharply distinguished. [And has little resemblance — *pace* Capra and Zukav — to Eastern mystical ideas which tend to deny the reality of this distinction.]

The answer of Wigner[35] and Peierls[38] [33] to the second question is that the measurement process is only complete when the result enters the "consciousness" or "knowledge" of the observer. Wigner tends to use the word "consciousness" and insists that only a "conscious" being — as opposed say to an inanimate device — can collapse the wavefunction. Certainly, if the device can be described by the laws of Q.M. (the time-dependent Schrodinger equation), it cannot collapse the w.f. since those equations are deterministic and the collapse is random. But Wigner's point of view has been assailed by those who ask where one is to draw the line in the animal kingdom between "conscious" and "non-conscious." We would all agree on humans as conscious, but what about chimpanzees, cats, frogs, insects, worms, bacteria? In my view, since the w.f. represents state of knowledge, any organism that can be said to "know" that which is contained in wavefunctions can be an "observer" in the sense of Q.M. Its state of knowledge of a system will be representable by a w.f.; and when that knowledge changes, the corresponding w.f. will collapse. Is a chimpanzee able to know in this sense? I don't know, since I do not know what goes on in a chimpanzee's mind. This answers the third question.

The fourth question is answered as we suggested above. Since the w.f. represents a state of knowledge, it "collapses" when that state of knowledge changes. As we have noted, this collapse, being non-deterministic, is not describable via the laws of Q.M. Thus we must conclude that the "process" or better "act" by which the observer's state of knowledge changes is not completely describable in physical terms.

One might worry, as some have, that the T.I. necessarily involves abandoning the notion of objective reality. I do not believe it does. One can show that the observations or knowledge of various observers (as long as they do not make mistakes in their measurements) must agree when compared with each other. This in my view suffices to show that we do not have a subjectivist theory here. One might ask whether one can speak of the true and objective state of a physical system apart from any observer's knowledge and measurements of it. I don't know, but certainly such a thing could not be the object of any human science that depended on measurement and observation! Since it is an element of such a science, it need not overly worry us that the w.f. does not provide us with such a description.

In any event if one is to avoid solipsism within the framework of the T.I. of Q.M. (as opposed to the M.W.I.), one is led to the three conclusions of the text.

The difference between the M.W.I.[39] and the T.I. is that in the former the w.f. never collapses; it just keeps on ramifying. Thus the observer has no fundamental role. It is a view which gladdens the materialist but should arouse the hostility of the positivist. Since these are often the same person, there is not much enthusiasm for the M.W.I. [There is a fallacious argument for the M.W.I. from quantum cosmology.[40] It is said that if one considers the w.f. of the whole physical universe, there can be no observer external to the system and hence such a w.f. will never collapse. In practice, of course, quantum cosmologists study w.f.s which describe the universe as a whole but not in every detail. They use variables which average over little lumps in the matter distributions like you and me. Moreover, even if one contemplates a wavefunction that involves *every* physical degree of freedom in the universe, it begs the question to suppose that it describes also the minds of all observers. Therefore *logically* we are external to the system described, though we are *geometrically* internal to it.] Actually, the observer in the T.I. could perversely refuse to collapse the w.f. but continue to carry around all of the components that correspond to results he did not obtain in his measurement. The real difference between T.I. and the M.W.I., then, and the only real room for "interpretation" in quantum mechanics, is whether one regards all those other "branches" of the world — the "paths not taken" — as being as *real* as the one experienced by the observer. This cannot be settled by experiment, only on the basis of "reasonableness." The T.I. asks us to believe in the reality of our own minds as more than complicated physical systems, as being capable of "knowledge" which is not merely a chemical process. This is not asking much since if it is not true, then what we "believe" about the world is just a question of chemistry and not very interesting. As Wigner[35] points out, moreover, we have more direct empirical grounds for believing in our own minds than in anything else. The Many Worlds Interpretation asks us to believe in a staggering number of "branches" of the world of which we can have no empirical evidence whatever.

REFERENCES

[6] St. Augustine, **Confessions**, Bk 11, Ch. 30. (I quote from The Image Books edition. [Transl. John K. Ryan, Doubleday, 1960]).

[7] **Ibid.**, Bk 11, Ch. 13.

[8] **Ibid.** See also St. Thomas Aquinas, **Summa Contra Gentiles**, Bk II, Ch. 35, P6.

[9] This indeed was a conception that did not originate with the Scholastics. St. Irenaeus of Lyons in *Adversus Haereses,* written between 180 and 199 AD, writes "For far removed is the Father of all from those things which operate in us, the affections and the passions. He is simple, composed of no parts, without structure, ..." English translation from **The Faith of the Fathers**, (see William Paley, "Natural Theology," contained in **The Works of William Paley** [Oxford: Clarendon Press, 1938], Vol. IV, p. 87). (See also St. Thomas Aquinas, **Summa Contra Gentiles**, Bk I, Ch. 18).

[10] St. Thomas Aquinas, **Summa Contra Gentiles**, Bk I, Chs. 21, 45 and 73. (Also Chs. 75 and 76).

[11] **Ibid.**, Bk I, Ch. 16, P7, and Bk I, Ch. 28, P6.

[12] "I am the Lord, and I change not," *Malachi 3:6.*

[13] **Summa Contra Gentiles**, Bk I, Ch. 15, P3.

[14] St. Augustine, **Confessions**, Bk 11, Ch. 13; St. Thomas Aquinas, **Summa Contra Gentiles**, Bk I, Ch. 66, P7.

[15] **Summa Contra Gentiles**, Bk I, Ch. 55, P2-3.

[16] **Ibid.**, Bk I, Ch. 77, P4.

[17] St. Augustine, **Confessions**, Bk 11, Ch. 13.

[18] Bernard J. F. Lonergan, S.J., **Insight, A Study of Human Understanding**, (Longmans, Green and Co., Ltd., London, 1958).

[19] J. D. Barrow and Frank J. Tipler, **The Cosmological Anthropic Principle**, (Oxford Univ. Press, 1986), p. 524. (Reference 4 of main text).

[20] See B. J. Carr and M. J. Rees, "The anthropic principle and the structure of the physical world," *Nature*, Vol. 278, p.605 (1979). (Reference 4 of main text).

[21] See J. D. Barrow and Frank J. Tipler, **The Cosmological Anthropic Principle**, pp. 252-3.

[22] This is also related to the so-called "flatness problem." See the paper by Alan Guth published in **Inner Space/Outer Space, The Interface Between Cosmology and Particle Physics**, (Univ. of Chicago Press, 1986), p. 287.

[23] See, for example, S. Bludman and M. Ruderman, *Phys. Rev. Lett. 38* (1977), or A. Zee, in **High Energy Physics, In Honor of P.A.M. Dirac's 80th Birthday** (ed. Mintz and Perlmutter, Plenum).

[24] Edad Gildener, *Phys. Rev. D14*, 1667 (1976).

[25] See ref. 19, Ch. 4.8.

[26] See R. Penrose, "Singularities and Time-Asymmetry," chapter 12 of **General Relativity, An Einstein Centenary Survey**, ed. S. W. Hawking and W. Israel (Cambridge Univ. Press, 1979), p. 630.

[27] Some ideas for explaining the existence of light along the lines of the approaches of Appendix D Part II are to be found in H. B. Nielson, "Did God have to fine-tune the laws of nature to create light?" **Particle Physics 1980** (ed. by I. Andric, I. Dadic, & N. Zovko. Proceedings of the 3rd Adriatic Summer Meeting on Particle Physics, Dubrovnik, Yugoslavia. North-Holland Publishers, Amsterdam, 1981). See ref. 28.

[28] Such a program has been pursued by H. B. Nielson and by J. Iliopoulos. Their ideas could also be regarded as an attempt to eliminate the arbitrariness of initial conditions as in "Attitude 3" discussed in sec. II B 1 of Appendix D, or a version of the "Statistical Ensemble" approaches discussed in sec. II C of Appendix D. Indeed these various approaches are akin to one another. For details of the Nielson and Iliopoulos ideas see H. B. Nielson and N. Brene, *Nucl. Phys.* B224 (1983), p. 396, and references cited in ref. 5 of that article.

[29] Conway, J. H., unpublished (1970). Discussed by M. Gardner in "Mathematical Games," *Scientific American 224* (1971), Feb., p. 112; Mar., p. 106; Apr., p. 114; *226* (1972), Jan., p. 104. See discussion by S. Wolfram, "Statistical Mech. of Cellular Automata," *Rev. Mod. Phys. 55*, (1983), p. 637 and references cited therein.

[30] This is discussed in A. Zee, **Fearful Symmetry** (Macmillan, 1986), pp. 281-283. He quotes Einstein as saying "What I'm really interested in is whether God could have made the world in a different way; that is, whether the necessity of logical simplicity leaves any freedom at all." (Of course, the "necessity" referred to is not a necessity.)

[31] J. Hartle, "Initial Conditions," published in **Inner Space/Outer Space, The Interface Between Cosmology and Particle Physics**, (Univ. of Chicago Press, 1986), p. 467.

[32] See reference 4 of the main text.

[33] For a semipopular introduction to the issues surrounding quantum mechanics see P. C. W. Davies and J. R. Brown, **The Ghost in the Atom**, (Cambridge Univ. Press, 1986) For a lucid but technical account see E. P. Wigner, **Symmetries and Reflections**, (Ox Bow Press, 1979), Ch. 12, 13, 14.

[34] See P. C. W. Davies and J. R. Brown, ref. 33, p. 71.

[35] See E. P. Wigner, ref. 33.

[36] See E. P. Wigner, ref. 33.

[37] **Ibid.**, pp. 176 and 179.

[38] R. Peierls, **Symposium on the Foundations of Modern Physics** (ed. by P. Lahti and P. Mitteltaedt, World Scientific Publishing Co., 1985), pp. 187-196.

[39] P. C. W. Davies and J. R. Brown, ref. 33, pp. 34-38 gives an account of the Many Worlds Interpretation.

[40] **Ibid.**, pp. 89-90.

The End of the Enslavement of Science to Philosophy

by

Paul M. Quay, S.J.

This discussion will concern two of the ways in which science was enslaved to philosophy very early on — and it will remind you of what happened to philosophy itself as a result. The discussion will sketch briefly what has been occurring recently to emancipate science from its bondage and then point out the new movement that is changing radically our way of looking at science. It will conclude with a brief mention, in the light of the new relationships between science and philosophy, of some of the more important problems that Catholic scientists and philosophers will have to face in the 21st Century.

I. THE ENSLAVEMENT

A. Though well known, yet it has been too little noted that the men who begot modern science are the same men who begot modern philosophy: Galileo, Kepler, Descartes, Huyghens, Boyle, Newton, and Leibniz. These individuals were in interaction with men more directly philosophical: Bacon, Hobbes, Gassendi, Henry More, Locke, and Spinoza. Yet these latter were in largest measure the disciples of the former group and had received the most crucially novel of their doctrines from them. As a result, science was born in chains, swaddled in bands of steel by these philosophies that proved to ill-suit it. Yet it was not until the days of Hume and Kant that this lack of suitability became wholly manifest. The new philosophies were, for a long time, not felt as chains. In the earlier days, they seemed rather the very essence of science's newfound freedom from a defunct tradition. For, the chief characteristic of the new philosophies was to take what *did* work marvelously well for science itself and to insist that it apply to the whole of reality. Let us recall a few details.

For Kepler, the only perfect knowledge was mathematical, not sensible; always quantitative, never qualitative. "Just as the eye was made to see colours, and the ear to hear sounds, so the human mind was made to understand, not whatever you please, but quantity."[1] The fundamental reality of the world was purely mathematical, primarily geometrical.

It was Galileo who was able to effect this mathematization of nature not merely in the orbits of the planets but in the sublunary world. He saw mathematics as the one language in which the book of nature was written. Hence, he made real bodies move through purely geometrical space, in a wholly actual, one-dimensional time (no longer a measure of transition between potency and act, but an interval of determinate length.). Such motion could be quantified at once and led to accurate description of the motion of projectiles. Galileo distinguished clearly enough between velocity and acceleration to be able to relate forces solely to the latter.

But Galileo raised no question as to the ultimate "why" of motion. He was satisfied to describe actual movements in detail. He did not ask what purpose is served or what final end is being sought. Since all physical reality is describable in the language of mathematics, he believed that discussions of purpose have no more place in physics than in trigonometry.

Galileo's experimental methods became highly analytic, in the sense that every being and process was split into tractable aspects which, once mathematically formulated, could then be reunited to form the ideal being or process, of which the sensibly observed one is but an imperfect exemplification.

Since the reality of the world was quantitative, primary qualities (such as size, shape, and movement) were to be sharply distinguished from secondary ones (such as color, odor, and tone). These latter were, for Galileo, only the effects in us of the primary qualities. To call a rose red is to apply to it an empty name, attributing to it our merely subjective reaction. The secondary qualities have, as such, no reality at all.

Finally, causality was seen solely in terms of forces, i.e., efficient causes of the motion of matter. Worse yet, Galileo introduced the fatal notion that sameness of cause implies sameness of effect.

This is clearly not the place to analyze Cartesianism and the problematic it established for the philosophy of the next three centuries. Suffice it to point out here that Descartes' philosophy sprang from his physics, and his physics from his mathematics. Having found a way to do geometry by means of algebra, he saw no obstacles to the total mathematization of the world. Once he had discovered the correct form of the Principle of Inertia, it was but one step to the uniformity of space implied in his greatest discovery: the Conservation of Momentum. Since he simply identified matter with extension, he declared the material substance of the world to be the uniform extension of limitless Euclidean space. Hence, the immaterial soul was not merely unextended but separate from the world of matter. For Descartes, the human soul subsisted *in* the body — the body now merely a machine activated and regulated by the soul from its seat in the brain. For this reason, the soul was no longer seen as the *form* of the body.[2]

Shortly thereafter, Huyghens stated that the causes and the effects of concern to physics were motions. Cause, moreover, is equivalent to effect in terms of work. The world had become a perfect machine, even before Newton had written its laws.

Later, while the philosophers were busy with the intractable problems the scientists' philosophies had generated, the scientists went their own way. Little interested in philosophy as such, they generally took for granted the mechanical universe. If they were religious men, they could praise God for this grand mechanism; if not, they could argue about the uselessness "of that hypothesis," as Laplace remarked of God.

B. Modern science became enslaved in another way: it was caught and put to the service of the atheisms of the Renaissance and the Enlightenment — despite the fact that the scientists themselves were, for the most part, devout and religious men. Indeed, much of their philosophizing had been done precisely to attack these atheisms or their kindred agnosticisms and deisms.

Yet science was seen at once, because of the novelty and power of its methods and results, to be useful against anything rooted in tradition. Such men of letters as Fontenelle and Voltaire grasped at once the implications of this newness of science. Since new, it was not the property of the Church. Scholasticism could not claim it, swaddled as science was in the new philosophies. It was patronized by the nobility, but they did not beget it. By paternity, science belonged to the bourgeoisie. Its vast powers for change lay in their hands as the perfect tool to be used against the social system they most resented and wished to eliminate: the aristocracy and the Church.[3] Nor should one overlook the appeal, not easily understood today, that a wholly mechanized universe had for those who wished to dispense with a God who revealed Himself in history as the Lord of history. In a justly famous passage, Butterfield wrote:

> The result was the emergence of a kind of Western civilisation which when transmitted to Japan operates on tradition there as it operates on tradition here — dissolving it and having eyes for nothing save a future of brave new worlds. It was a civilisation that could cut itself away from the Graeco-Roman heritage in general, away from Christianity itself — only too confident in its power to exist independent of anything of the kind. We know now that what was emerging towards the end of the seventeenth century was a civilisation exhilaratingly new perhaps, but strange as Nineveh and Babylon. That is why since the rise of Christianity, there is no landmark in history that is worthy to be compared with this.[4]

This new civilization, however, was *not* the result of science but of the revolt of the middle class against Catholicism — a revolt that was to lead to Marxism as well as to secular humanism. Renaissance irreligion spread in largest measure by drawing the apologists for religion onto its own grounds, away from faith into rationalism, where they made vain attempts to demonstrate the truth of the faith and the rightness of Christian morals to those who had chosen not to believe. Nor should one forget that great, even if temporary, loss of the virtue of faith effected by the Reformation. It was not the rise of the sciences that made people lose their faith. It was their loss of faith that found in the new sciences its excuse and justification.

Later, more fully developed philosophies took over still more of the scientific enterprise for their own uses. The Anglo-American empiricisms, first those of Locke and Hume and later those of the quickly naturalized Vienna Circle, offered themselves as the true philosophies of scientific achievement.

On the continent, Kant came to the defense of Newton against Hume's lightly disguised scepticism. His system, the first of the throng of German idealisms, was no more successful than Hume's philosophy in finding a way to genuine knowledge of the real world. Through this welter of subjectivist epistemologies, man, as observer and knower, had been excluded from the universe. His real being was nothing but the particular arrangement of the atoms within him, whose movements could not even be traced or identified as his.

The denial of the mind's power to know the world was the natural outcome of Descartes' split between the world of extension and the world of pure and unextended thought. Hume and Kant did little more than to manifest the impossibility of a successful way out of the Cartesian impasse.

Meanwhile, the new science had been incredibly successful not only in terms of its theories but in terms of practical applications to every aspect of control of the world. The contrast between scientific progress and the striking lack of progress in philosophy and theology led philosophers to search for the cause of such success in some method peculiar to science. Increasingly, the philosopher saw himself as called to (and limited to) establishing the basis for science's superiority in the superiority of its method.

Modern philosophy was, from its beginnings, a philosophy that was methodologically inspired and restricted to analysis of the problems of knowledge. Philosophy of science replaced the long tradition of the philosophy of nature. When the attempt was made to resuscitate the latter by the German Idealists, the disastrously ludricous results made palpable that nature was to be known only through science. The proper object of philosophy was the critical evaluation and improvement of the methods of science.

Scientists have not always been careful to dissociate themselves from their philosopher-patrons or from the warfare waged in their name by various reductionist philosophies, from the early ones of Hobbes and of the *Encyclopedia* to the dialectical materialism of Marx or the logical positivism of the Vienna Circle. Hence, modern science has often been presented as the only legitimate claimant to the title of valid knowledge. And, since no one could deny the intellectual power and practical effectiveness of science in its own domain, the intellectual atmosphere became increasingly stifling for those in nonscientific disciplines.

C. As might have been expected, science has been increasingly tied to the universities over the last century and a half. Yet now there are signs of a weakening of this bond to academia, as science has become a matter of business and industry, of national laboratories and DOD, of politics and economics — a shift that Marxists have been pointing to with ever greater vigor.

As a result, one no longer has to be an atheist or agnostic in order to prove one's scientific competence.[5] Many fine mathematicians, physicists, and other scientists of recent times have been believers. Many who are not are respectful of the faith of those who are. This will astonish no one who recalls how many believers are to be found among the great names in the history of science. Yet it is important to note because of the contrary popular opinion. It is important, also, because it shows that it is not their science that determines scientists' belief or lack of belief. They may well agree with one another about their science; their lack of agreement on religion must have some other source. Moreover, this source cannot be "the scientific world view" which they hold in common.[6]

In any case, it is now possible to point out in public the internal inconsistencies and self-contradictions of scientific materialisms of whatever variety without being automatically disqualified by the intellectual world.

II. THE SETTING FREE

A. Philosophy of science has undergone profound changes in the last twenty-five years. In the first place, logical empiricism, in all its varieties, has died. It could not obtain satisfactory answers to the "old" questions that had challenged it from its beginnings: e.g., how, in principle, can the collisions of atoms generate a theory of the collisions of atoms? How can entities defined solely in terms of quantitative properties be used to generate anything subjective and nonquantitative? If mind is the product of mindless processes, coming to be without purpose or aim, on what ground can one accept any mind's argument that such is the case?

Logical empiricism proved equally incapable of dealing with its own questions. Its attempt to reduce mathematics to pure logic not merely failed but was proven to be impossible. Its cardinal principle, which called for the empirical verification or at least confirmation of scientific laws and theories, turned out to be an endless generator of logical paradoxes and of violations of common sense. Even to show how to give empirical content to scientific terms or to find out whether the entities one or other theory postulated in its explanations really exist proved impossible. Time had to be eliminated from one's considerations and explanation of past events had to be treated as if it were the same thing as prediction. Furthermore, empiricism did not allow the questions that most people wanted to deal with even be asked. Finally, the surprise grew steadily, as science advanced so rapidly and generated ever new technologies, that empiricism should deny that we know anything at all of the real world by means of science.

But the *coup de grace* to logical empiricism was given by those philosophers who began to take seriously the history of science. Here we should recall that history and science had for three centuries been struggling with each other, each seeking to reduce the other to itself. Until recently, it was thought that science had swallowed history. Could not physics write down the equations that would yield, in principle, all the facts of history? It was believed that the cool reasoning of Laplace's hypothesized "ideal intelligence" could, given exact knowledge of the position and momentum of every particle in the universe at any one moment, calculate from the laws of physics everything that had happened or could happen in the history of the world.

Even the Romantics, in reaction against this view of the world, could not shake it loose — remember Nietzsche and the despair of the eternal recurrences. To make things worse, with the development of archeological and linguistic sciences, comparative religion, textual and form criticisms, historical-critical methods, etc., some historians thought to turn history itself into a science.

But such thought has been overthrown with the growing awareness of the historical nature of science itself. The continuing evanescence of the best established physical theories, theories that had seemed eternally valid acquisitions, led gradually to deep scepticism about any pretended rationality in science.

Soon, history seemed to have reduced science to nothing more than a time-dependent trait of Western culture, a trait making its appearance about 1600 and now in rapid decline, a trait, moreover, depending not on reason but on mere psychological and social determinisms. The views of the world from physics seemed to be mere fluctuations of thought and culture, of no greater relevance to truth than any other thoughts of human beings. Like soccer, science is a game indigenous to the West, easily transferable to other cultures, good for the entertainment or profit of some sectors of the populace but of no help in understanding the world.

Yet despite its success against logical empiricism and its great importance for bringing philosophers to the arduous task of looking seriously at the sciences they were supposedly analyzing, the historicism of Kuhn, Laudan, Lakatos, *et al.*, like one python seeking to swallow another that is swallowing it, has fared no better than its adversary. For, the historicists' final counsel was one of despair. They could offer nothing but a total historical relativism. But if there is no truth in science — only historically conditioned opinions — abandon Truth, all ye who enter here.

Rationalism, it is true, is still vigorous today. But the despairing rationalism of the present differs considerably from the optimistic one of the Enlightenment. The disintegration of all relics of reverence or even respect for state, the Church, and every institutional authority brought about in Europe by World War I and spreading to the rest of the world ever since has made the ground fertile for the irrationalisms of a new and despairing Romanticism. Among intellectuals not active in science itself, the "book of nature" is no longer readable even if they know some mathematics. Not only must its "text" be interpreted, always subjectively, but there is lessening hope of even finding the "text."

B. A healthier movement has now set in. There has come about gradually a recognition of the very real limits that science has imposed on itself in virtue of its own methods, objects, and purposes. Scientists themselves see clearly that, even if in some ideal future science should give us "nothing but the truth," it would never be in a position to give us "the whole truth."

Last August, at the first session of a dialogue of the Bishops' Committee on Human Values with scientists, philosophers, and theologians concerning the interactions of faith and the sciences, those of us in science were in complete agreement that there is no such thing as "the Scientific Method," that philosopher's stone of recent centuries that would turn the leaden dross of philosophy and theology and other disciplines into the golden certitudes of physics. It is now clear to all that modern science uses many methods in its search for truth about the world, some which are strongly empirical, some rigorously mathematical, some truly philosophical, in porportions largely determined by the interests and personality of the individual scientist. The magic method, so long sought from the time of Descartes, that would guarantee the success of the sciences and establish their superiority over all other ways of thinking about the world has been shown not only not to exist but to be impossible in principle.

The Neo-Platonic conviction that mathematical science yields the intelligible reality hidden behind deceptive sensible appearances is gone. For science seeks only to *describe* material things and to give the "how" of each event and process among them. It seeks no further "why" than some equally material efficient cause. Huyghens' point of view — enlarged, to be sure, to include nonmechanical long-range forces — remains dominant. But it is seen to be a defining limitation of the scientific field rather than a summary of all that is knowable.

Science seeks to find the quantitative aspects *in* or *of* time, space, and motion, not to grasp their complete reality even to their ultimate causes and apriori conditions of possibility. The achievements of Galileo and Descartes lay in their ability to abstract from the real condition of physical objects and to find the mathematical "forms" governing them all. Such abstraction, however, always leaves a residue, unexplained and not yet grasped by the science. It is no longer seriously thought either that this residue has been done away with or that it can be eliminated "in principle."

Similarly, there is now recognition of the essential multiplicity of sciences even within mathematics (e.g., algebra analysis, geometry). These are not only in rapid, often mutually independent, development but are often not even logically compatible. Thus, thermodynamics and statistical mechanics, both often needed for the solution of one single problem, are radically contradictory in their basic premises. The art of the physicist is to use both and to avoid letting the contradiction spoil his results. Indeed, from the days of Galileo, physics has never had any generally accepted theoretical unity. The fact that such disunity does not block physics' applications should not be allowed to disguise the fact that a single unified view of the physical universe, always just around the next corner, has never yet existed.

The classical materialist arguments, supposedly based on science, have been refuted. Thus, the argument of Laplace, concerning the calculation of the world's history, has been shown fallacious, even within its own context. For knowledge of all the trajectories of all particles through all time does not offer any principle of selection that would enable one to follow the history of, say, a particular dog, which remains the same animal for several years though the particles that compose it at any moment are soon scattered again. Knowledge of the particles does not give us knowledge of the behavior of particular systems formed from them. Similar and scientifically more important problems of identification of systems when all we know is their components and energy are to be found in quantum theory.

Finally, mathematics, which was for Descartes the supreme example of intelligible clarity, has developed a strange opacity. Old problems remain, more puzzling than ever before. Fermat was a contemporary rival of Descartes'; yet more than three centuries later his famous "Last Theorem" remains an intractable puzzle, never having been proved true, never having been found false, never having been shown to be undecidable or not to make sense. Other problems, less unbelievably simple but equally difficult, abound. Nor are new difficulties lacking. In our own days, Goedel's theorem has demonstrated the impossibility of removing a paradox from any mathematical system more complex than the simplest finite arithmetics.

C. Most importantly, the yoke of all these pseudo-scientific philosophies, from that of Descartes onwards, has been broken by phenomenology. Edmund Husserl's battle-cry, despite his own falling into the Cartesian trap, was return to the things themselves! He did not assert that mathematics is out of place in science but that it is wrong to identify the real with the mathematically expressible. His work has been greatly extended and recast in realist fashion by such contemporary scholars as John Compton, Patrick Heelan, and many others.

Here I come to what seems to me the essential novelty in the relations between modern science and philosophy: the tired and tiresome efforts to analyze science as method and mode-of-knowing are being abandoned at last for an analysis of the world itself — as known by our sciences and, simultaneously, as the given, ever-present life-world of our immediate experience, antecedent to all science and all philosophy, the world that contains both the scientist and his science.

Such phenomenological analysis — strange as it may sound to some — can not only decide on the validity of putative facts, but could save science from such embarrassments as Terrell's discovery in physics. For some 55 years, the best minds in physics took the equations of special relativity to show that an object passing an observer at nearly the velocity of light would appear to him to be shortened in the direction of motion. But with the work of Terrell, all that was undone. The equations were correct. But, when rightly interpreted, they showed that no object would appear to contract as it passed an observer but rather to rotate.

While speaking of relativity, it is good to recall that Aristotle's whole physics was based on the assumption of an absolute point of reference for motion (the center of the universe) and that Newton's physics postulated an absolute frame of reference, although with no privileged point to provide a center. Relativity has indeed "relativized" both these "absolutes" — but at the cost of taking the velocity of light in free space as absolute, i.e., as completely independent of the speed with which the observer of the light may be moving.

The need for interpretation of formulae in terms of the life-world, as well as in terms of other aspects of physics seems nowhere more manifest than in thermodynamics. Here, an infinite temperature is experimentally obtainable (albeit transiently and only in certain types of subsystem). But zero temperature is strictly and wholly unattainable. Yet negative absolute temperatures are attainable — and are hotter than the positive temperatures of our ordinary experience!

Everyone has heard that relativity has eliminated for ever the concept of the ether. There is no light-bearing medium, merely space. Yet general relativity has eliminated the Euclidean void and has given "empty space" a complex physical structure. In this structure, quantum theory would add a polarization of the vacuum, a quivering motion of the void, to say nothing of all the varied fields that propagate in this "empty" space. One doubts that Aristotle would have any problem with such a "void" as this.

From analyses of such aspects of science, not as logical structures but as assertions — true or perhaps false — about the life-world, then, one hopes for a more abstract and general and more soundly and broadly based philosophy, one at long last truly generated from one's science, not imposed upon it from without.

III. SOME PROBLEMS OF CURRENT INTEREST

A. REDUCTION

Metaphysical reductionism is that philosophical theory adumbrated by Leucippus and his successors: "Nothing exists but atoms and the void." In current lingo, whatever there is consists solely of quarks and fields or, more generally, is a compound of the fundamental entities of physics.

The principal thing to note is that if such a reduction is possible, then it must be strictly mutual. If a man is nothing but an interacting congeries of quarks, then quarks are nothing but the smallest (known or conjectured) parts of a man. One may use the latter description as validly as the former.

More interesting is the fact that some reductions of one theory to another have already successfully taken place. Thus chemistry has been reduced to physics — but not to the classical physics of the turn of this century. Rather, classical physics was itself recast by relativity and quantum theory, which latter especially borrowed heavily, without always realizing it, from chemistry. I would predict something similar for the eventual reduction of biology to chemistry. The chemistry to which reduction will be made, however, will not be our current quantum chemistry and physics but will be a "chemistry" redone from the ground up in the light of biological principles, introduced perhaps without realizing the fact as part of a necessary reworking of chemistry.

B. PARTS & WHOLES

The problem of parts and wholes can be seen as a subdivision of that concerned with metaphysical reduction. But there are interesting questions here, apart from any effort at reduction, questions of special interest both in physics and in biology.

For example, how can one understand the role of energy in the determination of what is a whole or a part? Too much energy applied at too high a temperature can dissolve any organism or molecule or atom. As Aristotle pointed out, the element of fire associates like with like by reducing all things to their ultimate components. Too much kinetic energy can turn an arm or a leg from an integral part of an organism into an independent, but soon dying entity. Other modes of energy-conversion can have analogous effects.

Contemporary phenomenology has been working hard on the question as to what may properly be said to be a whole, and as to what kinds of parts a whole may have. Such analysis may seem hopelessly abstract and useless. Yet, if it succeeds, it might have major importance for biology. Certainly, such questions lie at the basis of the problem of brain death: Are you dead if your brain is dead? Or are slime molds to be considered animals or plants or something else? Are the red blood corpuscles in the living body living with the life of the body or with a life of their own? And what of the germ cells before their union? More generally, is the universe best thought of by analogy with a heap of sand or with a living organism or in some other way? Does not the intrinsic dignity of the human person derive from the fact that he constitutes a true whole, distinguishable from all others, however much the other beings in the material creation turn out to be mere concentrations of the stuff of the world? Yet the human person cannot truly exist as he should unless he is a living member of the Church, the Body of Christ.

C. FINALITY

Science is now usually seen as simply incapable of dealing with either intrinsic or cosmic final causality — hence, as incapable of disproving the existence of final causes or of rendering them useless apart from its own methodologies. Purposes and goals do seem to be simply and necessarily absent from the inanimate world. Yet I think that final causes can be found in physics and indeed prove useful there — and this without introducing the "organismic" understanding of the world so strongly attacked by Fr. Stanley Jaki.

Any material being has many ways in which it might act upon the world around it. The entire range of these possible actions is determined by the agent's "form," its particular kind of being. But when it does so act, it acts in but one of those ways at any given moment. Whatever external influence determines or specifies its potentiality for action so that it acts in this way rather than any other of its possible ways is the non-rational analog of human purpose and, therefore, the final cause of the particular action.

Further thought shows this final cause to be a modification of the agent's own being ("form") by the actual presence of that upon which it acts when taken in conjunction with the entire system of which it forms a part.

A famous problem arises in quantum theory. For, it seems impossible, even when one knows all that is physically knowable about the agent and the system in which it is embedded, to predict, except in purely probabilistic terms, just what specific action will eventuate. I do not wish to say more here; but I think you can see that the problem has been shifted, at least in part, from metaphysics to epistemology — which suggests that the problem as usually propounded is not yet well formulated.

As to cosmic finality, let me say no more than that a weak form is obviously derivable from the mere fact of intrinsic finality: there exists a world of beings in gravitational, electrical, and other interaction, known and unknown, with one another. Their actions are specified accordingly by this overall system.

The strong form, however, is the one of primary concern to us all: is there a genuine purpose and meaning to the world? So formulated, it is evident that one is no longer asking about the final causes of physics but about true purpose, something knowable only theologically (or perhaps philosophically). One is asking whether there is a God who, as Supreme Intelligence, has a purpose in making the world and, if so, what it might be. One may doubt whether this is truly a problem for the philosopher. For what makes us think we could of ourselves discover God's purpose?

D. MIND-BODY

The mind-body problem has been and remains the central problem. Evidently, its resolution will depend upon the clarifications given to the three prior problem-areas.

All that I think is appropriate to note here is that this problem is often misperceived. We tend to place animals nearer to ourselves than to atoms. Yet the line between the material and the spiritual passes between us and the animals, not between them and the atoms.

Let me end by encouraging the younger among you to be grateful to God for the splendid philosophical opportunities now open to you, if this be your field of work, and to show that gratitude by making the most of these opportunities for the good of all. Science is now free, for the first time in history, to serve its true purpose: to make the world known to the philosopher no less than to the engineer in such fashion that he may use this knowledge to go through this world to its Creator.

FOOTNOTES

[1] *Opera* I, 31.

[2] The loss of the *Acta* of the Council of Vienne may explain why Descartes was never condemned for heresy. But I suspect that a deeper reason was that Catholics tended to forget, under the impact of rising rationalism, their own doctrine concerning the body, a doctrine whose crucial importance is only slowly being rediscovered in the face of the biotechnological revolution of the present day.

[3] It seems likely that this employment of science as a weapon against the Church by the rising middle-class was motivated in part by their resentment of the restraints the Church placed upon their mercantilist aspirations, especially by its condemnations of usury. One may wonder if today the swift advances in the biological sciences are not being used against the Church in a somewhat similar spirit by those who resent her teachings on sexual morality.

[4] Herbert Butterfield, **The Origins of Modern Science 1300-1800**, (New York: Free Press, 1957), pp. 201-202.

[5] Cf. the recent remarks of Dr. Freeman J. Dyson, Director of the Physical Sciences Division of the Institute for Advanced Studies at Princeton and one of the creators of quantum field theory, that "the main point" to see about scientists' attitudes toward religion is that "There is no consensus among us .... Many first-rate scientists are Catholics; many are Marxists; many are militant atheists; many are ... loosely attached to Christian beliefs by birth and habit but not committed to any particular dogma." "Science and Religion," *Religion, Science, and the Search for Wisdom: Proceedings of a Conference on Religion and Science September 1986*, ed. D. M. Byers , Bishops' Committee on Human Values, NCCB, Washington DC (1987), p. 48.

[6] Paul M. Quay, S.J., "Science and Religion: Response to Dr. Dyson," **Ibid.**

PART FIVE:
The Church and the Family

The Church's Message to United States Family Leadership
by
Msgr. George A. Kelly
President, Fellowship of Catholic Scholars

The State of The Question

The intended object of this lecture is the message of the Catholic Church to U. S. citizens of the 21st Century concerning marriage and family life. But there is a problem in relaying this message. A survey of 50 experienced family life experts brought the almost universal counsel that the Church's teaching first must be reintroduced to the Catholic community, which, given its present state of opinion, is in no position to preach to others. A recent study by George Gallup and Jim Castelli concluded that the Catholic Church "has lost much of its credibility on everything related to sex."[1] An official of Planned Parenthood, during the push to foist condoms on public school children in the hope of combating AIDS, was no less blunt. Joan Coombs simply declared the Church hierarchy "doesn't have a whole lot to do with the reality of Catholic lives."[2] These reports should not surprise us since academics as disparate as Richard McCormick, Andrew Greeley, John Tracy Ellis, and Roland Murphy have been hard at work for years liberating the faithful from the Church's sexual norms, which have been part of the Catholic tradition these two thousand years and whose observance is related to the salvation Christ promised to those who kept his word. The pressing question is: Why is there not more indignation in the right places over repeated statements by prominent figures that Church teaching on marriage is irrelevant?

Twenty years ago, Catholic academics hoped to solve all sorts of human problems by legitimizing the use of contraceptives. Contraception, we were told, would enrich and solidify marriages, diffuse tensions within marriage, delimit the growing reliance on abortion and help solve the population problems of the poor. Instead, as we know, our Catholic people are not notably happier, our divorce and abortion rates approximate those of the U. S. at large, and we have acquired in the meantime a surfeit of overcopulation among our young without benefit of marriage. A 1985 Gallup poll indicated that Catholics are now more tolerant of premarital sex than Protestants.[3] These developments have occurred with surprising serenity within the Church, considering the fact that we are dealing with sins that few people confess anymore and about which there is a grand silence among the Catholic clergy.

Let us place these issues where they belong, or should belong, for those who profess the Catholic faith. John Paul II (July 18, 1984) says that the roots of the Church's sexual morality are in the deposit of faith itself. Even the doctrine on contraception, so often scoffed at today by important clerics, is part of the "moral order revealed by God."[4] Three years after that 1984 statement, the Pope continued to insist that the Church's teaching on contraception was not a matter of free discussion among theologians. He scored their "leading the moral conscience of spouses into error."[5] A fortiori, the divine displeasure with fornication, self-abuse, divorce, adultery and homosexual lust must remain a matter of moral concern for faithful Christians, especially for those who have been appointed to preach and teach in Christ's name.

Apart from divine displeasure, there are human questions. The justification for the Catholic sexual revolution has been reduced to the much abused word "compassion" in favor of reducing feelings of guilt among those who engage in illicit sexual practices, for wives overburdened with too many children, for husbands denied their marital rights by puritanical or dictatorial spouses, for children reared in combative homes which allegedly are caused by sexual tension, for families groveling in poverty because of too many children, and so forth. Sociologists and psychologists were called upon by theologians after 1965 to "prove" the damaging effect of the Catholic sexual ethos on human lives.[6] But twenty years later and liberated though Catholics seem to be, dissenting theologians do not speak much about the growing social concern over the results of liberation: broken homes, children without mothers, children without fathers, children with illegitimate children of their own, mothers without husbands, surrogate mothers, test tube babies, slaughtered fetuses, men who want sex without marriage, women who want sex without motherhood, and a generation of young, including Catholics, taught not to frustrate their sexual impulses but live fully but safely, i.e., with condoms.

We also face what one politician called "the spread of filth campaign" — pornography, pimps, dirty movies, pederasts, peep shows, massage parlors, violence and dope pushers. And, of course, the growing rates of syphilis and now of deadly AIDS, a direct result of unnatural sexual activity, mostly among men. As these problems reach alarming proportions, popular revulsion against the libertinism, the voyeurism, or simply the anti-social excesses has not been translated into public outcry for sexual sanity, or for marital responsibility, or for the normalization of family life. Increasingly, the facts indicate that Catholics are following the practice of family life as it exists in the U. S., not the expectations of Christ in the Church.

From the Beginning

The point to be made here, I suppose, is that whatever the social situation, Mother Church must preach in and out of season God's word on marriage and family life even if unbelievers or not-so-faithful Catholics turn a deaf ear to its significance. Every culture makes what John Paul II calls "the human compromise" with God's ordained statutes concerning marriage. Usually the compromise levels off at the lowest common denominator of prevailing mores. Historically, Jewish prophets, then Christ, now the Church time and time again faced the hardness of people's hearts and their proclivity for lust, even for unnatural pleasures. Periodically, God's word on the subject did receive respectful hearing simply because sexuality's proper use was as vital to man's human development as it was to his eternal salvation. Church cynics and sybarites attribute the Catholic tradition to the worst features of Stoicism, Manicheism, Jansenism, and Puritanism. There is little the Church can do about distortion and misuse of the Christian code of sexual morals except to continue restating its own doctrine. The fundamental Christian world view sees sexuality as God-made and God-designed. Men and women, therefore, are to live their sexual lives in conformity to the nature of marriage as God intended it to be. Deny this proposition and Judaeo-Christian conversation about sex and marriage is almost impossible. In his two conversations with the Pharisees on the indissolubility of marriage, for example, Christ appealed to the way it was intended to be "from the beginning."[7] Even his disciples, taken back by his bald statement against divorce, thought that it might not be advisable to marry under those circumstances. Christ was not intimidated in the least by their reservations.

Whatever else is to be said about the Christian teaching on marriage or sex, therefore, must begin with Genesis (Ch. 2) and its reaffirmation by Christ himself. Who more authoritatively than Christ spoke of "two in one flesh" (i.e., monogamy), "what God has joined together let no one put asunder" (i.e., indissolubility), marrying another man's wife as adultery, lusting as adultery of the heart, the sinfulness of killing but of evil thoughts too (Mt. 5)? Where did St. Paul obtain the idea but from Christ that sexual immorality is antithetical to the demands of Christ's kingdom, whether it take the form of fornication, adultery, or homosexuality? Why did the early Church demand public penance lasting a lifetime for adultery and abortion, save that these were understood to be grave offences against Christ's own norms for Christian behavior? In those first centuries masturbation, contraception, sterilization, pederasty, and copulation with animals came under a similar censure. We speak, therefore, not of human traditions originating with unenlightened or ignorant people (a description that hardly fits the NT authors), but what God had deigned and joined from the beginning and for no man to deny or sunder.

If these reminders represent the negative side of God's word, they merely draw dramatic attention to his positive teachings on marriage and family life. Adultery is a grave offense against marriage because it contravenes the "till death do us part" commitment which marriage entails. In today's anti-family American environment, such long-term or irreversible commitments are counterculture. Yet if young couples on their wedding day do not believe in the bone of their bones that indissolubility is what Catholic marriage involves, they are in peril. Our parents knew this truth with their mothers' milk, but their grandchildren are not so sure, even after sixteen years of Catholic education. They are uncertain because many priests and religious have lost confidence in the human benefit of eternal promises.

Fr. Francis Canavan, S.J., capsulates the reason for the modern crisis in two sentences:

> One of the problems facing the American family today is a crisis of confidence, a loss of faith even on the part of parents themselves in the value of what they are doing. Women in particular are subject to an incessant barrage of propaganda telling them that they are sacrificing their very personalities by bearing and raising children.

He adds the advisory that the very idea of family is now suspect as a result of the psychological difficulty of committing oneself to marriage or parenthood.[8]

So, we may have to begin all over again, as John Paul II once reminded an audience, to reintroduce the world, and Catholics too, to the truth and the value of Christian marriage. This is what Paul VI tried to do with **Humanae Vitae** (1968) without much success. John Paul II attempted the same with **Familiaris Consortio** (1981), only to have his classic Catholic remarks scorned and turned aside in Washington, D.C., by prominent and so-called Catholic family leaders.[9]

The Christian Family: Nature and Mission

The distinctive note of Christian marriage is that it comes from God. It is not a human invention, but a postulate of God's created order. God calls his creatures to do many things, but the vocation to the married state is one of the most exalted. Why? Because marriage is a sharing not only in God's life but in his love, and in his creative power. A man and a woman married are called upon to manifest God's love by loving each other, the overflow of which results in the gift of God's life to others which once God gave to them. We tend today to speak of marriage in the language of the social sciences; yet the language of the Bible and of the Church is entirely different, more meaningful and more true to newlyweds' expectations and especially to those whose faith has taught them to look upon marriage as a sacred vocation. Men and women of true faith understand their relationship as ordained by God to the service of spouse, children, and society, not as a cohabitation absorbed in self-satisfaction or the mutual pursuit of riches or power. They see their marriage bed as a consecrated center of true Christian love, not a playground for egotistical pleasure seeking. Their home becomes "a little Church" dedicated to building up the mystical body, rich with little children so dear to Jesus, where God is worshipped daily, where the example of parents is reflected in the piety of their young as much as in their civilized development, whose home is memorable not so much for its artifacts and tools of amusement, not exclusively for eating, drinking, sleeping and merrymaking, as its only useful functions. In the truly Christian home husband and father complements wife and mother in the gifts brought to their common life and in the contributions they make together to the Christian manhood and womanhood of their children. It is not an arena of competition, domination or raw upward mobility where hardly any children are to be found, where husband and wife vie with each other in their distaste of the work of parenthood.

Thirty years ago I opened my **Catholic Marriage Manual** with the following paragraph:

> As a married man or woman, you have one of the greatest gifts — and one of the greatest opportunities to do good — that it is possible for human beings to possess on earth. In your sacrament of marriage you have a vocation from God — a special call by Him to you and your mate — to serve Him together in a holy sacrament until death. He does not expect you to do it alone. On your wedding day He walked away from the altar with you and promises you even now all the help you need from him to fulfill your role. And as if the satisfactions cf heartwarming companionship for life and parenthood were not enough, He assures you, as the Church states in her marriage ritual, "the greatest measure of earthly happiness that may be allotted to man in this vale of tears," as well as happiness with each other and your children in heaven forever.[10]

Does the Church really believe this? Of course it does. In **Familiaris Consortio** (No. 13) John Paul II, drawing on Tertullian, asks "How can I ever express the happiness of the marriage that is joined together by the Church, strengthened by an offering, sealed by a blessing, announced by angels, and ratified by the Father. How wonderful the bond between two believers, with a single hope, a single desire, a single observance, a single service!"

Most religious people, and not a few good pagans, have seen or been part of families which realized this dream. Most young Catholics leaving the altar hope it will be realized in them. Yet more often than not, particularly in these days of constant therapy or expectations of future affluence, young marrieds may not be particularly inspired by what they see going on in the lives of professed Catholics, or worse, they may look upon the Christian dream as downright silly or simply unworkable. Christ had a similar effect on his contemporaries, and he sounds pretty impracticable to the wise-acres of our day. So before couples ride the marriage train too far, they have to see again and again the Christian vision and be brought to recognize the hard rock reality that marriage is a sacred work. Reconciling opposite sexes takes work, having babies is the hardest labor of all, paying for their birth and their rearing involves a long life of work and of going without. Dealing effectively with pain, suffering, and death, with sin and the effects of sin calls for Christian character, and this entails a lifetime of prayer, penance, and piety. From an early age married couples need to be prepared to deal with these normal contests of life and with the temptations of idols, whether they be contraception, divorce, abortion, lust, consumerism, improvident marriages, especially by those of tender years, invalid marriages, parenthood denied, latchkey households, etc.

John Paul II once cried out "Family, become what you are."[11] But, how can this be if the family's head and heart, its husband and wife, are divided in their objectives or untrained in the skills required for living together or are earthbound in a marriage that was made in heaven. If the primary mission of the family is to become what God created it to be — an intimate community of love between a man and a woman at the service of life, of the Church, and of society itself — then the family and the Church must be reordered to make this a likely possibility. If the family is the primary society, the cell of both Church and State, then something more is required of these larger societies than lip service to its well-being. More is required, especially of the Church, than moralizations that sex belongs in marriage, that marriage is forever, that abortion is an abominable crime, that homosexuality is a form of idolatry. Everyone in the world, except the most isolated groupings, knows what the Catholic Church has to say about contraception, adultery, and divorce. The Church never stops its preaching on family life. She recognizes how easily lust takes over unless the sexual appetite is channeled toward the purposes God wrote into its structure "from the beginning." This discipline, however well-internalized by individuals, calls for social supports. Without support by Church and State, the family is easily overwhelmed by destructive forces from the outside. St. Augustine was quite right in his affirmation that "no one can be ready for the next life unless he trains for it now,"[12] but few of us remain in virtue long if everyone around us impresses on us a different life style, while our own value system remains unenforced.

Church Support System

So, whenever the Church preaches to the world, it is important that her own house be in good order. The Catholic community is never perfect of course, given the sinful nature of mankind. Still the Church has had remarkable success at times and in places bringing its faithful up to standards of belief and behavior first set by Christ himself. In the United States, for example, 75 per cent of our married couples thirty years ago and more than 80 per cent of our singles attended Mass every Sunday.[13] The network of agencies, social and religious, under Catholic auspices engaged in health, education and welfare was one of the largest private enterprises of its kind in the country. Two-thirds of our Catholics considered the use of contraception as mortally sinful,[14] and for the vast majority divorce of a sacramental marriage was unthinkable. One is reminded of how early Christians were described in the 2nd century letter to Diognetus:

> They marry and have children, but they do not kill them. They share meals but not their wives. They live in the flesh, but they are not governed by the desires of the flesh. They pass their days on earth, but they are citizens of heaven. Obedient to the law, they live on a level that transcends the law.[15]

Some moral choices have always been easy, made so by nature itself. It requires little effort to get people to eat or to mate. The instinct to live draws people to work and to take care of their health. But when it comes to sexual intercourse confined to marriage or to fidelity after marriage or to safeguarding the life of the unwanted child, individuals need training and support. No sane society legitimizes freedom of its citizens to do anything they want. Certain forms of behavior are necessary for the good of society itself, and certain evil deeds must be avoided because they inflict pain or injury on oneself or others. When malefactors disrupt other people's freedom or everybody's sense of well-being, constituted authority must assume the role of everybody's protector. From the vantage point of God's word, when evil is seen as sin and liberation from sin as one of the Church's responsibilities to preach, then it is the Church's role to form consciences and to mould a life style that makes virtuous living a little easier for everybody. The first step in that process, of course, is to make sure that Christians know what evils are sins and what sins are punishable by God and/or by the Church. The reason Christ was in disfavor with the establishment of history is easily explained: "I give evidence that its ways are evil" (John 7:7).

Even in Diognetus' time the Christian community did not distinguish itself simply by self-determination alone. Tossed afloat in a pagan empire, its faithful were sheltered in and by the Church. As Pope St. Leo the Great explained it: "Our faith is nobler and stronger because sight has been replaced by a doctrine whose authority is accepted by believing hearts, enlightened from on high."[16] Catholic Christians then did not hide from their culture, but they maintained their own life style dictated by the demands of their religious faith. They were able to do this because those demands were reinforced by the Church. Single-minded preaching, the penitential discipline, liturgical rituals, pious customs, parish missions, and canonical sanctions — all administered by a clergy that believed in the truth of the Church's message — helped shape and maintain what became known as "the Catholic way of life." The best Catholics attributed their *modus vivendi* to the Church's inspiration and to her convincing teachers who, oftentimes it must be admitted, prodded or penalized defective performance. Since the Church was dealing with the hand-me-down of God's revelation, she was not about to preach ambiguous doctrine about sin and salvation or have her faithful face contradictory choices in what pertained to their salvation. The faithful had to be taught to think with Christ and with the Church and to be socialized into going the way of Christ and the Church. Repetition became the educational tool not only of Jesuits but of Mother Church herself. Catholics liked what they were taught and the Catholic Church became the envy of the secular world. This secular world often did not like what the Church preached but, like Christ earlier, she did command respect for the strong family life she helped create. Whether they agreed or not, the outsiders recognized the force of Catholic teaching.

It does not require a compilation of statistics or bookish footnotes to suggest that Catholic teaching on sex, marriage, and family life has lost its force. Not only is John Paul II a lonely voice crying in the wilderness, but there are important clerics who wish he would stop talking about sex completely. Technology, they say, has separated sex from procreation, from marriage itself, even from heterosexuality.

It would only waste time to explore the smugness of those Catholic opinion-moulders who seem gratified that Catholic family life is now no different from that of other Americans. The decline of their religion as a cultural force in their lives, the election of self-interest and self-fulfillment over duty and commitment, the flight from generous parenthood, the alienation of the young from the Church, these effects are not simply the result of Americanization, but in large part of the abandonment by priests of their role to preach the gospel in season and out, popular or no, and to defend fidelity, fertility, and indissolubility as proper and God-given norms for all Catholic couples, newlywed or not.

The First Catholic Response

Obviously, the Church must once more address her own people with renewed seriousness. The general public, which has longer experience than Catholics with liberated sex, still listens when the Pope speaks. Witness the attention John Paul II's office received when the Holy See spoke out on surrogate motherhood and homosexuality. While the Secular City was acknowledging that the questions the Pope raised called for public examination and discussion, Catholic spokesmen could be heard telling fellow religionists that these statements were not infallible, were historically conditioned, possibly erroneous, that Catholics would make up their own minds anyway.[17] We have, therefore, a major catechetical task ahead of us, one that goes beyond questions of sex and marriage. John Paul II at one point expressed the view that a contraceptive mentality involved a break in a person's relationship with God. In the contraceptive world there is no place for God. Worshipping oneself, one's needs or fulfillment to the exclusion of God's dominion and providence is an old form of idolatry revisited. If contraceptive-minded spouses fail at preventing God's intervention in their married life, they frequently defy God in another way, either by aborting the baby he gave them or by resenting the baby God clearly wants them to take unto themselves. The contraceptive mentality finds justification for fornication, adultery, and homosexuality — all mortal sins. Those who use contraceptives also have low rates of Sunday Mass, rarely go to confession, do not confess contraception, and feel free to receive the Eucharist, a sacrilege by any normal Catholic determination.[18] These actions are superficial indications of how little the sacred in life, i.e., those things which appertain to God, touches the innermost core of their being. So the answer is not so much to persuade contraceptive or sex-liberated Catholics to give up their sinful practices, but to get them to make a true and sincere act of Catholic faith in God himself.

The entire daily prayer of the Church is directed to God the Father through His Son, Jesus Christ, asking for holiness here and happiness hereafter, grace to convert from sin, confessions of fear that by sinning we may suffer the loss of heaven and endure the pains of hell. The prayer of the First Sunday of Advent is oft repeated by the Church in different ways throughout the year:

> All powerful God increase our strength of will for doing good that Christmas find an eager welcome at His coming and call us to His side in the Kingdom of Heaven where He lives and reigns with You and the Holy Spirit.

In almost every Mass and daily office these are the Church's constant prayers. But they are hypocritical words if priests do not take them seriously. We fall, then, under the condemnation Christ reserved for the hypocritical teachers of Jewry — whose words were right but whose conduct and lifestyle belied their preaching (Mt. 23:1-3). When we the clergy are silent on or tolerant of sin (something which cannot be said characterized Christ or the Prophets or the great saints of the Church), we become cooperators in the very kinds of evil the Church says brings eternal damnation. Unless, of course, belief in sin or eternal damnation is no longer important. If not, grave questions of credibility not only about the Church but about Christ come to the fore. Those who make their act of Catholic faith sincerely must also fashion, even if belatedly, a Christian character and develop defenses against our natural proneness to evil, sexual evil being a major source of sinfulness for most of us. Habits of virtue must be inculcated by repeated acts of virtue, occasions of sin must be avoided, the sacrament of penance (not just unreconstructed reconciliation) must be reintroduced into our lives as a regular discipline, prayer to God must become meaningful, and struggling sinners must receive the support of their bishops and priests. If the pulpits are silent on sin, if lecherous clergy and rebellious religious continue to give bad example or bad counsel, if the word at the parish level is that easy annulments of sacramental marriages, even after twenty years and six children, are becoming as commonplace as no-fault divorce, we cannot expect anyone to take Church teaching seriously on any subject.

One of the words in the Catholic lexicon rarely used today is chastity. Often confused with continence or the absence of all sexual activity, chastity channels the sexual drive towards its proper use, as temperance directs people to use money, liquor, drugs, power in a virtuous way. Chastity is the opposite of lust, that unbridled attachment to sexual pleasure, pursued in or out of marriage, not out of love or as a good of marriage but with the wrong person or with the right person without regard to his or her wishes or through sadistic and indecent acts in pursuit of venereal pleasure.[19] Chastity does not come with the cutting of the umbilical cord and it surely does not come with puberty. Learning to use well our powers of body or of mind is a life-long process. It involves more than tales of birds and bees, more than charts of the ovaries and the testicles, more than repetition of old saws, such as "sex is good," the favorite phrase of modern text books. Chastity involves training of the will, as well as the mind, from an early age in anticipation of puberty, learning the do's and don'ts of behavior before these are really needed. Such training was not as difficult when there were four, five or six siblings in the one house — of different sexes — but it is still possible and today more than ever absolutely necessary. The Church must play its part for everyone's sake, including Christ's.

Twenty years ago the charge leveled against the Church was that she sent her people on "guilt trips." Removing guilt, even of the normally non-neurotic variety, became a crusade within the Church. Well, why not a sense of guilt for doing evil? The gangster who slits a throat with great aplomb and with a posture of internal calm is not sick. He is a social monster. More than ten years ago Karl Menninger wrote a book entitled **Whatever Became of Sin**? He knew sin was not in hiding and thought that the Church's doctrine of original sin was the only dogma of faith for which there was empirical evidence. Menninger really was asking not about sin, but "Whatever Became of Guilt?" that remorse following wrongdoing which always had been the necessary internal control of errant behavior.[20]   The Church never ceased sending her faithful on guilt trips. She is doing it all the time — today making them feel guilty about their racism, their anti-Semitism, their warlike attitudes, their sexism, and so forth. Since Vatican II we have rightfully created a Catholic climate which makes the faithful conscious of their failings as members of society. Catholics today often are embarrassed because they make a great deal of money or have voted against the Teamsters Union or joined the New York Athletic Club. Why are they embarrassed? Because they have acquired a sense of guilt about the violations of proper social norms, developed and preached by their bishops.[21]

But where anymore is there embarrassment when a Catholic politician leaves his wife and marries another or, though married, is known to have a girl friend? A young sixteen year old today has few qualms about discussing her active sex life on a street corner, nor about carrying condoms, nor about having a baby out of wedlock. Indeed we Catholics have almost begun to boast about our relaxed annulment procedures.[22]   How often anymore do we speak of motherhood? Or of the larger family, so praised by Vatican II and the last six Popes?[23] We have developed an easy tolerance of our sexual aberrations, but a shame too about those aspects of family life which once were the proud boast of the Catholic community. Since the fundamental mission of the Church is eternal salvation, the least we expect of clerics is that they begin once more to preach what the Church always considered essential to it. Sermons, lectures, seminars and conferences all over the Church with a coherent message built around the doctrines contained in **Humanae Vitae** and **Familiaris Consortio** are matters of urgent necessity if the Church believes what she preaches. The faithful may not, likely will not, be converted overnight, but vigorous preaching of solid Catholic doctrine will help establish the Catholic norms against which all Catholics are called upon to make the conscientious decisions for which they are responsible before God. Such preaching, if systematically enforced, will put an end to the poisonous view that Church teaching counts for nothing or is about to change. Determination of this kind, too, will restore Catholic pulpits and classrooms to those who fully believe what the Church teaches and Pre-Cana Conferences to couples who love children and live by the ideals of natural family planning which is Christian to the core.

The Second Catholic Step

Preaching and teaching by themselves will not renew the Church's family system in ways consistent with Christ's teaching or with revelation. We must restore pride in the Church as the Body of Christ — the one Sacrament of Salvation, true and Catholic. A great deal is made these days about community, usually from those who look upon the Church as People more than Christ's Body, who denigrate the so-called institutional Church and who seek to form small elite or disparate groups within the Church for the purpose of sifting out its cultural accretions the meaning of the pure gospel of Christ. Elites, by themselves, whether composed of academic activists or poor liberationists or just plain zealots for a cause, however much they serve personal needs, are not mass movements, unless they succeed as revolutionaries in dominating the institution. Frequently they are separatists who, far from creating it, fracture community. Examine what "break-through Catholics" did to the Church of Holland. See what academic elites have done to the religious communities in the United States. One hardly uses the phrase "religious community" any more, given the internal divisions among men and women originally vowed to a community that depends on the Church for its right to exist.

In the normal course of events community follows institution. It does not precede it. Wherever two or three are gathered to do a work together, there you have an institution, whether they are Christ and the Apostles in the upper room, Mother Teresa in a Calcutta boarding house, or the devil in his workshop. The family is such an institution and its Christian work is enhanced best by that other institution called the Church, the home where the family should find its best inspiration, its best encouragement, support, and protection. For all practical purposes this normally means the Catholic parish. Mr. and Mrs. Average Catholic admire the Pope on television and are still in awe at their bishop when he comes to confirm. But the parish is the House of God with which families regularly have direct contact. Most couples show little interest in activism, even for their pastor. But sleepers, too, need to sense the Church's presence in their lives, and this usually means contact with the local parish. One of the tragedies which ensued, once the success of the U. S. parish system was established, has been the demise of what came to be called "census-taking," but originally was known as home visits by the priest.

Thirty-one years ago as New York's new Family Life Director, I proposed to a Family Life Convention in Boston, a Famly Life Action Committee in every parish.[24] The time was ripe then but no one paid attention. Later we developed Cana Committees and CFM groups, which were eminently successful wherever they took root. They served as a leaven for the local parish making holiness in marriage respectable and babies a joy to possess. But bishops generally ignored them and when the Cana-CFM leadership decided they were a more modern Church than that represented by the Pope, these "cells" and the priests who shepherded them were looked upon as menaces to the institutional Church, dividing its membership and destroying its community.

Now we must begin all over again. Once upon a time we took poor immigrants, invented a Baltimore Catechism for them and a school system headed by singleminded and dedicated religious and moulded them into the finest body of practicing Catholics the free and modern world may have seen.[25] We still have immigrants, perhaps more in a ten-year period than ever, but millions also of half committed Catholics in need of recatechesis. This time we shall have to depend on the contributed services of lay Catholics who have been trained by priests who are themselves the graduates of proper seminaries. We now need elite laity and doctrinally sound priests who can translate in the 21st Century the Catholic faith as effectively as their religious counterparts in the 19th. But most of all we need a Cardinal to write a new **Faith of Our Fathers** and a series of modern Baltimore Councils, or whatever, which will just as effectively as their predecessors, make the Catholic faith live once more in the overwhelming majority of homes which claim the name Catholic.

The Church's Third Mission

But though the Church works better to shore up the family life of the baptized, it may not shirk its responsibility to deal with the family ethos of contemporary society, that which is wreaking havoc on the family life of more than Catholics. Couple-to-Couple Leagues, Base Communities, Charismatic Groups, Right-to-Life Associations, like the old Cana Groups and CFM, serve many Christian purposes, not the least of which is support and defense of involved Catholic families in an anti-family world. We need to encourage more of whatever associations deepen the faith of family members. But protective and defense mechanisms are not enough. For at least three hundred years Popes have been speaking about the Church's apostolate to the world and the world seems to get further and further away from its Judaeo-Christian roots.[26] The Second Vatican Council was supposed to place the Church in the middle of the world, with a view to its evangelization, at the least to make the world less hostile to religion. The most notable effect of these efforts seems instead to have been the secularization of the religious life of Catholics. The culture of the Western World is on a downward slide now that priests have removed their Roman collars, nuns their veils, and so many Catholic spouses are taking off their wedding rings. The only things people are advised these days to keep are their condoms.

What are we Catholics going to do about this situation? How do we reach over the heads of secular opinion-moulders and reach our fellow citizens? Fr. Anthony Zimmerman of Japan asks the startling question: When are we going to master the art of electronic communication? Save for Mother Angelica, we have had hardly any influence either in mass media production or distribution. Still, the problem goes beyond manufacturing a hundred Fulton Sheens, even beyond our giant universities, those great framers of secularist mentalities, which shape the thinking of opinion moulders in the *Washington Post,* CBS, the New York Art World, and the Rockefeller Foundation.

While the root causes of our neo-pagan environment may well be traced to those universities which spawn cynicism, skepticism and amoralism and to the media which market these vices,[27] the U. S. family must come to see that its most immediate enemy today is government. Breaking the ties that bind has become almost a national pastime, with government the ultimate and chief umpire. Whether the rubric be "freedom" or "privacy," whether the actors be the courts, the bureaucracies or the legislatures, the scales of justice are being tipped toward abstract persons and away from citizens' necessary and natural associations, of which the family is primary and most vital.[28] We have moved from divorce for cause to "no fault" divorce. The number of Americans living in non-marital "families" is increasing and the attempts to demaritalize the family are no longer camoflaged. In 1981, the name of the *White House Conference on the Family* was changed to a conference "on families" as a result of pressure from the homosexual lobby. Jimmy Carter lent Presidential respectability to the rejection of the nation's historic understanding of family as heterosexual and marital.[29] Catholics abet this process when they insist that a loveless marriage is a dead marriage and when Church tribunals discover belatedly that a sacramental marriage never existed after twenty-five years of common life and six grown children. One allegedly Catholic theologian goes a step further by defining marriage as "the ultimate form of friendship achievable by sexually attracted persons."[30]

The hitherto privileged position of the family to the meaning of a free society, recognized through the Christian era as untouchable by the State, as the primary educator of the young and their most important school, the ground and center of public virtue itself, is being challenged by those who ask: "Is marriage necessary?" The single most important buffer against State domination of personal lives is under fire by a government which wants more control of family failure, ignoring its own role in the denigration of the family. It is not surprising that the withering away of the family would be the objective of every socialist state, yet a similar end result is not impossible in an omnicompetent democratic state whose norms of governing are utilitarian and anti-religious. Affirming the importance of government to social well-being is not equivalent to endorsing a democratic government's domination of the family. Only sixty years ago (1924) U. S. bishops expressed outrage at the thought of Federally sponsored child labor laws, i.e., giving Washington authority to intervene in parents' decisions. Today contemplated laws to create children's rights against their parents hardly create a stir.

Nor are we embarrassed any longer when public law pretends men and women are the same. Common sense should dictate otherwise, but we remain strangely passive as government flattens roles and occupations, redefining the feminine in completely masculine terms — of office, rank, contest, achievement, success and failure. The stereotype of the oppressed housewife and mother appears everywhere as part of the orchestrated effort to persuade the American public that women are to be honored for the salaried work they do, not for their motherhood.[31]   One feminist theologian recently re-exegeted the NT to claim that it is Mary's role as Christ's first disciple that gives her special status in the Church, not the fact that she is Mother of God.[32]

The family unit, especially its intended permanence and procreative significance, is now looked upon by many as an oppressive structure for the simple reason that it involves a relationship with a lordly male "for better or for worse," and potential pregnancies over many years besides. The family is seen as oppressive, especially because it enshrines man-woman differences. By politicizing the complaints of frustrated feminists, organizations such as the *National Organization for Women* seek to use governmental power to gain for them what they are not likely to gain through the ballot box.

Indeed, many of the modern limitations on heterosexual marital life have come not by a vote of the people but by the fiat of a judge, an agency or a politician. No one in his right mind would deny a woman access to any public role or status available to all U. S. citizens on an equal opportunity basis. But the obliteration of all differences as between male and female, parents and children, able and unable, even at the expense of a family's pre-eminent rights? No physician may pierce a child's ear without a parent's permission but the same physician may pierce a child's vagina to abort a fetus without a by-your-leave to a parent. If it is a legal requirement of modern justice that varieties of species, sexes, abilities and freedoms be abolished, why is government so selective? Why are the voters rarely asked to sanction radical departures from traditional American wisdom? *Roe vs. Wade* as written would never have made its way in 1973 through the legislatures of the 50 states. ERA did not make it into the Constitution. And the last thing homosexual activists want is a vote on their status by the citizenry. Instead they have institutionalized homosexuality by terrorizing politicians.

Since the Church by Vatican II's decree is engaged more than ever in political affairs of nations, it would seem that its major effort should entail confronting the anti-family policies of what more and more takes on the coloration of Hilaire Belloc's Servile State.

Catechesis: The Truth, The Whole Truth

John Paul II has a favorite catechetical thrust: Catholics have the right to be taught the Church's authentic message whole and entire.[33] He repeats this demand because he knows that today Catholic teachers are frequently silent on those aspects of the gospel which many moderns are reluctant to accept. If culture tends to make cowards of us all, it makes us especially cowardly in our time about proclaiming vigorously the full Catholic doctrine and policy decisions on sex and marriage.

The following are a few areas which call for bolder teaching:

1. Motherhood

Some years ago after a sojourn in India on behalf of family planning, Germaine Greer, the early birth control advocate, gave a lecture in Dallas which shocked some of her friends. "I have gone to India," she said, "thinking there were too many of them and returned home deciding there were too many of me." The one-time author of the 1970 best seller **The Female Eunuch**, now 45 years of age and the author of a new book entitled **Sex and Destiny** (1983), complained that Western Society is anti-child. Without abandoning her advocacy of planned parenthood, Miss Greer nonetheless regretted her own barrenness: "I chose not to have a child when I could have. Then when I thought I could fit one into my life, I found I couldn't conceive."[34]

It is a strange anomaly of the present Church situation that so many Catholics today live by the norms of Germaine Greer the younger than by the norms which have characterized Catholic family life in any country where the Church was effective. It is only a generation ago that Catholic moralists instructed fertile Catholic couples who were capable that they fulfilled God's command to "increase and multiply" if they brought three or four children into the world.[35] Indeed, the better educated Catholics of that era were convinced of that demand and frequently had larger families, these couples described later in **Gaudium et Spes** (No. 50) as having "a generous heart." Today the expected 1.8 children from American marriages falls far short of what Christians usually meant when they used the word "family." Less than 10 per cent of young American women expect ever to have four children. Most will settle for two.[36] Consequently, if the American woman is likely to have the first of her two children in her early twenties and the last before she is thirty, there are serious marital and familial, to say nothing of moral, problems ahead for practically all Catholic marriageables. If the Christian woman's role is, as John Paul II says, an "irreplaceable value," what are we Churchmen doing to change a cultural mentality which dishonors motherhood as a vocation and makes it instead an exercise in self-satisfaction? What we have involved here, if we are speaking of people who claim the Faith, is a Catholic couple's relationship with God and attention to Divine providence.[37]

By way of conclusion to this section, something should be said about womanpower. Germaine Greer went to India and discovered the kind of power Indian mothers exercised in their local villages and in city neighborhoods, even as their husbands patrolled the civic community as if they were budding Rajahs. Most of us who grew up in Christian families could have enlightened her on this subject. Rare was the mother of a family who was not the heart and center of her home and of her parish. Catholic mothers were a power to be reckoned with because they knew who they were and so did their husbands, who generally were not the macho-male types feminists like to decry. As a pastor I could well have gotten along without the curates but would not have survived without the women — the single and the married — women who contributed most to the priestly ministry and to a large amount of neighborhood social action. The Eternal Feminine rocked the cradle and ruled the world, not the Female Eunuch. A generation ago the psychological affliction which imperilled our nation, according to writers such as Philip Wylie and psychiatrists like Edward Strecker, was not Ramboism but Momism — women in the home, women in the schools, women in the welfare institutions, and the rising influence then of women at work.[38] By 1960 the *National Catholic Welfare Conference* (predecessor of the USCC) was concerned enough to publish a booklet called *Father, the Head of the Home,* as if Catholics needed that reassurance from Washington, D.C.

When we speak, therefore, of womanpower we must make sure that it is not manpower that is sought as the special quality of woman and the emasculation of men which Streckers says began under "Momism." Nor does it help the cause of women as women to have "Femachos" speak for them. Women surely have the right to rival men in the public arena if they wish and if they can fulfill their marital and maternal responsibilities. But mothering is power enough for most women, especially if their men are accomplished in their own right and are satisfied with their role as fathers of the family. When elites speak of women hurting because their wants are unfulfilled, one should ask which wants and what women. Mary Joyce said it well: "Women need not hunger for authority when their special gift is for influencing everything. That's their best power."[39]

2. Fatherhood

St. Augustine, in addressing fathers, was wont to call them "my fellow bishops." He conveyed the idea that they were heads of their families much as the bishop is the head of the Church, with primary obligations in the family to teach, to rule, to sanctify. We speak glibly of marriage today as a 50-50 proposition when in truth it is the union of a 100 per cent man with a 100 per cent woman. Augustine was only building on St. Paul's formal dictum, "Man is the head of the woman as Christ is the head of the Church" (Eph. 23:5). Less than ten years ago Stephen Clark's monumental study **Man and Woman in Christ** reinforced what has been a Judaeo-Christian tradition "from the beginning," viz., that within the domestic community (we are not speaking of society generally) there are complementary roles to be played, with the husband responsible for the overall government of the family without the wife being his subordinate, and the mother responsible for all those areas which pertain to the internal life of the family, without the husband being voiceless. This division of labor is looked upon as God's creative plan for the family.[40]

If boys growing up suffered under "Momism," tending them to accept domination by women, they are taught by feminism to look upon women more as sex partners to be played with than as mothers who need their protection, support and leadership. Christian marriage with its propensity to child-bearing quickly roots the man in the father's role from the earliest days of his boyhood training. That very concept of manhood and fatherhood has been under attack in recent years — first from the business and professional community which demand commitment to the job more than to the family; from the economic system itself which has made the two income family almost a necessity to reach or maintain middle class respectability;[41] and from the ideology of feminism which legitimizes manly traits in women, while sanctioning a certain feminization in men.[42]

The Church does not need George Gilder (**Sexual Suicide**, 1973, **Men and Marriage**, 1987) to know that women by virtue of their mother's role are more important to society than men and a civilizing force of children and of husbands. Even a woman's more pervasive and more erotic sexuality is a superiority used to good advantage within the historic family. But deny the manly and fatherly role, or make it a matter of indifference, and it is the males who are liberated — to eschew what they think is the drudgery of home life, to distance themselves from commitment to one woman, to see sex as a toy, to turn homosexuality into another outlet for pleasure, to prove their virility not by domestic and social achievement but by sexual prowess.

If men to be men need fatherhood to fulfill their God-given manly nature, and as more than an incidental experience, women are most contented in the arms of a man whose love goes beyond sex to the care and protection of her children, on whom she can rely, making it possible for her to develop her own womanhood.[43]

It is important for the Church to defend and promote the child-centered family and the importance of men and fatherhood to that family. In their many economic proposals the Church should call for the revision of tax laws to allow families with dependent children to keep more of their income. Some way must be found to distinguish in our tax laws family oriented workers from child free careerists, with economic incentives favoring a family's single wage earner.[44]

3. Natural Family Planning

Never before in American history have Catholics had it so easy with regard to the necessities of life, even when one allows for the plight of the unemployed and the farm community. Never has there been more known about the natural spacing of births. Never has there been more practical help available for natural family planning. Never has the teaching of the Church been more clear, never better defended. Never has the moral bankruptcy of the contraceptive movement been so obvious nor the social ill-effects of its widespread use. Never before in the history of any country has there been less reason for those who profess faith in Christ and his Church to turn away from Catholic teaching on marital love and birth control.[45]

Yet, twenty years after **Humanae Vitae**, more than a half century away from **Casti Connubii**, the vast majority of married Catholics use contraceptives and natural family planning remains a step-child of the Church in practically every diocese.[46]

One other thing: The serious sins that most Christians are likely to commit from their earliest days involve marriage or sex and actions related to either. The sixth is not God's first commandment, but sins against marriage or sins involving lust are more commonplace than blasphemy, heresy, murder or treason. Furthermore, as St. Thomas Aquinas long ago demonstrated, untrammelled lust often leads to loss of faith:

> Blindness of mind, lack of balanced consideration, inconstancy, precipitation, love of self, hatred of God, excessive clinging to the present world, and horror or despair of the world to come.[47]

For this reason the Church has always preached moderation in the use of the sexual powers, insisting that Catholics be trained from their earliest years in the virtue of chastity.

The tragedy of our times is that sexual sins have been reduced to pre-moral evils or peccadillos, of little account in the formation of Christian character. Yet since sexual sins are of their nature seriously sinful, they have an important bearing on eternal salvation.[48]

4. Eternal Life, Salvation, Sin

The night prayer of the Church on Sunday reads as follows:

> Lord Jesus Christ, when tempted by the devil, you remained loyal to your Father, whose angels watched over you at his command. Guard your Church and keep us safe from the plague of sin so that we remain loyal to the day we enjoy your salvation and your glory.

Open the liturgical books of the Church at any point and you are likely to come across sentiments similar to these — a Christian prayer for eternal salvation and a plea for Christ's help in rising above our sinful nature to reach this beatitude. "God made us to know Him, to love Him, to serve Him in this life and to be happy with Him forever in the next." The penny Baltimore Catechism said it right. As we read in Hebrews 13:14, 11, "There is no eternal city for us in this life but we look for one in the life to come." The spiritual life of Catholics calls for a way of life that more and more is free of serious sin. Once the Catholic is in sin he is expected to reconcile with God through the sacrament still called Penance.

Are we turning away from our doctrine on sin to calm the guilt feelings of sinners without regard to Christ's express command?

Summary and Recommendations

In a few concluding words I would like to offer what seems to me to be the most important elements of the Church's agenda for the 21st Century, most important because they deal with the Church's family — the family life of middle class American Catholics, those great-great grandchildren of once poor and relatively unlettered immigrants, and the family life also of the new poor whose Catholicity is traditional but undeveloped and often marginal. Jesuit Joseph Fitzpatrick once phrased the Church's dilemma as follows:

> How can we do away with the poverty of thousands of families without destroying the deep and significant values which these families so often represent? This is an old and classic theme: the struggle to escape from poverty, disadvantage, destitution, only to realize that the very process which the poor man thought would enrich and ennoble his life has destroyed it.[49]

Is this not what has already happened to those Catholic great-great grand children?

When we address such a dilemma I presume that we speak only from our Christian givens, i.e., out of the truths about the family revealed by God through Jesus Christ, Our Lord, and communicated to us by His Church under the infallible guidance of the Holy Spirit through the voices of Peter's successors and the Bishops in communion with them.

Accepting these truths and the present U. S. realities, a number of things seem to propose themselves as worthy of consideration:

1. First, there must be a recatechesis of the faithful concerning the nature of Eternal Life and Christian commitment to the Church's way of achieving it. Eternal Life is the motivation and sanction of all Christian striving in this life and Catholics once more must come to value both the goal and the striving.

St. Paul spoke of it as follows: "There is no eternal life for us in this life but we look for one in the life to come" (Hebrews 13:14). Or, as he told the Phillipians (3:14-15): "I strain ahead for what is still to come. I am racing for the finish, for the prize to which God calls us upwards to receive in Christ Jesus."

And to the modern teachers who tell our young that the important Christian value is how they live this present life, Paul has this to say: "If our hope in Christ has been for this life only, we are the most unfortunate of all people" (I Cor. 15:19).

"Do you really believe this?" — an important question not unlike the one asked by Paul VI in his 1975 exhortation *Evangelii Nuntiandi* (No. 76) and by Christ in the Upper Room (John 16:31). Secularization has given our people an earthbound view of life. If this remains the case, there is little reason that they will believe anything else Christ and the Church have to say, unless it is to their convenience.

2. Secondly, we must recatechize our faithful on the Divine vocation of marriage, the central place of children and parenthood in that calling, and the vital importance (for Christians at least) of the sacred norms to fulfillment in this life and reward or punishment in the next.

To do this well the U. S. Bishops, perhaps in collaboration with the Congregation for the Doctrine of the Faith, must assess the present status of authentic teaching within Church institutions and initiate whatever remedial steps are necessary to see that correct teaching is the rule in the Church. Church membership is not a mere matter of affiliation, i.e., of personal choice. It involves commitment to the specific requirements of the Church. There is, after all, a content to Catholic commitment and for this to prevail authentic teachers are required. Furthermore, Catholic teaching must be reinforced down the line by Church committees, commissions, and curias. Uncertain voices existed in the Church of St. Paul (I Cor. 14:8), but after two millenia there is little reason for confused teaching under Catholic auspices, especially on family life, to continue. If the Church appears clearly as counter-culture on matters socio-political, why is John Paul II almost a voice crying in the wilderness on the morals of Catholic family life? We hear much these days of the seamless garment, but what is more intrinsically connected than the breakdown of the family structure and the contraceptive movement? Why do we permit teachings in our school systems which soft-pedal or deny the doctrines taught by **Vitae** and **Familiaris Consortio**?

Indeed, those of us in the teaching situation are no longer surprised how unmoved we have become over dissent in our midst and blase, too, when we hear again and again that the vast majority of Catholics reject the Church's sexual ethic. Is this their fault?

We need no reminders from our canon lawyers. We only need follow our liturgy to know whose fault it is. The 23rd Sunday in Ordinary Time, which restates our obligations under the Ten Commandments, calls upon Ezekiel in the Old Testament (33:7-9) and Matthew in the New (18:15-20) as reminders of what should be expected of the Church, especially of its pastors. They are to dissuade the flock from their evil ways. If pastors do not do this they are held responsible for the spiritual death of the wicked. And if the wicked will not take fraternal correction, even from the Church, then "treat him as you would a Gentile or a tax collector." These are Jesus' words, not those of a Curial bureaucrat.

Pastors of the Church are to preach and teach, to sanctify through the liturgy and the proper administration of the sacraments, and to govern the Catholic community. But their preaching is in vain if this community is ungoverned, i.e., if false teachers prevail without restraint and sacraments are administered sacrilegiously with no complaint from the pastors. In recent days political scientist George Weigel reminded bishops of St. Augustine's concept "tranquillitas ordinis," a negative concept to be sure, but one without which sinful men cannot live in peace. As Weigel phrases it: "Order keeps things from getting worse than they would be under conditions of chaos and anarchy."[50]

What is so different about insisting that only fully committed believers teach and supervise the Church's pastoral mission, especially among the poor whose family life is at the moment reasonably intact?

What is so heinous about quarantining the carriers of heresy, which is what "pick and choose Catholicism" really means, in a Church professing to proclaim Christ's truth? We are not dealing anymore with a sick situation calling for therapy. We are dealing with an evil situation which demands the corrective action of which Christ himself was the prime mover.

If we do not move in this direction with some semblance of deliberate speed, then the universal catechism, the one significant by-product of the 1985 Extraordinary Synod, will turn out to be another Church document filed and forgotten.

3. Thirdly, the Church should initiate a national crusade on behalf of *Natural Family Planning* — not only to teach our people how to be married and Catholic, when child spacing is incicated, but to educate the vast body of religious Americans what authentic married love is and why marriages based on this kind of love are more meaningful to them, more perduring, and more fruitful for both Church and Society. For the Catholic people alone NFP promises this much at least — a married life in conformity with God's law.

4. Finally, and this surely will be the Church's most arduous task, the Catholic community must bring its corporate influence to bear on the public institutions of our society, especially on the government, on the media, and on those who fashion the secular mind-sets of the country's public leaders. We are not speaking here simply of anti-pornography, anti-condom, anti-abortion activities, although we must not underestimate their importance as rallying points in a democracy of pro-family activists. There is the critical matter of freedom of religion. In the last forty years religionists have allowed themselves to be anti-established out of public life, with religion reduced to the status of public oddity. The approved, acceptable public role of an otherwise avowed religionist is capsulated in one affirmation: "I believe in Jesus Christ but . . . ." Here the adversary is government and its various subdivisions or bureaucracies. Nor any longer must we permit the media to trivialize or treat contemptuously the teachings and sacred authority of the Church. The recent pilgrimage of John Paul II to his American faithful appeared at times to be an anti-Papal crusade by the frequency with which dissident Catholics were called upon by media to explain away the Church and its Pope. The media would not have dared treat the Jewish, Black or Labor community with such cynicism. We surely need a well-supported Catholic League to defend Catholic interests, as Bnai B'rith, the NAACP, and the AFL-CIO protect the rights of their followers. We tend to shy at charges of censorship, of accusations aimed mostly at denying influence on the media to religionists. Why we have not by now an active role in the world of electronic communications is something of a mystery, especially in view of the success of Evangelical Protestants shoring up the faith of their flocks.

As a last point, we must draw on that segment of the Catholic university world which still is or wishes to be institutionally committed to the Catholic Church and its faith. One of the tragedies of our times is that the aspiring Catholic Harvards have become more Harvard than Catholic and of little use to the Church in confronting the neo-pagan and statist ideas that presently prevail in the higher regions of American society. What we must never forget is that there are a large number of Catholic scholars who believe in the truths of their faith and are quite willing to defend them. These are not the scholars quoted frequently on CBS or by the *New York Times,* oftentimes not even in *Origins,* the documentary service of the USCC.

If we can speak of the Catholic lay apostolate any longer, and we can if we mean "Catholic" as well as "lay," then pastors must give their support to these kinds of faithful and permit them to take the Catholic cause into the market place, where they, not clergy, will demand respect and get it, after they first fight for recognition.[51]

With a fully developed alternative to the present secularized organs of opinion-moulding, our Catholic parents can hopefully once more take pride in their Church and the quality of their family life, even if it is not mainstream secularized America.

FOOTNOTES

1 **The American Catholic People** (Doubleday, 1987) p. 183.

2 *The New York Daily News,* June 4, 1987.

3 1985 Gallup Poll.

4 John Paul II, **Reflections on Humanae Vitae** (St. Paul Editions, 1984) pp. 9-10.

5 English *L'Osservatore Romano,* July 6, 1987, p. 12.

6 Eugene Kennedy once argued that the moral distortions in Catholic Life were due to "people's acceptance of the Church's moral authority on the way they live their moral lives." (*America,* August 22, 1970, p. 87.) Jesuit Francis Buckley attributed them to "moral conformism and the acceptance of authority." (*I Confess* (1972) p. 53). Sister Marie Augusta Neal thought it improper to impose any "doctrine or values or commitment." (*Discovery Patterns Book,* 1969, p. 92). *Time Magazine,* September 3, 1971, p. 41, in a review of what was wrong with Catholic confession, stressed its disastrous effects.

7 Mt. 19:3 ff; also Mk. 10:2 ff.

8 *Human Life Review,* Spring 1981, p. 103.

9 CF. Fr. Henry Sattlers report, *Newsletter* of the Fellowship of Catholic Scholars, December 1982, p. 6 ff.

10 Random House, 1958, p. 3-4. Even George Gilder senses there is more to marriage than sex:

"Marriage is a sacrament, it's a sacred institution. Without this sanctity, it tends to become a kind of 'consumer contract' that can be revoked if both parties aren't satisfied or some better product happens to come along on the market." (*National Catholic Register,* November 23, 1981, p. 15).

11 **Familiaris Consortio,** No. 19.

12 PS 148 1-2; CCL 40, 2165-2166.

13 George A. Kelly, **Catholics and the Practice of the Faith**. (Paulist Press 1946).

14 CF. Andrew Greeley, *Chicago Studies,* Spring 1963.

15 Letter to Diognetus (usually attributed to Justin Martyr in the 2nd century), F. X. Funk, **The Apostolic Fathers**, 397-401. This citation is used in the Church's Divine Office of Holy Men and Women.

16 Second Sermon on the Ascension, PL 54, P. 398.

17 CF. *Origins,* May 28, 1987, pp. 21 ff.

[18] CF. *Notre Dame Magazine,* Summer 1987.

[19] CF. Henry V. Sattler, CSSR, **Sex is Alive and Well and Flourishing Among Christians** (1980), pp. 124-125. See his treatment of Sacramental Sexuality in Chapter 6.

[20] Karl Menninger in his book **Whatever Became of Sin?** uses rhyme to make a point: "At three I had a feeling of / ambivalence towards my brothers / and so it followed naturally / I poisoned all my lovers. / But now I'm happy: I have learned / the lesson this has taught / that everything I do that's wrong / is someone else's fault."

[21] For a full treatment of how every formation process works — and the role of the penetential discipline for Catholics, see George A. Kelly, **Who Should Run the Catholic Church?** (1976), Chapters 4 and 5.

[22] Report on a June 7-10, 1987, meeting of the NCCB at St. Mary's College, Notre Dame, Ind., at which an important prelate admitted the Church is granting divorces but had not yet admitted the fact. See also Bishop Edward Egan, former Judge of the Roman Rota, on the "Nullity of Marriage" in the *Newsletter* of the Fellowship of Catholic Scholars, December 1986 and March 1987.

[23] For a secular view see James H. S. Bossard with Eleanor Stoker Boll, **The Large Family System** (1956).

[24] Irving A. DeBlanc and Norma Scavilla, **Sanctity and Success in Marriage**, NCWC Family Life Bureau, 1956.

[25] George A. Kelly, **Catholics and the Practice of the Faith,** and Thomas Coogan, **Catholic Fertility in Florida**, Paulist Publications, 1946.

[26] CF. **The Lay Apostolate: Papal Teachings**, 1961, St. Paul Editions.

[27] The latest book trumpeting these concerns is Allan Bloom's **The Closing of the American Mind** (Simon and Schuster, 1987). The Rothman-Lichter studies of media bias can be found in **The Media Elite: America's New Power Brokers** (Adler and Adler, 1987).

[28] This subject is brilliantly covered in an unpublished paper of Donald Keefe, S.J., entitled "The Law and the Covenant," first presented on April 10-12, 1987, at a conference on Biotechnology and Law sponsored by the Institute for Theological Encounter with Science and Technology, Adamstown, Md. A number of other scholars have addressed the cultural tendency to downgrade the family. Brigham Young's Bruce Hafen has a first rate treatment in **This World** (Summer 1987), entitled "Custom, Law, and the American Family." Calling the family "the most valuable thing in people's lives" and a "mediating structure" between the state and individuals, Hafen argues that family life is "the source of public virtue — a willingness to obey the unenforceable," "a sense of obligation to interests larger than one's own." He traces the shift under governmental and legal pressures to the significance of marriage to individuals. Thomas Molnar's "The Target is the Family" *(Human Life Review,* Summer, 1987) covers the same ground — with special stress on the "sexual politicization' of the family in recent decades.

[29] A good review of the new literature redefining the family to avoid "perpetuating constrictive gender identities" is contained in the September 1987 issue of *The Family in America,* a Rockford Institute publication.

[30] See Dennis Doherty (Ed.), **Dimensions of Human Sexuality** (1979), p. 130.

[31] In article 19 of **Laborem Exercens** "Having to abandon these (domestic) tasks in order to take up paid work outside the home is wrong from the point of view of the good of society and of the family when it contradicts or hinders these primary goals of the mission of a mother." See also **Familiaris Consortio No. 23**. One Canadian study concluded that wealth tends to make men more conservative, women more liberal. Feminism was described as a "rich woman's hobby." *(The Family in America,* May 1987, p. 2).

[32] CF. Footnote 22.

[33] John Paul II to U. S. bishops, October 5, 1979, in *Pilgrim of Peace,* USSC publication, p. 119.

[34] See *Newsletter* of the Fellowship of Catholic Scholars, June 1984, p. 8. In her 1971 **The Female Eunuch**, she looked upon the family as "the prison of domesticity" and "patriarchy's chief institution."

[35] John Ford, Contemporary Moral Theology: Volume 2 — **Marriage Questions**. (Newman, 1963, pp. 420-421).

[36] *Statistical Abstract,* 1987, p. 65.

[37] **Familiaris Consortio No. 23**.

[38] Philip Wylie's **Generation of Vipers** and Edward Strecker's **Their Mother's Daughter** (1956).

³⁹ *National Catholic Register,* March 22, 1987. The initial ethnic family was "father headed and mother centered" in which the father generally exercised executive command while mother managed the household and oversaw the division of labor among the children. [Charles H. Mindel and Robert W. Habenstein (Eds.), **Ethnic Families in America: Patterns and Variations** (1976), p. 415].

⁴⁰ Servant Publications, 1980.

⁴¹ See George A. Kelly, **The Catholic Church and the American Poor** (Alba House, 1975), especially Chapter 2.

⁴² See Paul Vitz's April 1987 article in *Fidelity* and Stephen B. Clark, *op. cit., passim.*

⁴³ Mary Joyce.

⁴⁴ Charles E. Rice, **Fifty Questions on Abortion, Euthanasia and Related Issues** (1986), pp. 76 ff. It is of some interest that the Social Feminists who helped draft the New Deal — Secretary of Labor Frances Perkins, Women's Bureau Head Mary Anderson, and Mary Dawson of the Democratic National Committee — saw the achievement of a family wage as a solution to the country's most serious social problems. While working women were to be treated as equals to men in the marketplace, they were clearly an undesirable social development. The family wage would put an end to women's and child labor. *(The Family in America,* June 1987, pp. 3-4).

⁴⁵ This is the essence of a view propounded forcefully by John Kipplay in a letter to this writer.

⁴⁶ Cardinal Bernardin in his 1986 report to the U. S. bishops said as much: "In many dioceses it is not seen as an inherent part of marriage preparation or marriage enrichment, although the dimension seems to be improving." *(Origins,* December 4, 1986, p. 470).

⁴⁷ **Summa Theologica** II II, g. 153, a. 5.

⁴⁸ See Ronald Lawler, Joseph Boyle, and William May, **Catholic Sexual Ethics**, (OSV Press, 1985), pp. 64 and 214-215.

⁴⁹ Cited in George A. Kelly, **The Catholic Church and the American Poor**, (1975), p. 79.

⁵⁰ **Tranquillitas Ordinis**, (1987), p. 31.

⁵¹ Richard John Neuhaus' **The Naked Public Square** (1984), called "the book from which further debate about church-state relations should begin," calls for the development of a public philosophy which must be grounded in values that are based in Judaeo-Christian religion.

The Future of the Family —
Parents and Children in the Modern World
by
Helen Hull Hitchcock

"As the family goes, so goes the nation, and so goes the whole world in which we live." These words of Pope John Paul II, spoken in a talk during his visit to Australia, are prophetic words, for they contain an implicit warning of what is certain to happen if problems besetting the family are not immediately and intelligently addressed. It is a truism, in our society, that the family, as it has been understood throughout history, is in very deep trouble. So deep, in fact, that it is no longer possible to reach a consensus even on the definition of the word "family," as the ill-fated 1980 White House Conference on The Family (which had to change its name to White House Conference on Families) rather dramatically demonstrated.

It has been well understood by philosophers and educational and social theorists for more than a century that the role of the family has been central in transmitting to new generations of human beings those tacit assumptions about the just or proper of orderly relationships between human beings, assumptions about the relationships between children and parents, between members of a community or a religious group and the larger society — the government or nation, and finally, about the relationships of human beings with God and with the rest of the created order. It is this reality about the family's role in society which has made it a primary target of social reformers.

Nowhere has the recognition of the essential role of the family in transmitting basic cultural attitudes and central cultural assumptions which provide the basis for society been more strongly emphasized than in the 19th Century revolutionary social theories of Marx and Engels, who correctly saw that the outcome of the "struggle" to achieve their cultural revolution would be determined by the success of their attack on two fronts: on the faith of religious believers, and on the family, who transmits the faith.

Early Bolshevik revolutionaries accepted Marxist orthodoxy, and recognized that the dissolution of families — the disruption of the integrity of the family, of the natural interdependence among family members, and of the dependence of children on their parents for moral and religious formation — was absolutely essential to the future of the Soviet system. Bolshevik leaders of the early 20th century immediately instituted programs of universal mandatory employment of women and of forcing families to place their children in state-run day-care centers where children would be "properly" indoctrinated.

It is worth noting that many of the early Soviet projects were, in fact, abandoned for a time. Poorly planned, ill-staffed and under-financed day-care centers could not meet the stubborn resistance of parents, especially mothers, who refused to use them. The "sexual revolution" which early Bolshevik ideologues practiced and attempted to institutionalize also failed in the early years following the revolution — again, because of "grass-roots" resistance to the "new morality." It became apparent that the romantic libertarianism implicit in the "sexual revolution" was basically incompatible with the totalitarian Soviet system.

But the setbacks suffered by the Bolsheviks in the "restructuring" of Russian society were only temporary. As they settled their own internecine difficulties and as they achieved absolute control of the economic system, the resistance of families of religious believers was overcome.

Children — the most vital "commodity" of any State and the most essential to its future existence — *were* separated both physically and ideologically from their parents. The family as a powerful social and cultural force, as the "loom" on which the very stuff of the social fabric is woven, had been utterly dismantled and cast on the pyre of "social reform" ignited by the burning zeal of "expert" socialistic ideologues.

From our perspective we can see that the temporary frustration of the goals of early Soviet zealots was due more to trying to accomplish too much too soon than to their lack of money or organization. In the direct frontal assault on the family they encountered the resistance and recusancy of too many ordinary people — mostly peasants and middle-class people — who instinctively reacted to the assault on their families by refusal to collaborate in their own demise. For a time, religious persecution only made those *who were already believers* stronger.

That the setbacks were only temporary is attributable to two major factors: (1) state control of the educational system, which successfully eliminated the transmission of the ideas and principles and religious beliefs from parents to children, and (2) the adoption of Marxist-feminist rhetoric of "equality" — of the social, sexual and economic "liberation" of women — to conform to Soviet goals.

It does not take a professional sociologist or historian to observe that the ultimate "success" of the Soviet system — or of any utopian totalitarian ideologies — is finally predicated on how rapidly and completely it can accomplish the dissolution of the family as a cultural force, and with it the destruction of the moral and ethical assumptions based on religious belief. Thus it is not surprising that the chief targets of contemporary utopians and "liberationists" in the West are the Catholic Church and women.

The Catholic Church is a principal target because it is the single religious institution which has sufficient power, numbers and history to be a primary cultural force. It represents *all* of Christianity, and the Judeo-Christian cultural heritage, whose most fundamental beliefs about the very nature of human beings and of the world are, in essence, inimical to any form of totalitarianism. Its constant affirmation of the intrinsic dignity and worth of every individual human being radically contradicts any system which regards persons primarily as pawns to be manipulated by the State.

Social reformers target women because women are directly responsible for the formation of future generations — for the instruction and education necessary to the shaping of basic attitudes about human life and human love and of the world during the critical years of childhood when moral and religious beliefs become part of each child's permanent character.

So immediate and strong is the influence for good or ill of a mother over her child that no civilization, no cultural system, no system of religious belief can be destroyed without both deforming its women (who will refuse to "mother") and removing children from the influence of the family.

In order to overturn the existing social order in the shortest possible time, then, a war must successfully be waged on two fronts: faith and family.

If you, as a revolutionary "mastermind" can succeed in undermining the *religious* force in society, both from outside attacks (from the media, for example) and from corrosion from within, if you can succeed in confusing religious believers about the very nature of their faith and the meaning it gives to human life, and subvert a religion's claim of access to perennial, objective truth, half your battle would be won.

But the destruction of the continuity of the existing civilization would be complete only if you succeed in confusing and corrupting the women. If the women can be persuaded to deny their distinctive nature, to devalue their particular gifts and insights and power by which they participate in the divine plan for humanity; if you can foster within women a distorted notion of freedom and self-fulfillment which will cause them to lose sight of their natural dignty as female human beings, equal to but not identical with male human beings, whereby they will compromise their true selves in pursuit of a phantasm of "power" and a confused sense of "justice;" and where women will view the other half of the human race as "oppressors" and "victimizers" rather than as "help-mates," you will have destroyed the family.

Women, as well as men, would refuse to make the commitments and sacrifices necessary to the establishment of families and to the nurture and education of children. They would abhor the very idea of service, which is essential to establishing any viable community. Thus could be accomplished in a single generation what would take hundreds of years of political or philosophical theorizing by intellectuals.

Of course, your revolution need not be "bloody." The social order can be overturned quietly, as it has been in socialist Sweden. In an article on "comparable worth" ("Toward 'The Working Family,'" *Persuasion at Work,* Vol VII, No. 7), historian Allan Carlson notes the effect of radical-liberal and Marxist writings of the 18th and 19th centuries in a vision of society in which men and women have no separate roles. Rather than a child-centered family with sex-differentiated roles for men and women, a "working family" model was envisioned by Swedish social reformers.

As early as 1938, Carlson states, the report of a Parliamentary Committee on Women's Work

> emphasized the inevitability and necessity of women's labor outside the home, and the "right" of women to be paid-laborers despite marriage and motherhood. The Committee urged ... expansion in the number of day-care centers, the preferential hiring of women to remove the effects of past discrimination and an unspecified "new" wage system that insured women were paid as much as men. (p. 3)

It was not until the 1960's, when public debate on "sex roles" became a national passion that significant changes began to affect families. Grass-roots opposition to the proposed reforms was weak and disorganized, and the "experts" either pushed for women's "right to choose" between children and career, or advocated social reconstruction to eliminate the distinctions between sexes.

By 1968, the latter view won out, and Sweden's report to the United Nations on "The Status of Women" stated:

> A decisive and ultimately durable improvement in the status of women cannot be attained by special measures aimed at women alone; it is equally necessary to abolish the conditions which tend to assign certain privileges, obligations or rights to men.

By the end of the 1970's economic legislation virtually forced women into the "lifetime labor force" by making two incomes necessary to maintain a standard of living above the poverty line.

Carlson cites a report that by 1984 the full-time Swedish mother could "no longer be found among young women," and the number of children enrolled in government child-care facilities jumped from 60,000 in 1960 to 413,000 in 1980.

The negative "fallout" of Sweden's bloodless social revolution is now apparent. Sweden's birthrate is now less than 60% of the level needed to achieve "zero population growth," and the Swedish marriage rate is at the lowest in history. Carlson comments,

> Having drained marriage and childbearing of any moral and social significance, Sweden faces an increasingly sterile future. With the uprearing and character education of children largely socialized, creating a family and bearing babies make little sense in that land today. (p. 5)

In Paul Johnson's weighty and fascinating analysis of the world from the twenties to the eighties, **Modern Times**, we find a surprising contrast in the attitude towards the family in the astonishingly rapid reconstruction of post-war Germany and Japan. Speaking of Conrad Adenauer's role in the reconstruction of Germany, he notes that "the real antithesis to National Socialism was individualism, a society where private arrangements took priority over public, where the family was the favoured social unit and where the voluntary principle was paramount." (p. 581)

Moreover, his discussion of the reconstruction of Japan, Professor Johnson observes:

> What the constitutional reforms essentially did was to persuade the Japanese that the state existed for its citizens, and not vice-versa. It laid the foundations of a new and healthy individualism by encourag-

Johnson attributes the phenomenal industrial growth of Japan to a non-collectivist view of the industries themselves as "extended fami-lies," and the fact that relationships between corporations and workers are based on a familial model.

"As the family goes, so goes the nation and so goes the world in which we live."

The prophetic implication of the Pope's words is that whatever the family suffers will happen to "the world in which we live." If the family is destroyed, so will be "the nation" and the entire social order. The *reason* for prophecy is to jar human beings into action; to wake us up to the realities of our situation and to prevent us from following false "prophets" like lemmings into the sea of destruction.

There is, as you know, a contemporary intellectual fad with some very influential adherents called "futurism." Futurists claim to be prophets of "social evolution" and have, in fact, evolved a system of analysis of social and religious circumstances in order to formulate actual plans for the "redesigning" of "future history." Their analysis includes identifying "indicators" of the implementation of their designs, and from these indicators they prognosticate their timetables for achieving important developments or changes which will take place in the future. Then, working backwards, they base their schemes for establishing social policy for today.

Two self-proclaimed Futurists, Robert Muller, Assistant Secretary General for the United Nations Educational and Social Organization Council (ECOSOC), and Carl Sagan, popular astronomer and tele-vision personality, were key speakers at the 1985 convention of the National Catholic Education Association; and other disciples of "Futur-ism" led dozens of workshops and offered hundreds of books and publications to the 14,000 Catholic teachers (mostly women) who attended the convention. The title of the convention, "Catholic Educa-tion — Gateway to Global Understanding" (which was also the title of Muller's keynote address) is, when de-coded by Muller himself, down-right ominous. In his book **New Genesis: Shaping a Global Spirituality** (Image, Garden City, NY, 1984), Muller, a Catholic who calls himself a "cosmic optimist," stresses the urgency of restructuring society, and, of course, religion, to conform to a "global model."

In a pre-convention issue of the NCEA's publication, *Momentum,* [Dec. 1984] a very nearly haggiographic interview with Muller was published. In this interview, Muller states that he is himself "a very rich cosmos," and that "we know so much [about the universe] that we are probably of a divine nature," that as "cosmic beings, divine beings" we are at a "very marvelous point of the evolution of the cosmos where the earth is becoming conscious-of-itself."

Muller prophesies that the UN "will be considered someday as the paradigm of the New Millenium" because it is

> ... the first universal, global instrument humanity has ever had; the place where new ethical values for nations and humanity are being formulated; the central, permanent meeting ground of all human aspirations in which will be molded a peaceful, just, safe and happy future for the human race; an incipient brain of the human species ... keeping world conditions and phenomena under constant review ...; an incipient world nervous system which relays global findings and warnings to governments, local collectivities and the peoples; an incipient conscience and heart of humanity, which speaks for what is good and against what is bad for humans; the beginning of an important new story in evolution: the story of humanity as one family or one society living in one common home.

Muller's theme pervaded the convention. So did his idea that religion in the New Age must be purged of its "dogmatism, parochialism, and hierarchicalism."

Sr. Judith Bisignano gave a talk called "A Working Model of New Age Learning," and in a workbook for Catholic school children called "Creating Your Future" (published by the Kino Learning Center, with an introduction by Robert Theobold) she tells children:

> Futurists believe that contemporary society is witnessing the final breakup of the Industrial Age ... The Industrial Age has failed to provide everyone an opportunity to contribute to society. ...It has focused on the maximization of material welfare, on the short-range present, on a hierarchical, bureaucratic organizational structure, and on a divided world which has pitted manager against worker, teacher against student, parent against child.

> Futurists project that the coming New Age will be marked by possibilities rather than problems, by personable authority, by diversity, by cooperation, by systematic thinking, by enoughness, and by working in harmony with nature.

The workbook asks students to describe models of future "families," stressing "interdependence" rather than the "independence" characteristic of the dying Industrial Age. (Another Kino workbook designed for elementary school children was called "Living with Death." Among other chilling curiosities, it contained a blank page on which pupils are instructed to write an essay giving their personal views pro- and con- suicide.)

Another offering to teachers at this convention was a "teaching packet" developed by the Catholic Relief Services Global Education Office. It detailed the "infusion" method of teaching global awareness, in which every subject from math to religion is infused with "core concepts," among which are *Social Justice* [aimed at "transforming the structures which contribute to oppression and marginality"], *Change* ["the continual process of modification and forward thrust by which humans move toward their ultimate destiny"], *Transformation* ["the process by which persons, relationships and the structures of society are changed in order to serve human dignity and to bring God's creation closer to perfection"], *Empowerment* ["to enable people to design their own future"], and *World Order* ["the development of a just system governing communication, political, economic and social relationships within the global community"].

It may be a temptation to regard these "New Age" ideas as too fantastic or spooky to take seriously. But the tendency to implement the ideas of "experts" such as these through actual sweeping changes in social policy is far too serious to ignore.

In March of 1985 a conference called "Inventing the Future: Alternatives to Adolescent Pregnancy" was held in Fort Worth, Texas. The conference was sponsored by the National Organization on Adolescent Pregnancy and Parenting, the Sid Richardson Foundation, the Joseph P. Kennedy Jr. Foundation, and a national and a local unit of the March of Dimes. The approach to the subject of teen-age pregnancy was derived from "futurist" methods. In this approach, participants do not merely address problems as they exist, but give free rein to their imaginations in deciding what the future of the world ought to be like. Adolescent pregnancy was treated as a particularly unfortunate symptom of deeper social and cultural pathologies, which can be eradicated only by the most thorough-going revolutions.

Although most of the participants were professionals of one kind or another, the conference report revealed almost no interest in the basic facts of adolescent pregnancy. Unsurprisingly, the morality of out-of-wedlock pregnancy was never examined. But also omitted were statistical and medical facts of the topic. The entire approach to the study of adolescent pregnancy was in the form of "prophecy." The conference was divided into "teams," each of which submitted their own version of the "history of the future," which was published in the conference report.

One team proposed that a program of mandatory sterilization of all teenagers be instituted through school-based clinics and other agencies. However, the word "sterilization" was never used. The procedure was termed "immunization" against pregnancy, and it was intended to be reversible at some undetermined point in the individual's life when children were "wanted."

This team also offered the most elaborate prognostication for the future. In 1988, they predicted, "conservatives" will win a total victory in the United States, while China is demonstrating the effectiveness of the "five-year immunization against conception." The "Righteous Right" will succeed in getting an amendment prohibiting abortion passed in 1988, and will attack birth control, with the result that the adolescent pregnancy rate will soar "out of sight" and illegal abortions will flourish. Parents will take their children to Europe for "immunizations" against pregnancy, "immunization reversals," etc.

By 2000, the United States economy will be crippled by adolescent pregnancies; but Planned Parenthood will publish a report informing citizens of alternatives, and people will demand access to the "immunization" services available in Europe. Health clinics and sex-education programs will be implemented in all schools; and churches, including the Catholic Church, will support such measures.

In 2008, the newly elected president of the United States, a woman who is the child of a teen-age mother raised in a day-care center, with her homosexual male vice-president will make "conception immunization of all preteen boys and girls within the United States" mandatory, and the problem of adolescent pregnancy will disappear. Credit will be given to the "Women's Movement" for achieving this remarkable solution.

Although this example of one of the "team reports" is quite striking, the overall conference report made explicit commitment to "zero population growth," mandatory sex-education and "values clarification," parenthood as a privilege rather than a right. It favored sterilization as a form of pregnancy prevention and called for the abolition of "national government."

If you're beginning to get the feeling that we are being invited to sit at the head table at Balshazzar's banquet, you're probably right. For it is abundantly clear what is going to happen to our civilization if these "social engineers" have their way. It is also clear that, along with social engineering, we now have the technological capability of accomplishing the scenario of the "biological engineers" as well. Eugenetic theories accompany utopian proposals today as they have for the past hundred years; but only recently, with advances in genetic technology, has the capability of implementing even the most bizarre of these theories seemed imminent. As usual, the technological capabilities of humanity are rarely accompanied by equally potent moral capabilities. At the present time, the gap is growing wider and appears to be unbridgeable.

If anything, the complicity with these radical social ideologues of those who profess to be religious believers and on whom the world relies for moral and ethical potency puts human society at graver risk than that caused by frank secularism. It is clear, for example, that the NCEA's agenda means a good deal more than simply "leftist" political propaganda or dubious methods of religious instruction. Those who appear to dominate this organization have a view of the Catholic Church which requires nothing short of revolution at every level of its existence. For some of these leaders, the Catholic Church, through its school system, is primarily viewed as a world-wide institution which can be co-opted to effect certain social and political goals, while utterly destroying its religious mission in the process. The collaboration of the Catholic educational establishment with those forces which would tear apart the fabric of human society would seem to be an idea which could only exist in the mind of the "prince of this world." And yet, this collaboration has evidently begun.

The leaders of movements committed to the restructuring of society and its institutions are apparently gambling that the course they have chosen for the future of the human race will move ahead without effective resistance. The history of the past several decades gives them every reason to believe that this will be the case.

As Christians — as Catholics — we know that there is an antidote to the toxic fare which we have been invited to swallow. We know that the "antidote" is Christ Jesus, and that He offers Himself to us through His Church. We know that this, and *only* this, is a source of hope to our fallen world. We look to the Church for help in the time of trouble.

Over the past three years, Women for Faith and Family has received thousands of letters. Chief among the concerns expressed by the women who write to us are those involving their children.

The letters reveal a growing awareness — approaching alarm — that something is radically wrong with Catholic education in all its aspects, especially in the crucial areas of religious instruction and "family life" or "sex" education. They write of their experiences with their own children and their parish schools. They write of their grave concern that children are not receiving adequate moral and religious instruction in Catholic schools, and that the programs often actually undermine both Church teachings and the parent's relationship with their children.

The letters reveal that catechetical programs are widely regarded as deficient in presenting the authentic teachings of the Catholic Church and often downplay or omit altogether basic Catholic dogmas and doctrines such as the Incarnation and Virgin Birth of Christ, while emphasizing narrowly defined "Christian" participation in "social structures" with a decidedly leftist political cast.

Sex-education programs in the Catholic schools of today are almost uniformly deficient in presentation of ethical and moral issues. They often distort the Church's teachings on questions of sexual morality, advocate "values clarification," and emphasize the "right of individual conscience" over legitimate authority from either the parents or the Church. Concepts of "right" and "wrong" are to be based on "feelings" rather than any objective reality.

The many letters received on this subject indicate that Catholic parents recognize the strong influence of Catholic schools over their children, which many find to be predominantly negative. Parents can no longer rely on outside cultural support for Judeo-Christian moral principles. Furthermore, they fear that the Catholic schools may further erode, rather than reinforce, these principles.

For the most part, unhappy parents have been intimidated into silence when they attempt to question what their children are being taught, or have been ignored and marginalized. They feel almost helpless to anything about the situation, having unsuccessfully appealed to their pastor, their bishop or diocesan school officials. Although there are many exceptions, parents are also inclined to be silent not only because they want to avoid humiliation but because they fear "reprisals" against their children by resentful teachers or school officials.

Bishops, when they do not actively support this agenda, often do not exercise episcopal control even over their own school systems. Many otherwise good bishops may rely too heavily on the advice of the educational professionals in their school offices, who have a heavy investment of their own in the education establishment.

In one letter, a CCD teacher whose husband is a high-school English teacher and the parish "DRE," writes:

> Being a mother of five children ranging in age from 18 to 10½ [with the
> 18-year-old at Georgetown being challenged to "challenge" her faith

There are hundreds of letters like these. While they clearly show that the desparation of Catholic parents is exacerbated by their frustrated attempts to communicate with Church leaders, this contains a ray of hope in that it is clear that faithful Catholics are willing to battle against very uneven odds in defense of their Faith and their families.

Another letter shows that their efforts sometimes succeed [although, sadly, this is the only such letter in our files]. This mother had earlier written to get documentation about the teachings of Fr. Matthew Fox, whose books were being used as texts in the high-school her son attended.

Another notable exception to the remarkable passivity of many bishops to the problems confronting today's Catholic families is the recent (August 15, 1987) public statement of Bishop Anthony Bevilacqua on the subject of school-based clinics and sex-education. The detailed statement concerns both secular and Catholic schools. In it, Bishop Bevilacqua reveals the links between population control programs and organizations who promote School-Based Clinics, (SBCs). He is resoundingly critical of the NEA statement regarding "community choice" in the matter of SBCs which, he notes, "... demeans parental authority by placing it on the same level as the choice expressed by students and teachers and many other non-parents." He repeatedly affirms the right and duty of parents in the education of children, and commits his Diocesan Educational Department to redesign the sex-education curriculum. This curriculum, he writes, "... should focus on promoting communication skills between parents and their children, teach and reinforce the virtues needed to avoid pre-marital sexual activity ... and promote those traditional moral values and principles which are essential to live a good life and which are a part of our Catholic Faith." The bishop invites parents to be fully involved in these efforts to re-write the "sex-education" programs.

In this manner, Bishop Bevilacqua re-emphasizes the teaching contained in **Familiaris Consortio**, the Apostolic Exhortation of Pope John Paul II:

> The social role of families is called upon to find expression in the form of political intervention: families should be the first to take steps to see that the laws and institutions of the State not only do not offend, but positively support and positively defend the rights and duties of the family. ... Families should ... assume responsibility for transforming society: other-wise [they] will be the first victims of the evils that they have done no more than note with indifference.

The Pope's discussion of the *ecclesial* role of parents gives specific guidelines for the evangelical ministry of the Christian family. He emphasizes the need for family catechesis which, he says, is "absolute" because of "widespread unbelief or invasion of secularism [which] makes real religious growth practically impossible." The authentic catechesis which children can receive in the home constitutes the Christian parents' "original and irreplaceable" ministry of evangelization. And, in exhorting parents to instruct their children in prayer, he emphasizes that "... prayer constitutes the strongest incentive for the Christian family to assume and comply fully with all its responsibilities as the primary and fundamental cell of human society."

The introduction to the **Charter of the Rights of the Family** succinctly states the problem, and suggests the source of the solution:

> The well-being of families, strained today by the twin forces of individualism and state power, is acknowledged as the basis of any healthy society. In our day, because of the weakening of families, society is beset by a host of evils, from abortion and the suppression of parental rights in education, to chronic poverty and the neglect of the aged. ... [The Charter of Family Rights] constitutes a blueprint for building a healthy, humane society founded on the integrity of family life. For Catholics and for non-Catholics, it should serve as a source of reflection and a guide to action in bringing the values of the Gospel to bear on secular life.

It remains for us — Catholic men and women — to ask: What kind of future do we want for the world's children? What kind of society will they inherit from us? How can we prepare ourselves, spiritually and intellectually, to face with courage our task as Catholic Christians to preserve, protect and defend the Faith of our families? We must find answers to these questions. And we must be willing to *act*. For the *eternal* lives of our children — the *future* of the Church and of society — depend on us.

The Natural Institution of the Family (Marriage: An Office of Nature)

by

Dr. Herbert Ratner

Plants automatically lead good plant lives. They do not have the freedom to do otherwise. They are activated by tropisms which determinatively direct them to the good plant life: there is heliotropism in which one end of the seed grows toward the sun and geotropism and hydrotropism in which the other end of the seed grows toward earth and moisture. It is through these means that plants, though unknowledgeable of the ends, fructify and flourish and attain their ends.

Animals other than man also automatically lead a good animal life. They, too, do not have the freedom to do otherwise. They are activated through hierarchized instincts, which reflect the urge of all living things "to partake in the eternal and divine" in the only way possible to them by self propagation (Aristotle, **De Anima**, Bk. II, Ch. 4, 415a 25 - b 8).

Man, in contrast to plants and animals, does not automatically lead the good life. He has the freedom to do otherwise since he has free will, which makes him a decision-making animal. He is not activated but acts in the full sense of the word by deciding the ends and the means of his activity. Man's freedom to act is both his grandeur and his misery. His freedom permits him to be the greatest or the worst of all animals (Aristotle, **Politics**, Bk. I, Ch. 2, 1253a 30 - 35). His freedom makes it possible for him to rise above his animality and his mammalian nature but not escape from it or to drop below his animality and his social animal nature by controverting it.

Man's free choice is not left to itself. Though he is not compelled by tropisms nor instincts, man is not left adrift in directing his natural destiny. He has the natural inclinations of a mammalian and social animal. These are inclinations which in Pascal would correspond to his "simple pure ignorance." These natural inclinations can be confounded by higher education, which gives the illusion of a high order of intellectual and educational development but which, in reality, falls far short of Pascal's "learned ignorance." Some Catholics believe that a university education permits them to reject Magisterial teaching as if the conscience was a teacher not a pupil. As we have nouveau riche, we have nouveau intellectuals. Such Catholics have been educated out of their "simple pure ignorance" but unfortunately have not been educated into a "learned ignorance."[1]

Having the freedom to confound the guidance of his natural inclinations with an arrested education, man also has the freedom and capacity to complement these natural inclinations by virtue of his intellect. In reflecting on the experiences of life, he progressively uncovers the truths of nature enabling him to participate in nature's wisdom. He acquires ethical and moral teachings which, when true and applied, direct him to the good life. These teachings are the counterpart or the analogue of tropisms in plants and hierarchized instincts in animals. These teachings are accumulative as befits a species cognizant of its own intellectual history which can, through the power of language, transmit them to successive generations of mankind. Since man's ever deepening knowledge will never match God's knowledge, the accumulative process is endless. Accordingly what Cicero says about individual man applies to mankind over time:

> ... at first, at any rate, nature is marvelously hidden and can neither be observed or known; as we grow older, however, we gradually or rather tardily come, as it were, to know ourselves.[2]

In acquiring true ethical and moral teachings from a nature that "loves to hide," man must be cautious of obtaining only a partial view. By looking at nature wholly, not partially, one ultimately discovers norms of nature, norms which supply the script for nature's prescription to the wholesome life. There is a tendency for those who have great expertise limited to one narrow field to disregard man's widespread accumulative knowledge. This brings to mind Cardinal Newman's wonderful quotation from Francis Bacon, who, critical of the partial and incomplete knowledge of scientists and their excessive extrapolated claims, concludes:

> But of these conceits Aristotle speaketh seriously and wisely when he saith, "They who contemplate a few things have no difficulty in deciding."[3]

We observe this in the promotion of condoms as a solution to the problem of AIDS.

Man, however, with his fallen nature not only can go astray intellectually, but his perception of a natural ethic and morality is intrinsically circumscribed. Man needs the teachings of God as passed on to him in Scriptures, the Church, and the Vicar of Christ. These teachings, with the help of grace, confirm, fortify, enrich and transform the teachings of nature to help make good the promise of nature.

Yet many Catholics hold that the truths of the supernatural order do not harmonize with the natural order; that magisterial teachings conflict with that derived from reason; that the church's teachings on family and sex leave much to be desired when compared to the mundane.

Some, particularly those of an older generation, accept magisterial teachings on sex and family but only as a sufferance — a straitjacket — robbing them of many pleasures of life. They, however, obey them — some assiduously, some reluctantly — as a travail on the way to a good eternal life.

Some believe that church teachings on morals are not consonant with enlightened modern times and can be disregarded in the expectation that the Church, which moves slowly, will ultimately catch on and catch up and broaden its outlook and laws.

Some, like Siger of Brabant, the adversary of Thomas, believe that in reality there are two truths, that of faith and that of reason, which extracts from experience and modern science, including sociology. The latter have an independent status regardless of whether they are or are not consonant with Church teachings. In other words, the Church can be right theologically, but wrong scientifically.

Each forgets, however, that there are two revelations: one found in the Book of Scriptures and the other in the Book of Nature; one communicated through the Words of the Son (and His Vicar on earth), the other through nature from a lexicon written by the Father. However, the Father, the Author of nature, does not go about teaching one truth while the Son teaches another.

Accordingly, truths from the natural order obtained by reason have an intrinsic harmony with the truths of the natural order obtained by faith, resulting in a unity in which each help the other to a greater understanding so that together they complete the teachings necessary to achieve the good life, both temporal and eternal.

Jesus, for instance, tells us to love our neighbor. But Jesus does not instruct the mother how to love her closest and dearest neighbor, the newborn. Thus the mother is not told to nurse or breastfeed her baby. The Son, respectful of the Father, assumes that with eyes to see, with milk dripping from postpartum breasts, with hungry suckling lips rooting in search of the mother's teats, the woman can figure this out for herself.

In passing, it should be noted that the norm of breastfeeding is a striking example of a constant of nature not dissimilar from norms pertaining to sexual morality. The arguments that avant garde theologians use to justify a change in the laws of sexual morality can *a fortiori* be applied to breastfeeding. One can claim that breastfeeding is "historically conditioned," that "alternative life styles have developed," that "cultural and social conventions have changed," that "empirical social data" negate its value, that "advances of the behavioral and social sciences provide new understanding and insight," that "the importance of natural processes do not lie in their brute facticity," and that we now have "more accurate scientific information," all of which negates the norm of breastfeeding.[4] The fact remains, however, that after 37 years of permissive bottlefeeding, the American Academy of Pediatrics along with other international pediatric associations saw fit to reaffirm the norm and superiority of breastfeeding in 1978.[5]

It should be seen from the above that we have inadequately taught our Catholics that the truths of nature are one with the truths of the Church and that both are intended for our happiness not only in the hereafter but on earth as well. Having forgotten that philosophy is the handmaiden of theology, we have allowed God the Father, Creator of Heaven and Earth, to become the forgotten person in the Trinity. We profess belief in a Trinitarian God, but we are ignorant of or recalcitrant to the teachings the Father has revealed to us in nature even though we know by faith that God authored both the Book of Nature and the Book of Scriptures. In a sense, we ignore nature and tend to replace it with a sacramentalism, as if once grace is possessed, nature is irrelevant.

To be grasped is that, of the three fundamental institutions of man, the state is wholly natural in its origin, the Church wholly supernatural, but the family is both natural and supernatural. It is understandable, then, that the principles which are essential to marriage are those derived from nature, viz., fidelity and offspring. In its turn the supernatural institution, though not essential, adds excellency through the sacrament and bestows upon marriage grace which perfects nature and makes good the promise of nature.[6]

The battle for the survival of the family centers in good part around the explication of the family as a natural institution communicating nature's wisdom with its inherent power to persuade human reason and free choice. Nowhere is philosophy as handmaid to theology more applicable or pertinent. Philosophy has a persuasive influence with believers and non-believers alike. It can convince Catholics and all fellow human beings of the wholesomeness of the Catholic position on marriage.

Every pagan, then, even though he does not identify with God in a personal way and though he may profess that the world has resulted from the blind forces of an evolutionary process, is still exposed to God the Father through the Book of Nature. That is why many pagans have a stronger and healthier family life than many Catholics, despite the absence of the sacrament and the advantage of supernatural grace. Even some communist countries have a greater dedication to the traditional family than that shown by many western democracies with a Catholic heritage. It is also true of many primitive societies.

The following are some highlights, briefly sketched, of nature's teaching on the family as the normative mode of reproduction.

A. The Normative Mode of Reproduction

Each species of living things has a mode of reproduction which is characteristic of the species, the end point of which is to turn out progenies capable of fending for themselves. In most species of birds, for example, the mode is seasonal monogamy since it takes only one breeding season to turn out young mature enough to fend for themselves. In man the maturing of the newborn to young adulthood is of long duration and while one progeny is maturing another comes along prolonging the parental obligation and bond. Furthermore, man is a social animal and the relationship of parents to progenies and others in the extended family continues through adulthood. Accordingly, the mode of reproduction characteristic of man is a life long monogamy as exemplified by the traditional family. Were we to ask a social engineer to blueprint *de novo* the specifications of a species with the following prime properties: a social animal with a widespread division of labor necessitating a diversification of qualities, talents, bodily gifts and personalities of its members, the result would be identical to that found in nature. The primary diversification of its members would be achieved genetically by creating two sexes, male and female; the secondary diversification would be achieved by one's position in the family constellation and by other environmental influences.[7] By its socializing influence, the traditional family is the microcosm which readies children for the macrocosm of a double sexed society.

One of the great historical challenges to nature's norm for the family was initiated by the Communists following the Russian Revolution of 1917. The Communists moved to destroy the traditional family by ridding the Russian people of what they took to be bourgeois values and mores. Their action was guided by August Bebel, a disciple of Marx and the author of two Communist classics on woman which held that the distinction of the sexes was primarily cultural. His books popularized positions that were identical to the feminist position a century later. Bebel believed that "marriage is sexual slavery" and "free love must be absolute." Marriage was virtually wiped out by unilateral divorce. Such divorce was automatically accomplished by one or the other spouse mailing a postcard of notification to a central agency. The outcome of this experiment was so devastating that by 1936 the Communists found it imperative to return to traditional and family morals.[8]

It is no surprise, then, that the traditional family is one of the most enduring and resilient realities of human history.[9] Aberrations and deviations, innovations of one sort or another, come and go, but they never thrive or last. The traditional family has a habit of burying its undertakers. For example, the decade of the 1960's saw the rise of communes and communal family life with their sharing of sex partners and children. But this was short-lived. By the late Seventies, monogamy and traditional family life were making a comeback in these very same communes.

Nature has a vested interest in the traditional or monogamous family: the reproductive mode of her highest creature, man. Though we think of nature as Mother Nature and credit her with all that motherhood implies, she has an inescapable shortcoming that circumscribes and limits her merciful motherhood. She is a stern teacher and disciplinarian who expects us to heed what she says or suffer the consequences. Mother Nature doesn't plead with us, doesn't cajole us, doesn't bribe us. Mother Nature says: "These are my ways. They are good. They are wise. Follow them." When nature is ignored or transgressed by free wheeling man, she fights back. In a brilliant characterization a 12th century theologian, Alain de Lille, referred to nature as the "Vicar-Regent." Following him, 14th century Chaucer referred to her as "the Vicar of the Almighty Lord." The notion of nature as a Vicar General is a realistic and dynamic concept of nature which recognizes man as an integral part of biologic nature and the universe "tied within the divine mind by an indissoluable knot."

Since a Vicar General is one with his or her superior — in the case of nature the oneness is with God — and given nature's nature, no appeal is possible in nature's tribunal. The inability to appeal finds expression in an old anonymous saying: "God always forgives, man sometimes forgives, nature never forgives." A 1956 Nobel Laureate in internal medicine, Professor Dickinson W. Richards, writing as a modern physician, expressed this thought as follows:

> ... there is increasing evidence that man is not controlling nature at all but only distorting it. ... his powers have extended so far that nature itself, formerly largely protective ... seems to have become largely retaliatory. Let man make the smallest blunder in his far-reaching and complex physical or physiological reconstructions, and nature, striking from some unforeseen direction, exacts a massive retribution.[10]

On a world wide basis we are observing nature's retribution to man's experiment with sexual promiscuity. It is of long historical proportions and accounted, in part, for the collapse of the Roman civilization. The retribution has now culminated in response to today's sensate society with its widespread dissociation of the unitive from the procreative. The name of nature's retribution is the "Acquired Immune Deficiency Syndrome — AIDS."

The forerunner of this retribution is found in *Rolling Stone* (March 4, 1982) which features articles on "The Pill, VD/Why Sex Isn't Fun Anymore." In one article the author, Steven Levy, with remarkable insight, concludes:

> Of course, we cannot pin all the blame for this sexual counterrevolution on birth control and the failure of The Pill. There are other factors, and taken, altogether, they may seem like some wrathful deity is exacting revenge for our decade-long orgy (p. 28).

This deity, of course, is Mother Nature whose norms are not negotiable, and as Vicar General, has no choice but to retaliate against those who are in revolt against her teachings. In the past when one recommended abstinence and faithful marital monogamy as the protection against nature's wrath, the advocates of abstinence and monogamy were told "to keep religion out of it." However, in the past year nature's message on AIDS has been so persistent that atheists, pagans, public health physicians and others alike are "preaching" abstinence and monogamy.

B. The Family as the Primary Teaching Unit

Parents are primary teachers. The profound formative influence of the first six years of life is universally recognized. During these preschool years the primary teaching function of the family is not the elevating of the I.Q. but the nurturing of emotional maturity. Its work is to temper emotions, to order the emotions to proper ends, and to lay the foundation for cultivating the cardinal virtues. Without emotional stability the best of human intentions are thwarted and the way is open to divorce, alcoholism, drugs, juvenile delinquency, precocious and faithless premature genital sex and other indices of a sick society.

Because love holds together the delicate membranes of human society and is the basis of our relationship with God, the chief need of the child is to experience love leading to a healthy self-love and to be able to love others as he has learned to love himself. Since love is taught essentially through a one-to-one relationship, nature sees to it that the vast majority of babies come one at a time, so that each child has his or her private tutor of love. For this task nature has selected the mother. As a female her capacity to care for the newborn is unique.

Although the human male and female share a common nature and its attendant equality, dignity, freedom and personality, man and woman are not identical in soma and psyche. They differ in bodily parts and psychologic dispositions, in the balance of hormones that give rise to natural inclinations, and in the interplay of the two components of the intellect: understanding and reason — the intuitive and the discursive. These differences set the female apart to be the primary caretaker of the newborn.

Since nature fashioned the mammalian female to be the prime nurturer, the key to the woman's special qualities is the infant — the *raison d'etre* of nature's formation of woman as woman. T. S. Eliot, echoing Aristotle, states the principle: "The end is where we start from." A woman's task requires of her a certain congruence, complementariness and reciprocal fitness with the infant, for the natural togetherness of the nursing couplet is far more than a lactary relationship. Nature finely attunes the woman to the total physiological and psychological needs of the helpless, inarticulate, withal responsive human being — the baby. This makes possible a two-way affective connaturality which, with or without cognitive knowledge, generates an interpersonal, loving relationship.

The soft, smooth skin of the infant bespeaks the soft, smooth skin of the woman. As we, out of solicitude, envelop the baby in soft, smooth coverings, so, also, with even greater solicitude, does nature. What baby, if given a choice, would prefer to be cuddled and cherished by a rough-skinned, hairy and stubbly male? Touch, the most fundamental of the senses, and a major means of communicating love, is facilitated in man by furless skin, and is enhanced in the woman and infant by their mutual tactile softness. Both Aristotle and Aquinas point out that the correlation of soft skin and intelligence reflects the gnostic function of touch:

> ... In respect to touch we far excel all other species in exactness of discrimination, that is why man is the most intelligent of animals. The difference to touch and to nothing else accounts for the difference in natural endowments; men whose flesh are soft are well endowed (**De Anima** Bk II C. 9, 421a 20-25).

> ... In those who have bodies of better disposition, their souls have a greater power of understanding, wherefore Aristotle says, that it is to be observed that those who have soft flesh are of apt minds (**Commentary** ibid lect. 19, N-484).

If these philosophers are correct, and much modern thinking is supportive, the intelligence of each member of the nursing couplet is superior to that of the adult male. No one exceeds the infant's prodigious ability to learn, nor the mother's ability to understand, a function that outranks and outreaches the reasoning mind.

The infant's ability to hear only high tones bespeaks the woman's soprano voice. This explains why adults, universally, raise their voices to get a baby's attention, and why males are conspicuously unsuccessful in lullabying babies to sleep. Furthermore, since hearing matures earlier than vision, the mother's voice is familiar to the baby. During the last trimester of its gestation, the child in the womb hears its mother's voice daily. This probably explains why the most effective and earliest stimulus to elicit a smile from the baby is not the face, but the female voice.

The scent of the baby bespeaks the discriminatory olfactory acuity of the mother. As the lover desires to smell good to the beloved, nature wants the baby to smell good to its mother. In the early postpartum period, some mothers' olfactory ability is so enhanced that they speak of a unique fragrance emanating from the baby. Often, they liken it to the fragrance of roses. This heightened olfactory ability enables the mother to identify her newborn by smell. With even more certainty, the newborn is capable of recognizing its mother by smell within a few days after birth.

The infant's need to have the mother's face in focus bespeaks the woman's protruding breasts, unique amongst primates. The human face is the most expressive of all animal faces and is the major source of the infant's security during its long immobilized dependent state. Research shows that the newborn is responsive to the face from birth. The response is initially elicited by the eyes and forehead, and, subsequently, by the full face. This coincides with the focal length of the newborn's vision which is about nine inches, a measure that approximates the distance from the baby at the breast to the mother's eyes and face. In contrast to the perceptual ability of primates whose young are mobile and clinging, the eyes of the immobilized infant, during the early months of nursing, are steadily fixed on the mother's face. When the Psalmist pleads to God to turn His "shining face" upon him, he echoes the acceptance the nursling seeks from its mother, its source of security.

The infant's need to be held, carried and comforted bespeaks the woman's cradling arms, arms that contrast significantly with the throwing arms of the male. The difference is not only evident in sports, but is even seen in the way children carry their books: boys at their sides; girls in front of them with flexed arms. The girls' inclinations to encircle and encompass foretells the future cradling of the nursling close to heart and breast in an initiation of a bosom friendship.

The infant's inability to communicate verbally and conceptually bespeaks the woman's ability to communicate through a modality of "feeling": of knowing and loving through the intuitive, the poetic, the experiential and the affective. These non-conceptual modes of communicating result in a preternatural form of knowledge, a primary knowing common to all but most necessary in the intercommunication of the nursing couplet. In Pascal's words, ". . . the heart has reasons of its own which reason does not know."

The natural togetherness of woman and infant constitutes a predominantly spiritual, sensorial gestalt. It is the infant's need to survive and thrive that preordains the special characteristics of the woman *qua* woman.

Unisex is a great slogan. But it goes counter to the remarkable gift nature has bestowed upon woman. She is the infant's spiritual womb, the womb with a view. If it can be said nature abhors a vacuum, it probably can equally be said that nature abhors a unisex.

C. Fidelity

All mammals are automatically faithful to their young by determinative instincts. Human mothers, on the other hand, have free will and can accept or reject motherhood in whole or in part. Since mammalian newborns are dependent upon mothers for nourishment and nurture, nature implants in the mammalian mother the basic motherly characteristic of fidelity. This faithfulness carries over to her spouse, to her church, to all of her activities. She is even faithful to such organizations like the March of Dimes, who exploit this trait by making her feel needed.

The most damaging effect of the increasing trend toward working mothers, who leave the home to work during the baby's formative years, is the relinquishment of the child to a day care center[11] where the child is raised as if it were part of a litter of offspring. If nature intended young children to be raised in litters, they would have come in litters. This is an example of how we must read nature for the guidelines of family life.

Major authorities now universally agree as a result of studies of the past fifteen years that, for the optimum personal maturation of the child, the child needs the full-time attention of the mother or a full-time mother substitute during the first three years of life.[12] Young women must appreciate that their life span in developed countries is now over seventy-five years. Not everything in life has to be accomplished in the early years of marriage. There is enough time for career fulfillment after children are off to school. And dedication to children in their dependent years accelerates their independence and, in turn, liberates parents for additional activities.

More than that, the mother infant relationship, which in the natural order is the child's first sustained human association, becomes the prototype of the child's future relationships with others. If the child experiences the fidelity of his prime caregiver especially when it is during the period when his needs are greatest and which when met engenders in him security, confidence and trust, that example will remain with him for life. It becomes the pattern on which all future friendships are based, a pattern which even paves the way to his relationship with God. The fidelity of the mother to her child fortifies the child's natural inclinations to the fidelity he possesses as a social animal. In its absence insecurity and distrust abounds and affects him all through life.

D. Maternal Attachment

It has been demonstrated that immediately following childbirth (and for some days or weeks thereafter) the mother is in a unique psycho-hormonal state which is propadeutic to her maximal attachment to the newborn, an attachment which has lasting qualities. This attachment or bonding process is analogous to the imprinting phenomenon found in lower animals, an imprint which lasts until the young mature and have no further need of the mother. Breastfeeding, started immediately after birth, is nature's normal and foolproof mode by which this attachment is fostered and intensified. It converts mother and infant into bosom friends.

Obstetrical technologies,[13] imposed on normal childbirth, intercept and disrupt nature's subtle processes with loss of nature's beneficence. It is now believed that disruption of the normal attachment process has led to an increase in child abuse, premature use of the nursery school, demands for day care centers, and, in general, to an increase of parental indifference and parental delinquency. Nature cannot forgive; it can only retaliate.[14]

Catholic maternity services, from not appreciating God the Father's script, succumb to obstetrical technologies as avidly as secular maternity services. Actually, the great medical advances rooted in the restoration of nature's norms and the recapture of nature's wisdom in developed countries have originated primarily not with Catholics but with non-Catholics. These advances include natural delivery, the elimination of *routine* episiotomies (as if God was not able to make a functional perineum for man), rooming-in, birthing centers, home deliveries, breastfeeding, and maternal-infant coupling to enhance maternal attachment.

Several years ago at a medical convention a Jewish friend of mine, a professor of pediatrics at Northwestern Medical School, knowing that I was a convert to Catholicism said to me:

> What puzzles me about my study is that the incidence of breastfeeding is no different in nuns' hospitals than in secular hospitals. I cannot understand it. I thought the nuns would have a greater feeling and respect for God's wonderful creation.

Apropos of this, we have reprinted a remarkable homily of Jeremy Taylor, the great 17th century Anglican theologian on "The Duty of Nursing Your Child in Imitation of the Blessed Mother."[15] In it, he terms the refusal to breastfeed a sin against nature. Some contraceptionists are now asking if artificial contraception is a sin, why is not the artificial feeding of newborns also a sin.

Women today who are rediscovering their womanhood and nature in the area of childbirth and child rearing are turning more and more away from technology which attempts to override nature. In the 1870s, when the baby carriage was invented, there were perceptive physicians who said: "The baby carriage is no substitute for a pair of strong loving arms." Today, mothers carry their babies in slings of one kind or another. They prefer to keep their babies close to their bodies because therein lies the baby's security. When in touch with their mothers, babies are in touch with the world; when not in touch, they are out of touch with the world.

E. Is There a Family Size Optimum for the Rearing of Children?

The difficulty in raising an only child is generally recognized. Parents find themselves without previous experience at child-rearing and without the salutary effect of siblings on the lone child.

In the face of preoccupation with the alleged "population explosion," where social engineers are urging limitation of family size to one or two children by fiat if necessary, some prominent scientists (e.g., Rene Dubos and Erik Erikson) have warned of the dangers of taking the small family as the norm for man. Erikson writes: "Just as sexual repression characterized the Victorian era, so repression of the urge to have children may characterize the future."[16] Psychiatrists, he continues "... can easily overlook how much some modern persons who are practicing systematic birth control may need enlightenment in regard to what they are doing."

The elimination of larger families would short-circuit the rich diversity of the human race. There is not only the primary diversity of man at the genetic level due to intermingling of chromosomes from the two sexes, there is also a secondary diversity which occurs through differences in family constellation. These are multitudinous, viz., eldest, middle and youngest children develop different personalities traceable in considerable part to their relative position within the family.

One internationally recognized pediatrician (Sir James Spence, a Protestant who believes in birth control) argues for five children as the minimum family size necessary for the optimum rearing of children.[17] My own belief is that the minimum optimum is three children. The third child sharply increases the probability that the children will not all be of one sex, thus better preparing siblings for a two-sexed society. Again, the third child protects against polarization along the lines of sex, age or dominance. Moreover, the third child dramatically multiplies and enriches the dynamics of family life.

Earlier I referred to Russia's experiment with the family in which its man-made plan which goes counter to nature's plan ended in failure. Later, I referred to another challenge to nature — an ongoing one of long duration — man's disruption of the unity of the unitive and pro-creative. To that Nature counter attacks with sexually transmitted diseases culminating in a new disease, AIDS. The third experiment is China's present arithmetical approach to "overpopulation" — the one child family. Not being satisfied with the great headway it made educationally which virtually eliminated premarital sex and postponed marriage age into the late twenties, it opted for the one child family. Had China consulted me on their problem, I would have said as I did in 1982: "Better one family with five children than five families with one child each."[18] But China hadn't consulted me. The returns of its experiment are now coming in. True, the size of the population is being reduced, but China is now producing a generation of "brats":

> Eight years after the world's most populous nation put its controversial family-planning program in effect, limiting most couples to one child, one of the most conspicuous results has been the rise of a generation of "little emperors," which in the West would be known as spoiled brats.
>
> Many only children are so doted upon by their families that they become timid, overbearing, lazy, self-indulgent or contemptuous of physical labor, officials said . . .
>
> Newspapers constantly warn adults against indulging in the "4-2-1 syndrome," in which four grandparents and two parents pamper an only child.
>
> *(The Philadelphia Inquirer 7/27/87)*

> PEKING UPI — Doctors are concerned that China's "one couple, one child" family-planning policy is producing a generation of fat, spoiled children.
>
> According to the New China news agency, doctors are worried about the growing number of overweight youngsters, many of whom are pampered by their parents with calorie-packed goodies like chocolate, sugar and high-fat meat.
>
> *(The Chicago Tribune 1/28/86)*

A more disturbing consideration, however, is the kind of society that will exist when the second generation of single children appear on the scene. These children will have no aunts, no uncles and no cousins. When their grandparents die and later their parents, they will have no blood relations, unless they marry and have a child of their own. If they don't marry, who among their relatives will be there to pray for them when they die? What a radical transformation of China's society! Does this foretell a move to a state ruled animal colony? And there is a further point to be made. Family counselors report that marriages of only children or eldest children are the most difficult. What will be the consequences?

F. The Value of Children

Young couples getting married today are nowhere more ignorant than in their failure to appreciate the significance of children in marriage. Family life programs including Catholic programs stand under special indictment for neglecting to inculcate in couples the gift, the pleasures and the value of children. Kierkegaard said: "The trouble with life is that we understand it backwards but have to live it forwards." Our goal should be to educate the young so that they understand life as they live it forward and thereby help them make prudential judgments. The greatest regret of American married women toward the end of life is that they hadn't had a child or hadn't had more children. Authentic prudential judgment is based on objective reality, not an evasion of reality. It is not a circumventing of reality so as to make it conform to one's subjective desire. Secularized prudence is overly concerned with the price to be paid not the value received; it is overcautious in regard to dangers or risks. True prudence approaches judgment-making with a trust in the providential order and includes hope in the final decision. The following are some reminders of the objective reality associated with marital decisions.

1. Children are a gift biologically as well as theologically. Man is a relatively sterile animal. Couples flock to birth control and family planning clinics in their twenties but switch to sterility clinics in their thirties. Babies for adoption are at a premium. Test tube babies and surrogate mothers measure their plight.

2. The time-span from age 38 to age 58 or from age 58 to age 78 is no longer and no shorter than the span from age 18 to age 38. But that which gives pleasure in life tends to differ for the respective age groups. What seems more of a chore and intrusion in one's personal life when one is young becomes far less a chore and intrusion as one grows older. Children become more and more important to a person with advancing age. The joys of grandparenthood are well known. Children are seen as a blessing where once they may have been viewed as a hardship. In countries with sharply reduced birth rates we are now hearing of the sufferings of a grandparentless society. Even death itself becomes more bearable when the dying are surrounded by loved ones. One does not go through life feeling always like a teenager or young adult, yet what one does in these earlier years may preclude the joys of later life.

Certainly God does not expect the young couple to embark on marriage preoccupied with grandparenthood and death, but God does expect a couple to avoid doing what would rob them of the happiness which should come with the later stages of life. In this context, couples should be attentive to the core principle of **Humanae Vitae** of preserving the integral oneness of the unitive and procreative aspects of marriage. D. H. Lawrence makes the point poetically: "We are bleeding at the roots, because we are cut off from the earth and sun and stars, and love is a grinning mockery, because, poor blossom, we plucked it from its stem on the Tree of Life, and expected it to keep on blooming in our civilized vase on the table."[19]

3. The choicest gift one can bequeath to a child is not material possessions but another brother or sister.

4. Parents do not live forever, and children have each other after their parents pass on. At family reunions the children, now uncles and aunts, have the opportunity to pass on family stories which give the grandchildren a sense of roots, of their unique heritage.

5. Children mature parents more than parents mature children. For most adults parenthood is the road to maturity. It is capable of converting the selfish into the unselfish.

6. The large family is the best preventive against the loneliness which is so all-pervasive in modern society. One can go on.

A persuasive case can be made for having children early in marriage and spaced with the interval which nature ordinarily arranges in the breastfeeding mother, an interval of approximately two years. This affords each child a life's orbit wherein he can more readily relate to his brothers and sisters. This point has been elaborated in the following passage from "Man Against Nature: Nature's Subtleties and Nature's Prescription":

> Nature's prescription not only shortens the obligations of the pre-school period, (1) it brings youth to child-bearing and the arduous early child-rearing years, (2) it permits children to grow up with more intimately shared lives, (3) it closes the generation gap between parent and child, particularly valuable in the adolescent years, (4) it lengthens the joys of parenthood and grandparenthood, (5) it allows for leeway in case of obstetrical misfortunes and tragic events, (6) it gives parents the opportunity to reexamine their goals while reproductive options are still available, and (7) it rids the couple of the fear of an unplanned pregnancy with each love act, permitting them blissfully to ignore birth control for nine years or more during the period of greatest sexual activity.[20]

If the ecologic era bears any message it is this: when nature is treated well she reciprocates. Nature is for us, not against us. All she asks is that her highest achievement, man, be tractable to her teachings — that he be responsive, not rebellious. By following nature's prescription, man not only protects himself against his worst enemy, himself, but he regains his best friend, nature, the nurturer and guide to a happy life on earth.

REFERENCES

[1] Blaise Pascal, **Pensees**, Fr. 327, Ed. Ernest Rhys, Trans. W. F. Trotter, Everyman's Library.

[2] A Cicero Character in **De Finibus** v. 41.

[3] John Cardinal Newman, **The Idea of a University.**

[4] H. Ratner, "Nature, Mother and Teacher: Her Norms," *Listening* 18:197-199, Fall 1983.

[5] Canadian Paediatric Society and the American Academy of Pediatrics, A Joint Statement. "Breast Feeding: A Commentary in Celebration of the International Year of the Child, 1979," *Pediatrics,* 62:591-601 (Oct.), 1978. Reprinted in *Child and Family,* 17:244-62, 1978.

[6] Thomas Aquinas, **Summa Theologica**, Third Part (Suppl.) Q. 49, a. 3. Reprinted in *Child and Family,* 16:112, 1977.

[7] Marcy Sneed, Editor, **Human Life: Our Legacy and Our Challenge**, Chpt. 1 The Face of Man: Tomorrow's Unborn, Yesterday's Dead, Herbert Ratner, M.D. and Helen Deitz, Ph.D., Part One: The Youngest Member of the Human Family: A Biography, © 1976 McGraw-Hill, Inc.

[8] Nicholas S. Timasheff, "The Attempt to Abolish the Family in Russia," *Child and Family* 16:242-252.

[9] C. Levi-Strauss, "The Family," In H. A. Shapiro (Ed.), **Man Culture and Society**, Oxford University Press, 1971.

[10] P. Talalay (Ed.), **Drugs in Society**, Johns Hopkins Press, Baltimore, 1964, p. 34.

[11] H. Nagera, "Day-Care Centres: Red Light, Green Light or Amber Light," *Child and Family* 14:110-136.

[12] T. Hellbrugge, "Early Social Development and Proficiency in Later Life," *N.A.M.T.A. Quarterly* 4:6-14, (Spring) 1979. Reprinted in *Child and Family* 18:120-130, 1979.

[13] H. Ratner, "The History of the Dehumanization of American Obstetrical Practice," **21st Century Obstetrics Now!**, NAPSAC, Inc., Chapel Hill, NC, 1977, pp. 115-46. Reprinted in *Child and Family,* 16:4-31, 1977.

[14] H. Ratner, **Medicine: An Interview by Donald McDonald**, One of a Series of Interviews on the American Character, Center for the Study of Democratic Institutions, The Fund for the Republic, Santa Barbara, CA, May 1962. Reprinted in *Child and Family* 11:4-14; 100-10; 276-86; 363-75, 1972.

[15] J. Taylor, "The Duty of Nursing Your Child in Imitation of the Blessed Mother," **The Whole Works of the Right Rev. Jeremy Taylor, D.D.**, Heber-Eden Edition, London, 1865, Vol. II, pp. 72-81. Reprinted as "The Duty of Nursing Children" in *Child and Family* Reprint Booklet, The Nursing Mother: Historical Insights from Art and Theology, 1969, pp. 19-29.

[16] Erik Erikson, Quoted by Virginia Adams, "Erikson Sees Psychological Danger in Trend of Having Fewer Children," *The New York Times*, Aug. 4, 1979.

[17] J. Spence, "The Purpose of The Family," In **Purpose and Practice of Medicine**, Oxford University Press, 1960. Reprinted in *Child and Family*, 8:26-35, 1969, p. 26.

[18] Herbert Ratner, "The Family: Nature's Institution," in C. Anderson and Wm. Gribbin (Eds) **The Family in the Modern World**, © by The American Family Institute.

[19] D. H. Lawrence, **Sex, Literature and Censorship:** Essays, Harry T. Moore (Ed.) "A Propos of Lady Chatterly's Lover," Twayne Publishers, New York, 1953, p. 104.

[20] Herbert Ratner, "Man Against Nature: Nature's Subtleties and Nature's Prescription," *International Review of Natural Family Planning*, 2:11-7, 1978. Previously published in *Child and Family*, 8:290-1, 1969; 9:2-3, 99-101, 1970, and reprinted in a *Child and Family* reprint booklet *Child Spacing*, 1982.

Social Implications of School-Based Clinics

by

Rita L. Marker

School-Based Clinics (SBCs) have been in the center of controversy sweeping the country. The controversy, however, has not prevented large organizations from endorsing their support. On the fourth of July, 1987, close to eight thousand members of the National Education Association, the nation's largest teachers union, endorsed contraceptive distribution to students at school health clinics.[1]

It is this "service" — birth control for children and abortion referral in the case of "contraceptive failure" — that has engendered the heated debate about SBCs. But there is also a growing awareness that SBCs have the potential to mold the minds, attitudes, and values of future generations.

Recognition of SBCs' historic potential was given at the Third Annual Conference on School-Based Clinics held from October 5 through 7, 1986 in Denver, Colorado. The conference titled "SBCs on the Move" was sponsored by the Center for Population Options (CPO), a major organizer of SBCs.

"You are in the forefront of a movement that's going to have a great impact on this country," said James P. Comer, M.D., director of Yale University's School Development Program, in his opening remarks to conference participants.

Explaining that the school is strategically located in both the developmental and the physical life of children, Comer said:

> It is the ideal place to expose them to all they will need to function well as an adult. People who provide services — people who are caretakers — are in a position to form an attachment — to bond — with children. This bond will enable school personnel to motivate and teach children and will play a decisive role in a child's growth and development.

It is this decisive role and the values those playing the role will impart that are the core of the SBC controversy.

On the surface, SBCs promote an image of primary health centers offering a broad range of services at "middle, junior and senior high schools ... as part of the school day"[2] for the purpose of solving such diverse problems as school absenteeism, low self-esteem, teen pregnancy, and unemployment. SBC organizers "seek to improve the overall physical and emotional health of adolescents. ..."[3]

A strong emphasis is placed on the need to improve self-esteem and self-reliance among teens and, although people of very differing views may agree that enhancement of these qualities is laudible, the means and measurements of a teen's self-reliance differ considerably.

Planned Parenthood and SBCs

Sixty-three years ago, Margaret Sanger wrote: "The civilized world is coming to see that education cannot consist merely in the assimilation of external information and knowledge, but rather in the awakening and development of innate powers of discrimination and judgment."[4]

Sanger, who founded the American Birth Control League (which, in 1942 became known as the Planned Parenthood Federation of America[5]), was particularly concerned about educating for change — change to "remodel the race."[6] "Through sex," wrote Sanger, "mankind may attain the great spiritual illumination which will transform the world. ..."[7]

Educators were to play an important role in her vision of a remodeled race and a transformed world; thus, among the plans of Sanger's organization was a program to include "enlightenment of the public at large, mainly through the education of leaders of thought and opinion — teachers, ministers, editors and writers — to the moral and scientific soundness of the principles of birth control and the imperative necessity of its adoption as the basis of national and racial progress."[8]

Sanger espoused the belief that such education would "tend to develop the powers of self-direction, self-reliance, and independence in the individuals of the community instead of dependence for relief upon public or private charities."[9]

Her organization, since its inception, has been vitally interested in education to change society. A Planned Parenthood publication of the mid-1960s dealt with incorporating family planning into the school curriculum, noting, "... a broadly representative committee with commitment should be able to establish the beginnings of a national program of school curriculum in population and another in family planning which, with the support of educators and the public, will eventually find acceptance. ..."[10]

Although these educational plans had been in place for years, the real breakthrough enabling Planned Parenthood to pursue its goals more aggressively did not occur until the late 1960s and early 1970s when federal funding became available for family planning services.[11] Such funding enabled Planned Parenthood affiliates, in some cases, to double staff size and greatly expand existing programs.[12]

Special emphasis on birth control to teens followed the infusion of federal money. By 1978, Planned Parenthood of Rochester and Monroe County in New York State had been granted $102,000 to "develop a special program to cope with teen pregnancy. [The] package included workshops, writing of curriculum for teaching human sexuality. ..."[13]

During this time, however, the involvement in high schools was limited to providing education, information, and referral for birth control services with a number of approaches initiated, using such innovative techniques as the "Youth Information Project" in which teens trained by Planned Parenthood carried supplies of literature, foam, and condoms to dispense to classmates in school hallways and restrooms.[14]

New York City high schools displayed posters announcing Peer Sex Education with such catchy words as the following:

If you think I.U.D. is a note
to someone you owe money to ...
If you think vacuum aspiration
is G.E.'s newest model electric broom ...
Then you need a visit to Room 122,
The Peer Sex Information Center.[15]

Planned Parenthood also suggested yearbook advertising as a way of getting a "foot in the door." A youth publication of Planned Parenthood described a program developed by Sandra Rand, working with the Los Angeles Regional Family Planning Council, as "highly recommended," explaining that such advertising was one way of reaching teenagers with contraceptive service information.[16]

An early attempt by Planned Parenthood to establish an in-school birth control clinic failed in Washington, D.C. It was acknowledged at the time that, to reach students, services other than family planning also had to be available.[17]

In some parts of the country, opposition to SBCs occurred when it became known that Planned Parenthood was involved in the program.

In 1980, an attempt was made to establish the Health Advocates Program (HAP) in Snohomish County, Washington. Preliminary publicity for HAP emphasized a four-fold approach addressing the issues of drugs, alcohol, nutrition, and pregnancy. HAP team members contacted local community organizations for endorsements and area school administrators with a prepared curriculum and an offer of professionals willing to provide services in area schools. HAP materials contained no mention of Planned Parenthood's involvement in the program.[18]

Planning for the program proceeded until, several months before the scheduled program opening, a community resident began contacting school officials, church leaders, and key residents in the area with information documenting Planned Parenthood's sponsorship of the program and a Minnesota-based foundation's funding for the HAP experiment. Parental and community opposition to Planned Parenthood's involvement and community concern that an attempt was being made to deceive parents about the program's intent caused cancellation of the program.[19] Such experiences led Planned Parenthood to play a less visible role in SBC organizing.

Washington, D.C.'s Planned Parenthood entered into the SBC arena again in 1985, but only after careful groundwork and only after enlisting the support of such well-known personalities as Jesse Jackson and Camille Cosby. Great care was also taken making Planned Parenthood appear to be but one member of a coalition of groups sponsoring a clinic offering "comprehensive health services" to teens.[20]

Planned Parenthood's image as part of the community has been carefully sculpted. A prime target for image building as well as for integration into the community has been the agency's aggressive courting of the religious community. Recognizing that "churches are a powerful force in communities all across the nation ... involved in a variety of issues, from voting rights to nuclear disarmament,"[21] the community service director of Planned Parenthood of Washington, D.C. urged church enlistment into teen pregnancy programs.

Novel approaches, such as "Teen Pregnancy Prevention Sundays," were introduced in area churches. Sermons and scriptural references were used which addressed teen pregnancy and "reflecting the particular denomination's own orientation toward it."[22] Prior to the special Sunday events participating congregations were to sponsor human sexuality training programs for parents and teens. Presentors for the programs were Planned Parenthood staff members.[23]

Center for Population Options Plays Lead Role

The established leader in the SBC movement is the Center for Population Options (CPO). Established in 1980, CPO "seeks to educate adolescents about family planning and reproductive health through media projects, school-based clinics, and other efforts in order to reduce unintended teenage pregnancy." With a full-time staff of 16 and an annual budget of $830,000 the organization also operates the International Clearinghouse on Adolescent Fertility and a Resource Center on adolescent sexuality and pregnancy.[24] The Houston, Texas, based Support Center for School-Based Clinics is also a CPO project.

Although attempts are made to downplay the family planning component of the clinics, CPO inludes "adolescent sexuality and reproductive health care as one [*sic*] of the major goals of the program, including the provision of family planning services."[25]

Involvement in abortion advocacy is also included in CPO's agenda. Among the organization's 1986 board members was Karen Mulhauser, former executive director of the National Abortion Rights Action League (NARAL).

In early 1986, a CPO quarterly published an announcement urging participation in a march sponsored by the National Organization for Women (NOW) "to demonstrate the majority support in this country for keeping abortion and birth control legal."[26]

The most blatant display of CPO's abortion advocacy, however, was a joint effort undertaken by CPO and Catholics for a Free Choice. (Catholics for a Free Choice bought a full page ad in the *San Francisco Chronicle* the day of Pope John Paul II's arrival in that city. The ad quoted the Pope's words from his Latin American trip, "No to the artificial prevention of fecundity! No to abortion! Yes to Life." Following the quote, the ad carried the announcement that the Pope has " carried this dangerously irresponsible message" when "motherhood kills where women are denied any choice at all."[27])

In August of 1986 Judith Senderowitz, CPO Executive Director, and Frances Kissling, President of Catholics for a Free Choice, joinly signed a letter written on CFFC letterhead expressing concern that "support among teenagers for abortion rights has dropped 20 percentage points since 1969."[28] The letter continued:

> The Center for Population Options (CPO), is concerned about this anti-choice trend in our teenagers ... CPO is also asking CFFC to help them gather information about anti-choice activities and materials. The results will be available to the pro-choice community for its internal information and may serve as a tool for future programming.[29]

Connections with Planned Parenthood are also evident. Joy G. Dryfoos, chair of CPO's Board of Directors, is the former director of research at Planned Parenthood's Alan Guttmacher Institute. Dryfoos, in her address to the Denver conference participants, made it clear that the SBC controversy is more than a mere skirmish. "To the dispassionate observer," she said, "this might be a fascinating game — the 'battle for the morals of the children' — and a never ending debate. ... But there are no dispassionate observers. ... You have to defend what has to be done. ... The fight goes on."

Sources of Funding

Costs of waging the battle described by Dryfoos are high, and those promoting SBCs have been cultivating the sources to meet these expenses.

Much of the cost of overall promotion, planning, formulation of strategies, and "technical assistance" (how to approach the school board, deal with the media, respond to the community, handle the controversy, and get initial approval for limited services) is handled by CPO with initial funding for local SBCs' establishment and operation coming from both government funds and private foundation grants.

Federal family planning money, available under Title X of the Public Health Service Act, was used to establish San Francisco's Balboa High School Clinic. Stephen Purser, Health Program coordinator of San Francisco City and County, explained that use of Title X money is appropriate for SBCs since "if you look around at the school-based clinics around the country, approximately 30, 40, and sometimes 50 percent of the services offered in these clinics is family planning." Based on this high level of family planning activity, Purser plans to obtain half of continuation funds for SBCs from Title X. The remaining half of the funding will come from the City of San Francisco.[30]

Awareness of the source of SBC funding helps clarify what services will be provided at a specific location. For example, Title X funding *requires* the provision of family planning services for teens although parents may be unaware of or opposed to such services.

According to John W. Nields, Jr., "Clinics receiving Title X funds are to further Congress' paramount goal of stemming the epidemic of teenage pregnancies and are *not* to notify parents over a request for confidentiality by the adolescent."[31] (Emphasis in original)

In addition to Title X money, SBCs have obtained governmental funding from state maternal and child health (MCH) block grant funds and from the Early and Periodic Screening, Diagnosis, and Treatment Program (EPSDT), a state-administered program to screen and treat

Medicaid-eligible children under the age of 21.

The costs of operating an SBC are high, with annual budgets running from a low of $25,000 (for one clinic running on a part-time basis) to a high of $1.9 million (for another clinic which operates at several sites). According to the former program administrator of a St. Paul, Minnesota, program, an average of $90,000 is needed annually to maintain an established program.[32]

With such large amounts involved, clinics cannot rely on only one source of funds for continued operation. One SBC, for example, receives funding from 15 different sources of revenue, combined from public and private coffers.[33] Foundation funding, though, is often instrumental in helping SBCs gain initial approval. In this way, school boards do not need to approve both the concept of SBCs and the use of scarce school dollars for clinic implementation.

By late 1986, there were 71 operational SBCs, 80 potential sites, and 20 locations targeted for opening with a three-year funding commitment from the Robert Wood Johnson Foundation.[34] By August of 1987 the SBC count exceeded 100 locations.[35]

The Robert Wood Johnson Foundation's interest in school health programs goes back a number of years. In 1982, it also funded 20 programs through what it called its Program to Consolidate Services for High-Risk Young People. The Ford, W. T. Grant, Rockefeller, Kaiser, and Harris Foundations also have played significant roles in such areas as data gathering, development, and clinic establishment. The Hewlett Foundation's major emphasis has been on support for development of SBCs in junior high schools.[36]

Foundation funding, though, is generally provided only for new programs. After clinics have been operational for several years, they are expected to generate their own continuation funding for operation and expansion. SBC promoters recognize this and, therefore, are seeking better ways to ensure the use of tax money to underwrite SBC costs.

According to Joy Dryfoos, "Public funds, particularly from state departments of maternal and child health, social services and education, are being sought in order to expand existing programs to more and more schools and to start new clinics in other communities.[37]

Special strategies for reaching legislators were discussed in a general address to the Denver conference called "SBCs: Capturing Public Funds," in which Paul Shaheen, executive director of the Michigan Council for Maternal and Child Health, suggested ways to get SBC funding approved by legislatures:

> Prevention is the name of the game. Cost containment is the only thing legislators are concerned about. You have nothing to offer but cost containment. It's a question of marketing. ...
>
> We follow a strategy that says, "Go to the conservatives." Prevention is a conservative concept so when we wanted to get family planning, I went to the middle of the Republican party and said, "Gee, guys and ladies, you say your welfare roles are growing too fast and you say you don't like abortion. Well, neither do I. But you've got a four to eight week waiting list at your family planning clinics. People don't stand around and wait. They find things to do with those four to eight weeks. ..."
>
> We used the most conservative physicians we could find. ... They

go to their conservative friends and say "This isn't a question of politics. This is a question of human pain and suffering."

Legislatures in a number of other states have considered funding SBCs. Washington, Connecticut, Minnesota, North Carolina, California, and Oregon are among those who have introduced or enacted SBC legislation.[38]

A bill that would have provided 200 million federal dollars for SBCs was introduced in August 1986. The "School-Based Adolescent Health Services Bill" (H.R. 5377), co-sponsored by congressmen Henry Waxman, George Miller, and Chester Atkins, was designed to give $50 million for each of four years to non-profit public and private agencies with priority given to those with a "track record in primary care service delivery to adolescents or undeserved populations."[39]

Agencies receiving funding from the legislation would have been required to provide services within or adjacent to schools or in such locations which would better serve the needs of qualified adolescents served by the project. Those receiving a grant would have been required to provide family planning services and other "health care services" mandated by the program to all "qualified adolescents." A "qualified adolescent," according to H.R. 5377 was defined as "any individual between the ages of 11 and 18 who lived in the school district or districts served by the project."[40]

These requirements could have been interpreted as requiring an SBC to provide family planning services and education to 11 and 12 year-old children without parental knowledge or consent if the children were not attending the school where the clinic was located. This would, in effect, have removed parental rights from even those parents who, out of concern for their children, had chosen to send their children to private, rather than public, schools in the area.

Although H.R. 5377 and its companion bill in the Senate (S. 2757) failed to win approval in 1986, similar proposals will be introduced. Congressman Miller and others attempting to garner public moneys for SBCs rely heavily on winning approval for the clinics as cost-effective programs. According to Miller, "School-based services have demonstrated that they can provide valuable prevention and intervention services which effectively reduce health problems, as well as non-health related school problems, such as school dropouts. What is also clear is that they can save a great many tax dollars."[41]

Family Planning for Teens

The promise of savings in money and human potential is held out to the public as *the* reason for SBCs. But is the promise backed up with facts?

Past expenditures for family planning services to teens and the impact of such expenditures give some indication of a gap between promise and performance.

Stan E. Weed, director of the Independent Institute for Research and Evaluation, and Joseph A. Olsen recently completed studies on the impact of federally funded family planning services for teens. The study was prompted by rising trends in reported teen pregnancies at the same time large federal expenditures were being made to fund family planning services for teens.

Weed and Olsen found that, from 1971 to 1981, the number of teen family planning clients increased five-fold (from 300,000 to 1.5 million clients) while federal expenditures rose by 4,000 percent (from $11 million to $442 million). The rationale for such expenditures had been a projected decrease in teen births, abortions, and pregnancies. However, the pregnancy rate for 15 to 19 year-olds increased from an estimated 95 per 1,000 in 1972 to an estimated 113 per 1,000 in 1981, and, although the size of the teen population was virtually the same, the number of abortions performed on teens rose from 190,000 to 430,000 annually during the same time period.[42]

Even though more and more teens were using family planning services, the decline in births to teens was due, not to a decrease in teen pregnancy, but to an increase in teen abortion. According to Weed, family planning programs for teens "are more effective in convincing teens to avoid birth than to avoid pregnancy." He further stated, "Birth avoidance can certainly be accomplished by resorting to abortion. Unfortunately, that is not what the effort was set up to do nor the basis on which it was funded."[43]

SBC Cost Effectiveness

As with previous family planning programs for teens, SBCs are set up and funded on the basis that they will reduce teen pregnancy, and statistics are used to justify expenditure of public funds for the clinics. The statistical game has become so much a part of the SBCs' organizational scenario that CPO has developed a special handbook and software package "to help you compute the cost of teenage childbearing in *your* community."[44]

Statistics gleaned from the use of such tools as well as statistics obtained from other sources present data supporting the *need* for intervention. They do not, however, provide any meaningful data proving the effectiveness of SBCs which have been in operation.

Although the SBC experiment has been going on for over a decade, a sampling of statements and studies by SBC advocates themselves makes it abundantly clear that there are *no* reliable statistics to prove that SBCs reduce teen pregnancy.

As Joy Dryfoos wrote in 1985, "School-based clinics have been credited with improving students' health, lowering their birthrates, raising their levels of contraceptive use, and improving their school attendance. However, there have been few reliable studies of these programs. Improved program evaluation will be useful in helping these clinics retain their financial and community support."[45]

In mid-1986, a flurry of articles appeared in newspapers and magazines citing a study which purported to prove the effectiveness of SBCs. However, the study, conducted by Zabin, Smith, and Hirsch did nothing of the kind. In fact, the only concrete "finding" was that the study had proven nothing. While the authors stated there was "an *apparent* [seven month] postponement of first intercourse among high school students exposed to the program for three years,"[46] (emphasis added) they further noted the following methodological problems with the study — problems that rendered the study useless:

1. The high level of student transfers and reassignments during the year made it difficult to follow the same students throughout the study.

2. The collection of behavior-reflecting data was difficult thus hampering "before" and "after" program comparisons.

3. Schools within the system differed so significantly that control schools, although used in the study, could not be compared directly with program schools.[47]

In addition, the reported results were based upon school populations *as a whole*[48] and so comparisons were not made between individuals who used the program and those who did not.

This latter fact makes it possible, if not probable, that even the "apparent" seven month delay in first intercourse may have been the result of averaging *earlier* initiation of sexual activity by program participants with later first intercourse by those who had no program participation.

In an article about the study, the study's authors stated, "a longer period of time than that involved here is probably needed to achieve and to measure the full impact of intervention such as these."[49] But, even while admitting the need for further study to measure the impact of such programs, the study's authors recommended that younger children (those under 7th grade level) be placed in family planning programs "before young people develop behavior that places them at risk of early post-pubertal conception."[50]

It may be significant to note that the study's principal investigator, Laurie S. Zabin, was chairperson of Planned Parenthood's Alan Guttmacher Institute during the time in which the study's conclusions were being formulated.[51]

Additional articles by the study's authors have promoted the unsubstantiated "need" to reach very young children with family planning stating: "Future projects must find out how much earlier young people might profitably be reached with similar education initiatives because our baseline data suggest that junior high may be too late to affect sexual onset for about half of these boys and girls, or, indeed, to reach the sexually active among them in their high-risk period of exposure."[52]

While admitting that studies on existing SBCs likely show that such interventions are not working, the authors conclude that it is because such interventions occur too late. No consideration is given the more obvious conclusion, that such interventions will not work no matter when they are initiated. The stage, therefore, is set for trying to make the program work by reaching a different "target" population — very young children.

Asta M. Kenney, associate for Policy Development with the Alan

Guttmacher Institute, wrote in the spring of 1986: "Some might judge them (SBCs) successful simply on the basis of their rapid proliferation and students' heavy use of their services. In several areas, 75 percent or more of students have availed themselves of clinic services. Nonetheless, solid data on the health impact of these clinics are scarce." Kenney further noted that CPO, recognizing that better data on school-based clinics is needed, has announced it has undertaken an evaluation of seven SBCs. The study will be completed in 1988.[53]

An article appearing in the Summer 1986 issue of *Family Planning Perspectives* admitted the non-results of SBC evaluations: ". . . the lack of important information in both of the data sets used by these articles [referring to articles published in the same issue] continues to leave frustrated those who are looking for research findings on which to base sound decisions about school programs and policies that will reduce teenage pregnancy."[54]

Speaker after speaker at the Denver conference called for record-keeping and statistics, leaving no question that, currently, there is no proof that SBCs accomplish the purposes for which they are established and funded.

And yet, even in the face of such lack of proof of SBCs effectiveness, the call continues to go out, urging establishment of additional clinics for even younger children. In a general session of the Denver conference, Gerald Kitzi, executive director of Kansas City's Adolescents Resources Corporation, said: "In middle and junior high school is where these young people have to be reached." But Kitzi, whose corporation runs three SBCs, cautioned that reaching this age group will be difficult and more expensive since the students are not motivated.

Other speakers made references to the great amount of time and effort needed to reach adolescents who do not want to attend family planning clinics. Such students, according to SBC professionals, must be educated to understand that they need the services. This, indeed, does present a challenge to the clinics. How can children be convinced that they need what they do not want?

Creating the Need

The first high school clinic offering family planning services began in Dallas, Texas, in 1970[55] but Minnesota's Maternal and Infant Care (MIC) Program, established in 1973 in St. Paul, is best known as the "pioneer" of the SBC movement.[56]

The St. Paul clinic, originally set up to offer care to pregnant teens, soon shifted its emphasis to pregnancy prevention by providing birth control counseling for students. Students, however, were reluctant to attend the clinic. Ann Ricketts, program administrator, explained the reluctance, saying: "There was no question why someone was going in there." This led to a quick expansion of services to include weight control, sports physicals, and other types of programs to encourage students to visit the clinic.[57]

There can be no doubt that the raison d'etre of SBCs is family planning. But, as the St. Paul and the early Washington, D.C. experiences demonstrated, a clinic limited to family planning will not attract teens.

Clinic workers use a number of means to attract students, thus introducing them to the concept of "responsible" family planning. The most widespread method is the routine health assessment during which all clinic participants, male or female, are provided with a questionnaire or a "psychological evaluation" asking about current and planned sexual activity.[58] Wording on such questionnaires is done in such a way as to presuppose eventual teen sexual activity. Chicago's Du Sable High School Clinic, for example, asks, "Have you started having sex?"[59] Students who answer affirmatively or who indicate that they may be planning to become sexually active are provided with birth control (by referral, prescription, or actual provision) and followed up thereafter.

All SBCs counsel students regarding the use of birth control. The majority (52 percent) prescribe contraceptives.[60] Students must then go to another location to have the prescription filled. While this other location may be as close as the pharmacy across the street, the added effort is, according to SBC professionals, a problem for poorly motivated students. The ideal situation, according to SBC advocates, exists in only 28 percent of existing clinics where the actual contraceptives are dispensed on school premises.[61]

The remaining 20 percent of SBCs refer students to nearby family planning agencies.[62] In such cases, student initiative is required — initiative that SBC professionals feel is lacking. Although clinic staff members often make the actual appointments, the students must arrange to go for the appointment. It is this "extra step" that is viewed as requiring too much of the students, since they often fail to keep the appointments.

The lack of interest on the part of the target population has led to SBCs adopting what they refer to as "aggressive and creative approaches" to sell the idea of birth control to teens.

One New York social worker makes videotapes of boys as they are breakdancing or playing basketball then offers them the opportunity to see themselves on tape. To view the tape, however, they must go to the local family planning clinic where the videoscreen is set up and where they must also take part in a talk about "sexual responsibility."[63]

Incentives are also used to motivate students. In an effort to assure that students make regular return visits for family planning, one school administrator has suggested offering points toward field trips as a way of rewarding students for keeping follow-up appointments.[64]

Follow-up is described by SBC workers as a major challenge. Since students often did not directly request birth control services in the first place and since, therefore, their interest in such services is minimal, they must be reminded again and again to return to the clinic. Often such reminders are given by clinic staff contacting students in their classes, requesting that they visit the clinic. Because clinics also offer other services, this presents no problem according to Joy Dryfoos since "classmates do not know why the student is being asked to come to the clinic."[65]

It is the unmotivated "high risk" teen who must be given the most attention to both initiate birth control and to make certain that the method is used correctly. At times such a teen may use any number of excuses to avoid the use of birth control. Barbara Ann Taylor, a nurse practitioner in a St. Paul, Minnesota SBC, suggests that clinic professionals be very flexible in approaching such students. To illustrate her point, Taylor told Denver conference participants how one student said that she could not take the Pill since she had never been able to swallow pills. "If the excuse is 'I can't swallow pills,' " said Taylor, "let them practice swallowing pills by using Tic Tacs." Taylor explained that this is the type of student one must "see as often as necessary to reinforce and follow up. This may be daily at first."[66]

Family Planning and the Classroom

The influence of the SBC and its promotion of family planning for teens is not confined to the clinic location. Attempts to reach students occur in the classroom as well. As a way of linking education and clinic services, clinic staff often conduct sex education and family life classes in the school "so they have ample opportunity to encourage the students in the classroom to attend the clinic."[67]

A particularly "creative" approach to convince teens to use birth control has been developed by Peggy Brick and Carolyn Cooperman. Their 1986 Planned Parenthood publication, *Positive Images: A New Approach to Contraceptive Education,* is based on the belief that programs must be unequivocal in supporting the use of birth control for teens. It includes the following lessons:

> "Creating Positive Images: Advertising for Contraception," in which students design sample ads promoting contraception. By doing such an exercise students must look for the most positive and the most marketable aspects of birth control. The attempt to "sell" the concept of birth control by means of the sample ad helps students overcome any negative ideas about contraceptives they may have had in the past.
>
> "Condom Comfort," designed to give students the opportunity to create original instruction sheets illustrating effective condom use, provides students the information essential for use of the condom.
>
> "Putting Birth Control into Romance," offers students the chance to create an original romantic scene incorporating the use of contraceptives into the language of romance.[68]

"The manual can be used to integrate contraceptive education into the more traditional academic curriculum," says its authors.[69]

CPO has also developed a curriculum called *Life Planning Education: A Youth Development Program.* The program, which presents birth control as a right and a responsibility of teens, includes a visit to a family planning clinic among the classroom activities."[70]

Another activity, the "Myth Information Game," helps students differentiate myths from facts. For example, the myth, "A teenager needs parental consent to get birth control from a clinic," is replaced by the fact, "Family planning clinics ensure the confidentiality of their services. That means they don't have to tell *anyone* in order to provide birth control to teenagers."[71]

The *Life Planning* curriculum is sold to school districts as a program integrating "traditional sexuality education with vocational preparation ... appealing to both teenagers and program sponsors because it places delaying parenthood in the total context of future preparation."[72]

Integration of clinic and classroom is an important element in the success of SBCs. Asta Kenney suggests the following ways to accomplish this: (1) full-time rather than part-time clinic staff so the same people will always be available, and (2) classroom presentations by clinic staff to strengthen the bond between clinic and classroom. This, says Kenney, "helps build students' confidence in the clinic and improves their knowledge about health matters."[73]

Such a meshing of the classroom and the clinic pressures all students to accept clinic services.

Parental Consent — Fact or Myth

Parental involvement and parental permission for a student's receipt of clinic services are often highlighted during initial publicity for SBCs, but, in practice, parental rights are considered virtually non-existent.

The St. Paul clinic explains that "a parental permission slip is necessary for students to obtain general health services." Such services include treatment of sore throat and provision of aspirin and similar medications. However, according to the St. Paul clinic, "the Minors' Consent Law in Minnesota states that minors have the right to seek confidential services without parental consent."[74] "Confidential" services — those for which parental consent is *not* required — include family planning.

A book for health professionals who treat young people explains:

> The Supreme Court has held that contraceptives must be made available to minors and that states may not prohibit such access in the interest of legislating morality. ... Title XIX (Medical Assistance), Title XX (Aid to Families with Dependent Children) of the Social Security Act, and Title X of the Family Planning Services and Population Research Act of 1970 require that participating states provide family planning assistance to eligible minors who desire such assistance without regard to marital status, age or parenthood. Parental consent and/or notification is not required or allowed.[75]

In most clinics, parental permission is requested for providing an entire array of services. The permission covers all of the years a child may attend the school and may not list all services available. In New York City, even members of the Board of Education were unaware of family planning provision until two years after the city's SBCs had been in operation.

According to Marion Schwarz who had been instrumental in getting SBCs in New York schools, there had been no announcement of the family planning component, since clinics were not compelled to "itemize every service."[76]

Board of Education President Robert F. Wagner, Jr. said he had known of the family planning component and implied others should have assumed its inclusion. "Anyone who believes comprehensive health care for sexually active adolescents does not include birth control is crazy," he said.[77]

Abortion referrals are generally offered by SBCs, as are pregnancy tests.[78] Here, also, while one may assume such could not be done without parental permission, parents need not be informed.

In areas where a parent specifically notifies the school that a child is not to receive family planning services, the SBC may make it clear to parents that "the student will be referred elsewhere for services."[79]

Programs have been approved in some locations after SBC organizers agreed to omit birth control services. This "concession" on the part of SBC professionals has been erroneously viewed as a "victory" by the family planning opponents. In reality, once an SBC is in place, students will receive family planning counseling, education, and referral.

Cleveland, Ohio, is one example of such an empty victory for those opposing SBCs. Attempts over the last several years have been made to obtain approval for actual dispensing of birth control at the existing SBCs. Although the permission for on-campus provision of contraceptives has been denied, clinic staff refers students for family planning.[80]

What is "Family Planning"?

Family planning is generally perceived to be synonymous with contraception, however, it is more accurately considered interchangeable with "birth control" or "fertility regulation."

Within the context of SBCs, what is meant by "family planning?" Does it refer to the "full range" of fertility regulation as often described by Planned Parenthood and similar organizations? Such groups customarily refer to four general methods of "fertility regulation" — abortion, abstinence, contraception, and sterilization.

Do SBCs provide abortions? The abortion issue is addressed by clinic professionals with a denial that abortions are done by SBCs. There is little doubt that this denial is accurate. SBCs — at least for now — do not actually do abortions. Space is limited. Equipment to perform surgery is not available on the premises. SBCs do, however, refer for abortion. In just one New York City clinic last year, 70 percent of students receiving positive pregnancy test results were referred for abortion.[81]

CPO expressed great concern in early 1986 over possible passage of a Title X amendment which would have barred funding of clinics that perform or refer for abortions. Following the failure of the amendment, CPO announced: "The long battle is over — for now. ... If passed, the amendment would have had the effect of immediately defunding virtually all current Title X grantees."[82] SBCs are recipients of Title X funding.

Although various laws have been passed to ensure that parents are notified of a child's planned abortion, such laws have been challenged in state after state. Minnesota's Parental Notification Law was the most recent law to fall after being deemed unconstitutional by Federal District Judge Donald D. Alsop who said he could find no factual basis for holding that the law "on the whole furthers in any meaningful way the state's interest in protecting pregnant minors or assuring family integrity."[83]

Recognizing that 90 percent of SBCs provide pregnancy tests[84] and that no state requires parental consent before a minor can obtain an abortion, it would be incredibly naive to think that SBCs do not assist teens in obtaining abortions.

This abortion link was made clear in an article in *Family Planning Perspectives* where it was stated: "One problem cited by clinic personnel is the lack of public funding for abortions in most states, which severely limits the options of the low-income young people who typically use school health clinics."[85]

Abortion, then, is obviously considered within the range of "family planning" or "fertility regulation" options. What about abstinence? Is this method of family planning given any great degree of promotion? The answer would appear to be, "No."

Abstinence as a means of family planning receives short shrift from SBCs, being presented as an "option" that is rarely chosen. "Abstinence is often not a realistic choice," according to Dr. Alwyn T. Cohall who works at New York's Louis D. Brandeis High School clinic.[86] Contraception fares much better as a method of choice.

Contraceptives such as the condom and diaphragm are introduced to students — even those who are not clinic participants — in novel ways. One school has designated a room for health education giving students in the health education classes an opportunity to see the room's display of condoms and diaphragms during general health education sessions. But these methods of birth control are not the most popular among students. The Pill tends to be the birth control method most often used by teens attending SBCs.[87]

It is worth noting that the largest manufacturer of the Pill is the Ortho Company, one of fifteen professional companies in the Johnson and Johnson "family,"[88] the "family" that is the sole contributor to the Robert Wood Johnson Foundation, SBCs' greatest source of foundation funding.

Use of the Pill presents potentially grave health risks, particularly for girls whose parents are unaware of their use. Most young people are unaware of the details of their family medical history. Yet a family health history is important in assessing the risks for Pill users.

Among teen users, the effectiveness of the Pill is very low, providing an average pregnancy-free interval of only 19.3 months.[89] Such lack of effectiveness may well be, in part, due to the lack of parental knowledge that a teen is taking the Pill.

Since parents are still required to give consent for a minor's treatment for such illnesses as upper respiratory infection or various other conditions, a parent may consent to a medication, prescribed by a family doctor or dentist, that reduces the Pill's effectiveness. Such medications, commonly prescribed, include antibiotics (rifampicin, ampicillin, and tetracycline) or barbiturates, phenylbutazone or phenytoin sodium.[90]

A minor's attempts to conceal Pill taking from parents may also lead to variation in time of day when the Pill is ingested. The Pill's effectiveness is reduced if it is not taken exactly as prescribed. According to the detailed package insert, the Pill "must be taken exactly as directed and at intervals not exceeding 24 hours ..." since taking the tablets at the same time each day will maintain "proper amounts of medication in your system."[91] The requirement that the Pill be taken at the same time each day presents a number of problems for teen users. Teen schedules are irregular. For this reason, the teen who plans to take the Pill in the morning will, if she sleeps in one day, miss the time when the medication should have been taken. No parental reminders will be given. Likewise, scheduling to take the Pill in the evening will probably involve carrying them in her purse or pocket.

Sterilization, the fourth type of fertility regulation, had not been mentioned in reference to SBCs until lately. However, in recent months, concern from the black community has been expressed about the obvious trageting of minority areas for SBC services. This concern has led to alarm regarding the possible connection of SBCs and sterilization. Chicago's Auxiliary Bishop Wilton T. Gregory warned: "I would not at all be surprised if, in the future, more drastic measures [to control births among the poor and minority groups] are considered and proposed, perhaps even as drastic as sterilization."[92] Similar concern was expressed by Dr. Gwendolyn C. Baker, a member of the New York City Board of Education. Dr. Baker, a black Protestant, said: "Then in another 10 years it will be sterilization. Why? Because 10 years ago we wouldn't have talked about contraceptives — it would have been so out of line."[93]

How "out of line" is the possibility of sterilization for teens? It is probable that, currently, sterilization of teens is not being promoted, but the potential for pressure on young, poor students, particularly those who may be considered "ineffective contraceptors," is very real.

Few constraints exist to prevent such pressure. Perhaps the greatest roadblock to sterilization for minors is the fact that federal regulations provide that, under no circumstances, is federal reimbursement available for sterilization of anyone under the age of twenty-one.[94] However, only nine states forbid sterilization for minors in all circumstances.[95]

A few state statutes expressly permit minors' consent to sterilization. Among these states are Oregon (where the age of consent is fifteen and over)[96] and Rhode Island (where consent may be given by a minor if necessary to "preserve health").[97] Minnesota has no specific statute covering sterilization of minors. However, state family planning centers must notify a minor's parents when advising sterilization.[98]

Planned Parenthood has stated that the "right of everyone to have *full access* to fertility regulation information and services applied equally to young people, *including those in the adolescent age group (10-19 years)."*[99]

Of the four types of family planning services, contraception and abortion have become customary services of SBCs; abstinence is described as unrealistic. Can the last of the four, sterilization, be far behind in the offerings of family planning "options" available to teens through SBCs?

Implications for the Future

SBCs cause far more problems than they attempt to solve. Some of these problems are immediately evident (for example, health hazards resulting from Pill use by growing girls, usurping of parental rights and responsibilities, costs to taxpayers of ineffective programs). However, SBCs pose other grave threats to the health and lives of children.

Reference to the growing problem of AIDS has been lacking in SBC literature, training programs and conferences until the end of 1986, even though the same activity that leads to pregnancy can lead to AIDS. The situation changed dramatically following the Surgeon General's report calling for AIDS education which "must start at the lowest grade possible."[100]

Immediately the "safe sex" campaign was on, with "experts" ready to provide children with such sage advice as ". . . safe sex can still be plenty of fun."[101] For over a decade, teens had been told: "If you're 'sexually active,' be responsible. Use family planning." Yet the teen pregnancy rate has continued to rise. In the next decade, if teens are told: "If you're sexually active, have 'safe' sex," we can expect that this approach will be even less effective in preventing AIDS than the teen family planning approach has been in preventing teen pregnancy.

Condoms are notoriously ineffective in preventing pregnancy. *Contraceptive Technology 1986-1987,* a well-known handbook on birth control methods, ranked the condom's effectiveness at 10 pregnancies for 100 women for one year. Since a woman is only fertile for, at most, only one-fourth of her cycle, during the majority of times condom intercourse occurs, conception is not even possible. Since the AIDS virus can be transmitted at any time in the cycle, there is theoretically a minimum 40% chance of AIDS transmission using "safe" sex. The possible failure rate of condoms, in preventing the spread of AIDS, was estimated even higher in a Minneapolis television station report. Explaining that "there are those who say condoms provide a false sense of security," the report noted that they "could have a failure rate up to 50 percent."[102]

While teachers unions are issuing recommendations that "schools make condoms available to students in grades seven through twelve in efforts to combat the AIDS epidemic"[103] medical publications are noting the high incidence of defective condoms. A recent article noted that the FDA had "recalled 41 lots of condoms because of a leakage rate greater than four per 1,000" but had approved "an additional 163 lots with an 'acceptable' average failure rate of 3.3 per 1,000."[104] Even if children were to use condoms "correctly" — and they won't — and even if there were not a failure rate due to storage time, damage in shipment, etc. — but there will be — there would still be up to a 3.3 per 1,000 failure of the condom itself.

But it appears unlikely that SBC staffers will back away from promoting condoms. The "safe sex" promotion gives SBCs another angle from which to push for support.

While there have been leaders courageous enough to speak out, they have received vehement opposition. Bishop Anthony Bevilacqua of Pittsburgh in an August 15, 1987 statement said: "It is not a responsible action to use the devastating disease of AIDS as an excuse to promote methods of artificial birth control. It is not responsible to suggest that the main concern in expected sexual activity is to 'be careful.' "[105] For days following his lengthy and well reasoned statement, Bevilacqua was bitterly attacked by letter writers to Pittsburgh newspapers.

New "Norm" Established

SBCs have the potential of causing grave harm to the family, especially harm brought about through the already recognized denigration of parental rights and responsibility.

Teen sexual activity is being raised up as a new model to emulate. According to a recent article in *Ob-Gyn News:* "Health professionals and counselors can gain a greater understanding of teenage pregnancy by acknowledging that sexual activity among American and many European teenagers is now the norm, not an indication of social deviance."[106]

A "norm," as defined in the dictionary, is "a rule or authoritative standard; a model." The shift from accepting teen promiscuity as "inevitable" to promoting it as a "model" has begun. If such a trend continues, teens who are not sexually active will be viewed as "abnormal." Acceptance of such a condition will finalize the acceptance of moral chaos as the model for society.

This attitude will have an untold impact on the family lives of future generations. A 1978 study found that premarital sexual attitudes and behavior are closely related to extra-marital attitudes and behavior. Thus, the assumption that, although one has been involved in sexual activity prior to marriage, one will remain faithful and nonexploitative after marriage seems to be false. In effect, the premarital activity sets the stage for viewing sex as acceptable outside the context of marriage.[107]

Marriages which accept the new norm will be based on the "ideal" of fulfillment of sexual desire, not on such values as love, fidelity, or strong family ties. Fulfillment of sexual desire will be evaluated by society with the same criteria for both the married and the unmarried, where promiscuity and infidelity are seen as normal so long as they do not lead to the birth of an "unwanted" child or the contracting of disease.

An additional concern about possible ramifications of SBCs should be considered. New attitudes about sex and birth control were viewed by Margaret Sanger as ways of transforming the world. But this transformation has another element as well.

Speaking at a recent conference of the Hemlock Society — an organization whose primary purpose is the legalization of death by choice — Dr. Joseph Fletcher, the "father of situation ethics," reminisced about the days when both he and Margaret Sanger joined the Euthanasia Society of America "thus linking the two causes so to speak — the right to be selective about parenthood and the right to be selective about living." Fletcher explained: "We've added death control to birth control as a part of the ethos or life style of our society."[108]

In two states, legislation has been proposed recently which would give teens the right to sign "living wills" directing the withholding of treatment and care if they should become severely disabled.[109] How long will it be before "life planning" assistance from SBC professionals includes not only family planning but also death planning, both types of planning under the guise of personal choice, personal responsibility, and, of course, the right to privacy?

Conclusion

Information about SBCs — their origins, their current activities, and implications for the future — makes it apparent that, if allowed to continue unchecked, SBCs will launch society into a time of even greater social upheaval and health hazards than we are now experiencing. Faced with the enormous resources available to and the tremendous amount of misinformation circulated by SBC advocates, what can be done?

The following four-fold approach can begin to change the current trend:

1. *Awareness of SBCs and their implications.* A vague understanding that there is something "not quite right" about SBCs is insufficient in dealing with SBCs. When faced with statistics and what, on the surface, sounds like a well-reasoned argument in favor of SBCs, it is necessary to have accurate information to help others develop an awareness of the actual and potential problems with SBCs.

2. *Early opposition to SBCs.* Opposition to SBCs has come from a number of sources ranging from minority groups concerned that emphasis on minority-area schools aims at reducing the black population[110] to outspoken statements from members of the Catholic hierarchy.[111]

Such opposition, however, has generally been expressed in response to announcements that an SBC is being considered in a community — announcements that are not made *until* all essential support for the program has been put in place. By the time the public becomes aware that an SBC is being considered at least a year of work has already taken place building support from individual school board members, school administrators, and key community leaders.

Even the collection of information on student health needs in the area — often viewed publically as the first step in the SBC process — is far down the list in the organizational agenda. A recently published guide to implementing SBCs suggests that *before* information on health needs is obtained, a small select planning group already will have obtained initial funding and developed the clinic's philosophy.[112]

The most effective opposition to SBCs, therefore, usually takes place before public promotion of such a program begins. To influence decision-making, it is necessary to contact school board members, community leaders, and legislators, explaining the need for unequivocal support for teen chastity before the need to combat a proposed SBC is apparent.

In areas where SBCs have already been introduced, concerned individuals can exert pressure to bring an end to such programs, replacing them with programs promoting sexual abstinence as a positive value for teens. Such pressure can take the form of becoming involved in the actual structure of program planning through school board membership, or it can take the form of helping the community recognize that existing programs are ineffective in achieving the results for which they were formulated and funded.

By opposing SBCs, individuals are refusing to be part of a most demeaning and patronizing attitude that has developed over the years, leading some to believe that a person who is young, poor, or a member of a minority class is incapable of saying "yes" to self-esteem and self-control.

Becoming involved in the public process and the development of public policy is not an option but an obligation. Opposing SBCs, recognizing their danger to the family and to individuals is not enough. The need to take action in protecting the family was clearly spelled out by Pope John Paul II in **Familiaris Consortio**:

> Families should be the first to take steps to see that the laws and institutions of the state not only do not offend, but support and positively defend the rights and duties of the family. Along these lines families should grow in awareness of being "protagonists" of what is known as "family politics" and assume responsibility for transforming society; otherwise families will be the first victims of the evils that they have done no more than note with indifference.[113]

3. *Acknowledgement of the need to address very real problems.* There *are* problems facing teens and their families. Today's teens are pressured to be sexually active. Families are challenged as never before in society. Mixed messages are the order of the day. The message, "Don't, but if you do ..." is confusing and has led to teens getting little or no support for chastity.

Once we have acknowledged our negligence in working to support teen chastity and family life, it is time to stop the hand-wringing and get on with open and frank discussions about the benefits of chastity and healthy family life. In order to do this parents and teachers must be educated. The greatest lack of education related to sexuality is not an unawareness of sex itself, nor is the greatest problem the timidity that some parents and Catholic educators may experience in discussing sensitive issues. By far, the greatest problem today is an unawareness of or lack of understanding of the Church's teachings on sexuality and family life. How many parents, how many Catholic educators have read **Humanae Vitae** and **Familiaris Consortio**? Often, there is more concern about what the media will say about Catholic approaches and Catholic beliefs than about what Jesus would say about the seeming inability to live the truth in order to become a light to others. Without knowledge of, love of and a willingness to live the truth, attempts to promote healthy family life and the benefits of chastity will be empty, gimmicky and doomed to failure.

4. *Willingness to promote programs unequivocally offering chastity, not as one of many options, but as the norm for teens.* Programs of this type must offer the concept of abstinence not only from the stance of a set of prohibitions, but from the perspective of the positive value of abstinence for unmarried people. In so doing, we can show teens — all teens — the respect they deserve by recognizing that they are capable of chastity and have a right to encouragement to be chaste.

Are there such programs available? Yes, but until recently no mention of them has been made by the media. This situation has led to the public assuming that people who oppose SBCs and the birth-control-for-teens approach have done nothing to address the problem of teen pregnancy.

One such program — the Teen Aid Program — has been available through the Human Life Center for several years. A recent *Time* magazine article described the Teen Aid Program as confronting value-free teaching by urging "youngsters to 'resist the tide' of sex-saturated culture" by helping students "sharpen their 'refusal skills.' " The article noted that the Teen Aid Program involves parents by sending home summaries of lessons.[114] Teen Aid and its approach is growing rapidly, with 25 affiliates in the U.S. and Canada.

Similar teaching tools for public and religious education, from full curriculum materials to teen pamphlets and brochures stressing the benefits of chastity, are available and need to be more widely publicized.

CPO's Joy Dryfoos was correct when she called this "the battle for the morals of the children." It is most definitely that, and we must engage in that battle. If we do not, the real losers will be our children.

NOTES

[1] Most Reverend Anthony Bevilacqua, "The Questions Raised by School-Based Health Clinics," *Origins,* vol. 17, no. 12 (Sept. 3, 1987), p. 188. Hereafter cited as Bevilacqua.

[2] Sharon R. Lovick and Wanda F. Wesson, *School-Based Clinics: Update* (Washington, D.C.: Center for Population Options, 1986), p. 3. Hereafter cited as *SBC: Update.*

[3] Elaine M. Hadley, Sharon R. Lovick and Douglas Kirby, *School-Based Health Clinics: A Guide to Implementing Programs* (Washington, D.C.: Center for Population Options, 1986), p. 9. Hereafter cited as *Implementing Programs.*

[4] Margaret Sanger, **The Pivot of Civilization** (London: Jonathan Cape, 1923), p. 229. Hereafter cited as **Pivot.**

[5] Gina Johnson, Johanna Pugni, *Echoes from the Past* (New York: Planned Parenthood Federation of America, 1979), no page listing. Hereafter cited as *Echoes.*

[6] **Pivot,** p. 243.

[7] **Ibid.**, p. 244.

[8] **Ibid.**, p. 254.

[9] **Ibid.**, p. 255.

[10] Dorothy Millstone, ed., *Family Planning, Population Problems and the Secondary School Curriculum* (New York: Planned Parenthood — World Population, 1966), p. 18.

[11] *Echoes.*

[12] "Planned Parenthood Beginnings — Affiliate Histories," compiled by Mrs. Alan Guttmacher for the Margaret Sanger Centennial Celebration, 1979 PPFA Annual Meeting, Houston, Texas, November 15, 1979, p. 90.

[13] **Ibid.**, p. 91.

[14] "Getting It Together: A Publication of the Youth and Student Affairs Program of the Planned Parenthood Federation of America" (New York: Planned Parenthood Federation of America). vol. 5, no. 5, July 1975, p. 8.

[15] **Ibid.**, vol. 6, no, 3, February 1976, p. 6.

[16] **Ibid.**, vol. 7, no. 3, March 1977, p. 3.

[17] National Family Planning and Reproductive Health Association (NFPRHA) 14th Annual Meeting; Washington, D.C.; March 5-7, 1986; School-Based Family Planning Clinics" workshop. Remarks of Sharon Robinson of Planned Parenthood of Metropolitan Washington, D.C. Hereafter cited as NFPRHA Meeting.

[18] "Parents Concerned about Health Advocates Program," *Snohomish Tribune*, 1/21/81.

[19] "New School Borders Set in Snohomish," *Everett Herald*, Jan. 28, 1981, p. 3A.

[20] NFPRHA Meeting.

[21] Brenda Rhodes Cooper, "Mobilizing the Religious Community," *Planned Parenthood Review*, vol. 6, no. 2, (Spring, 1986), p. 21.

[22] **Ibid.**, p. 22.

[23] **Ibid.**

[24] *Population: Briefing paper on issues of national and international importance* (Washington, D.C., Population Crisis Committee, December 1985), no. 16, p. 3. Hereafter cited as *Population.*

[25] *SBC: Update*, p. 4.

[26] *Issues and Action Update: A quarterly concerned with the prevention of adolescent pregnancy* (Washington, D.C.: Center for Population Options), 5:1 (Winter 1986), p. 8. Hereafter cited as *Issues and Action.*

[27] *San Francisco Chronicle*, Thursday, September 17, 1987, p. A6.

[28] "Dear member" letter signed by Frances Kissling, President of Catholics for a Free Choice, and Judith Senderowitz, Executive Director of the Center for Population Options, August 7, 1986.

[29] **Ibid.**

[30] NFPRHA Meeting. Remarks of Stephen Purser of the San Francisco Department of Public Health.

[31] Testimony of John W. Nields, Jr., Esq. before the Subcommittee on Family and Human Services of the U.S. Senate Committee on Labor and Human Resources' Hearing, "Parental Involvement with Their Adolescents in Crisis: The Federal Government's Response," February 24, 1984.

[32] Joy Dryfoos, "School-Based Health Clinics, A New Approach to Preventing Adolescent Pregnancy?" *Family Planning Perspectives*, 17:2 (March/April 1985), p. 74. Hereafter cited as "New Approach."

[33] **Ibid.**

[34] Support Center for School-Based Clinics 3rd National Conference: "SBCs on the Move," Denver, Colorado; October 5-7, 1986. Closing remarks by Sharon R. Lovick. Hereafter cited as Denver conference.

[35] Jean Seligmann, "A Challenge to School Clinics," *Newsweek*, August 10, 1987, p. 54.

[36] "New Approach," p. 73.

[37] **Ibid.**, p. 70.

[38] *Congressional Record*, Proceedings and Debates of the 99th Congress, Second Session, August 8, 1986, vol. 132, no. 108. Congressman George Miller, California; School-Based Adolescent Health Services Bill. Hereafter cited as *Congressional Record.*

[39] *Clinic News*, (Washington, D.C.: Support Center/Center for Population Options), vol. II, no. 3 (October 1986), p. 1.

[40] Proposed legislation: H.R. 5377, 99th Congress 2nd Session, "To amend the Public Health Services Act to establish school-based adolescent health service demonstration projects," Section 2110 (2) (E) and (3).

[41] *Congessional Record.*

[42] "Curbing Births, Not Pregnancies," *Wall Street Journal,* October 14, 1986.

[43] **Ibid.**

[44] Center for Population Options "Dear Colleague" letter signed by Katia Segre, Resource Center Coordinator. Received, October 1986.

[45] "New Approach," p. 70.

[46] Laurie S. Zabin, Marilyn B. Hirsch, Edward A. Smith, Rosalie Streett and Janet B. Hardy, "Evaluation of a Pregnancy Prevention Program for Urban Teenagers," *Family Planning Perspectives,* 18:3 (May/June 1986), p. 22. Hereafter cited as Zabin.

[47] **Ibid.**

[48] **Ibid.**, p. 124.

[49] **Ibid.**, p. 125.

[50] **Ibid.**

[51] *Population,* p. 1.

[52] Laurie S. Zabin, Marilyn B. Hirsch, Edward A. Smith, Rosalie Streett, Janet Hardy, "Adolescent Pregnancy-Prevention Program: A Model for Research and Evaluation," *Journal of Adolescent Health Care,* vol. 7, no. 2, March 1986, p. 86.

[53] Asta Kenney, "School-Based Clinics: A National Conference," *Family Planning Perspectives,* vol. 18, no. 1, January/February 1986, p. 45. Hereafter cited as Kenney.

[54] "Sex Education and Sex-Related Behaviors," *Family Planning Perspectives,* vol. 18, no. 4, July/August 1986, p. 150. (Editorial, unsigned.)

[55] Douglas Kirby, *School-Based Health Clinics: An Emerging Approach to Improving Adolescent Health and Addressing Teenage Pregnancy* (Washington, D.C.: Center for Population Options, 1985), p. 5. Hereafter cited as *Emerging Approach.*

[56] **Ibid.**

[57] Elizabeth Stark, "Young, Innocent and Pregnant," *Psychology Today* (Oct. 1986), p. 33.

[58] *Emerging Approach,* p. 8.

[59] "Psychosocial Evaluation." Questionnaire obtained from Du Sable High School and in use there according to a letter written by Louise Kaegi, February 21, 1986.

[60] *SBC: Update,* p. 9.

[61] **Ibid.**

[62] **Ibid.**

[63] *Issues and Action,* p. 6.

[64] "New Approach," p. 73.

[65] **Ibid.**

[66] Denver conference. Remarks during "Teens and Unintended Pregnancies" workshop.

[67] "New Approach," p. 73.

[68] Peggy Brick and Carolyn Cooperman, *Positive Images: A New Approach to Contraceptive Education* (New Jersey: Planned Parenthood of Bergen County, 1986), p. 41-50.

[69] **Ibid.**, p. 3.

[70] Carol Hunter-Geboy, Lynn Peterson, Sean Casey, Leslie Hardy and Sarah Renner, **Life Planning Education: A Youth Development Program** (Washington, D.C.: Center for Population Options, 1985), p. 173. Hereafter cited as **Life Planning.**

[71] **Ibid.**, p. 161.

[72] Center for Population Options "Dear Colleague" letter signed by Debra Haffner, Director of Information and Education, Received, 1986.

[73] Kenney, p. 44.

[74] "Information about the St. Paul School Health Clinics," from Healthstart, St. Paul, Minnesota, 1986, p. 11.

[75] James M. Morrissey, Adele D. Hofmann, Jeffrey C. Thorpe, **Consent and Confidentiality in the Health Care of Children and Adolescents: A Legal Guide** (New York, The Free Press, 1986), p. 63. Hereafter cited as **Consent and Confidentiality**.

[76] "9 New York High Schools Dispense Contraceptives to Their Students," *New York Times,* October 6, 1986, p. 1.

[77] "Contraceptive Policy Is at Center of Dispute," *New York Times,* Oct. 13, 1986, p. 14.

[78] "New Approach," p. 73.

79 NFPRHA Meeting. Remarks of Stephen Purser of the San Francisco Department of Public Health.

80 Telephone Interview, October 28, 1986.

81 "Sex a Health Issue at New York School Clinics," *New York Times,* October 15, 1986, p. 1. Hereafter cited as "Sex a Health Issue."

82 *Issues and Action,* p. 1.

83 "Abortion Rules for Under-18's Upset by Judge," *New York Times,* Nov. 8, 1986, p. 6.

84 *Emerging Approach,* p. 7.

85 "New Approach," p. 73.

86 "Sex a Health Issue."

87 *Emerging Approach,* p. 8.

88 *Hospital Purchasing News,* vol. 9, no. 11, November 1985, p. 35. (Advertisement)

89 "Correlates of Effective Contraception among Black Inner-City High School Students," Laurie Zabin, Edward Smith and Marilyn Hirsch from the Dept. of Gynecology/Obstetrics, The Johns Hopkins University School of Medicine, Baltimore, MD. Final Report, prepared under Grant from National Institute of Child Health and Human Development, p. 7.

90 **Physicians Desk Reference** (Orandell, New Jersey: Medical Economics Company, 1984), 38th Edition, p. 1432.

91 Package insert for Triphasil-21, Wyeth Laboratories, Philadelphia, PA, Issued 8/22/84

92 "Birth Control at School: Pass or Fail?" *Ebony* (October 1986), p. 42.

93 "New York Schools Assailed on Sex Plan," *New York Times,* October 9, 1986.

94 **Consent and Confidentiality**, p. 71.

95 **Ibid.**, Appendix: State-by-State Table, p. 149-250.

96 **Ibid.**, p. 225.

97 **Ibid.**, p. 229.

98 **Ibid.**, p. 198.

99 *The Human Right to Family Planning: Report of the Working Group on the Promotion of Family Planning as a Basic Human Right* (London: International Planned Parenthood Federation, November 1983), p. 17.

100 "AIDS Classes in Grade School Urged by Surgeon General," *San Francisco Chronicle,* October 22, 1986.

101 "Sex Education May Now Be a Matter of Life and Death, But How Do You Tell an 8 Year Old about AIDS," *People Magazine,* November 10, 1986, p. 73.

102 *KSPT TELEVISION 10 P.M. News,* St. Paul, Minnesota, Week of February 19, 1987.

103 Bevilacqua, p. 188.

104 Eric Justice, "Condoms: Playing 'Russian Roulette'?" *Medical Tribune,* 9/23/87, p. 1.

105 Bevilacqua, p. 188.

106 "Encourages Physicians to Accept Teenage Sexual Activity as Norm," *Ob-Gyn News,* August 1-14, 1986, p. 18.

107 L.H. Bukstel, G.D. Roder, P.R. Kilmann, J. Laughlin, and W. Sotile, "Projected Extramarital Sexual Involvement in Unmarried College Students," *Journal of Marriage and the Family,* 1978, 40, p. 337-340.

108 Hemlock Society Third National Voluntary Euthanasia Conference, Washington, D.C.; September 25-27, 1986; "Is Rational Suicide with Assistance Justified?", general session.

109 Massachusetts S. 487, "An Act Relative to a Patient's Right to Refuse Medical Treatment," failed to pass in 1986. Oregon's S.B. 812, Draft J as amended is currently pending.

110 "Chicago School Clinic Is Sued," *New York Times,* October 16, 1986.

111 Birth Control at Boston School Clinics Puts Catholics at Odds," *New York Times,* Oct. 13, 1986, p. 14; "Bernardin seeks Senate rejection of contraceptive funds," *National Catholic Register,* Sept. 7, 1986; "Preventing Teen-Age Pregnancies," *Origins,* Sept. 18, 1986, vol. 16, no. 14, p. 252-253; Bevilacqua, pp. 187-190.

112 *Implementing Programs,* p. 10.

113 Pope John Paul II, **Familiaris Consortio**, November 22, 1981, Article 44: The social and political role.

114 "Sex and Schools," *Time,* November 24, 1986, p. 57.

The State of the American Catholic Laity: Propositions and Proposals

by

Joseph A. Varacalli

This paper starts from the assumption that the Catholic Church in the United States is presently bordering on an out-and-out civil war between "orthodox" and "heterodox" factions. "Orthodox" Catholics are defined as those who affirm the legitimacy of both the Catholic conception of the Magisterium and of what Avery Dulles in his **Models of the Church** has termed the "institutional" model of the Catholic Church. Heterodox Catholics are defined as those Catholics who, in accepting a unilinear evolutionary understanding of the future of the Catholic Church that posits the ultimate supremacy of "individual" conscience," reject both the conceptions of the Magisterium and of the institutional model. It is important to point out two things about the definitions just offered. First of all, they are "religious" and not "political" definitions. Put another way, an "orthodox" or "heterodox" Catholic may be either politically liberal or conservative (although empirically there is a tendency, respectively, for orthodox religious and conservative political orientations and heterodox religious and liberal political orientations to be positively associated with each other). Secondly, each definition allows a considerably wide spectrum of alternatives to coexist within it. "Orthodoxy" includes not only traditional "propositional literalists" but "neo-orthodox" writers who accept modern social scientific and humanistic methods to obtain traditionally religious doctrinal conclusions. Conversely, "heterodoxy" includes those who range from having no use whatsoever for the concepts of the Magisterium/institutional Church to those who consider such allegiances to be "optional" or non-binding in the exercise of the Catholic faith.

Proposition Number One: The American people as a whole are a religious people. They range from being authentically religious to moderately religious with the latter ripe for further conversion.

Based on a scale of eight items (feeling that God loves you, engaging in prayer, attending religious services, reading the Bible, having a religious experience, participating in a church social activity, encouraging others to turn to religion, listening to religious broadcasts) a recent and sophisticated nationwide survey, **The Connecticut Mutual Life Report on American Values in the '80s: The Impact of Belief**, identifies 45 million or 26% of the 174 million Americans 14 years and older as either "highest" (10%) or "high" (16%) in their religious commitment. The **Report**

> ... identifies a cohesive and powerful group of Americans, approximately 45 million strong, as "intensely religious" ... the effect of this group is spreading across the nation ... The study also identifies a large pool of Americans of all ages who can be considered "latently" religious, and therefore susceptible to a call to faith. Approximately three of every four U.S. citizens describe themselves as religious and say that religion would become a more important factor in their lives if they knew they had only six months to live. Our findings suggest that the increasing impact of religion on our social and political institutions may be only the beginning of a trend that could change the face of America.   (p. 7)

It is important to stress that social science research indicates that the United States is considered to be much more religious in orientation than Western Europe. According to a 1976 international Gallup poll, 56% of adult Americans consider religion to be very important to them, compared with 27% of Western Europeans. (quoted in **Report**, p. 9) The writers of the **Report** offer the following assessment as to why American society has maintained its high degree of religious orientation:

> We live in a relentlessly egalitarian society that encourages self-interest and mobility of all types ... One reason so many people may cling to religion in the United States is that it provides some measure of order in their lives, some restraint on the cultural injunction to pursue happiness, or in some cases, hedonism, to its farther limits. One recent in-depth study, for example, suggests that Americans regard religion as a code of conduct, without which 'there would be no reason not to sin and their lives would fall apart.'   (p. 11)

The **Report**, furthermore, clearly demonstrates a significant difference in religious involvement and intensity between Protestants, Catholics and Jews. 33% of Protestants rank either "highest" or "high" in religious commitment with the figures for Catholics and Jews being 15% and 3% respectively. 23% of Protestants were labeled "moderate" in religious commitment with the figures for Catholics and Jews being 28% and 16% respectively. Finally, 34% of Protestants were scored either "low" or "lowest" in religious commitment with the figures for Catholics and Jews being 56% and 81% respectively. Assuming that the figures for Catholic Americans were much higher twenty-five years ago (not a terribly risky assumption), the important question is why is this the case today. Catholic heterodox tend to stress the inevitability of a lessened (or, as they would prefer to say, "transformed") religiousity given the socio-economic mobility of American Catholics over those years. Orthodox Catholics tend to argue that much of the loss in religious fervor was unnecessary but caused by the self-weakening of the Catholic institutional network. Catholics, the orthodox maintain, self-consciously "lowered their shields," allowing secular and liberal Protestant influences to make a significant impact on Catholic identity. The net effect of this, following the logic in Dean Kelley's **Why Con-**

servative Churches Are Growing, is that the Catholic Church in the United States has herself been fueling a movement toward her own self-destruction.

Proposition Two: The American value system is conducive to authentic religious expression; however, it is much more in line with Protestantism than with Catholicism.

Accepting the rough consensus of most sociologists, one can argue that the following list represents the major values of American culture: achievement and success, activity and work, humanitarianism, efficiency, practicality, progress, material comfort, equality, freedom, conformity, science and rationality, nationalism and patriotism, democracy, individualism, ethnocentrism, education, male supremacy, romantic love, monogamy, heterosexuality, religion-in-general.[1] A few caveats are in quick order. First of all, the list is only a rough consensus and there is room to quibble over this or that value (e.g. "male supremacy"). Secondly, it is clear that the present value system of the United States has changed somewhat from the days of colonial America. Today Americans are perhaps, following the thrust of **Habits of the Heart**, less work-oriented, more concerned with material comfort, less "community-centered," and more "self-centered." However, it is important to point out that most social scientists stress that it is *continuity not change* that best characterizes the American value system over time. This is clearly the argument in Ben J. Wattenberg's **The Good News Is The Bad News Is Wrong** and the important community study of Muncie, Indiana, **All Faithful People** conducted by a team of researchers headed by Theodore Caplow. Where there is change, it is mostly *socio-economic class specific*. That is, roughly speaking, it is mostly upper middle class young urban professionals ("Yuppies") or what certain sociologists have called the "new knowledge class" who have embraced values that differ significantly from early Protestant colonial America, or, in the Catholic case, from the "Catholic ghetto." Put another way, different subgroupings within American society can embrace or reject subconstellations of the American value system. Finally, a modern society like the United States contains more values than does a relatively simple, pre-modern, homogenous community. This translates into both greater choice for the individual and a greater chance of being caught in an identity crisis or value-conflict. "Choice," following the logic of Peter L. Berger's **The Heretical Imperative**, is "structured into" the modern American context with important implications for the individual who is both American and Catholic.

The foregoing analysis says nothing or little about the question of the compatibility of the American value system with religion. The argument here is that there is no intrinsic reason why the American values previously listed can't coexist peacefully with religion. It is taken-for-granted by a large majority of historians and sociologists of religion that most of the present array of American values actually find their origin in Protestant Christianity. "Individualism" may or may not be still tied into Protestantism; for most Americans it is, for the secular elites it is not. "Materialism," to use a second example, may be tied into a world-affirming "social Gospel" or it may simply degenerate into the "American Dream" of materialism pure and simple. "Nationalism" may be tied into an authentic (Judaic-Christian "common-denominator") American Civil Religion as discussed by Robert Bellah, or it may simply represent what Will Herberg thought to be a transcendentaless "American Way of Life." The social science evidence points to the reality that for most Americans — including a significant and increasing percentage of American Catholics — these values are still coupled and contained within a Protestant referent. Many liberal Catholic intellectuals like Andrew M. Greeley (**American Catholics Since the Council**) and Jay Dolan (**The American Catholic Experience**) do not so much as deny this as they redefine the Catholic heritage through an acceptance of a unilinear "evolutionary" model to fit their own apparently preferred model of liberal Protestantism.[2] It is only the new knowledge class of pure secular humanists that has shed the Protestant referent. However, the degree to which these originally and still Protestant values can be successfully contained within Roman Catholicism without corrupting the latter is a serious question. In other words, the question is whether American Catholics can be "Protestant" or "American" in their civil dealings in the outer society (something, by the way, I find desirable) and still be "Roman" or "Catholic" in their internal relationship to the Church and Magisterium.

Proposition Three: A secular humanist "new knowledge class" is attempting to eliminate religious values from the public sphere of American life.

It is the perception of many neo-conservative sociologists that a new social class is starting to dominate America's public institutions. Furthermore, this class is spreading and institutionalizing anti-religious, or, at best, non-religious values throughout American society. In part this new class's strategy is to eliminate any legitimate religious voice from public policy-making, or, more accurately, when that religious voice happens to disagree with any item on the new class's agenda.[3]

This new social class has been termed by numerous social scientists, including Peter Berger in his essay "Ethics and the Present Class Struggle" and Michael Novak in his **The Spirit of Democratic Capitalism**, as the "new knowledge class" — an elite class of workers in what can be termed the "knowledge industry," an industry that is comprised of those who derive their livelihoods from the creation and manipulation of symbols. The knowledge industry would include, most prominently, the science-based industries (electronics, computers, etc.), the information industry (the mass media), the public sector of government (public policy and research), and the educational industry (especially those involved in higher education). These types of occupations tend to both draw and develop individuals with value systems that are either anti-religious, areligious, weakly religious, or, at very best, religious in a distinctly "liberal" way. Such individuals tend to emphasize the rational, the this-worldly, the material, the modern. They tend, by virtue of their self-perception as the bearers of the most "modern" forms of knowledge, to look down upon *any* manifestation of tradition, especially traditional religion. In public life, given their belief in their own ability to "socially engineer" modern arrangements, the new knowledge class proposes solutions to "social problems" and modes to further enhance the materialism that is their penultimate concern. In doing so, the new class often consciously or unselfconsciously violates traditional religious tenets. It should be pointed out that this class has a definite vested interest in "socially engineering" modern society: the more social programs, the more jobs, power, money, and status will accrue to this class. In the private sphere of life, this class, in part because of their rejection of the "absolute moralities" associated with traditional religions, tend to, at best, tolerate, to, at worst, propagate "liberated" life-styles. The new knowledge class, liberal across the board, in short, is the most modern class in human history and represents the vanguard of a moral revolution that can be termed secular humanism.

The new class has attempted to disenfranchise believing and traditional Protestants, Catholics, and Jews through a specific and very "narrow" interpretation of the constitutionally-based "separation of Church and state." The "wall of separation," for the new class, sunders not only religious institutions and the institutions of the state but also religiously-based values and public policy. Any appeal to a traditionally religious based value used to buttress an argument for this or that public policy option (anti-abortion, pro-tuition tax credits, a moment's silence of prayer in school, etc.) is for the new class a "violation of the separation of Church and state." Of course, if the new class happens to be in agreement with a so-called religiously based position (e.g. the Catholic Bishops on nuclear weapons, the Catholic Bishops on the morality of the American economy, Jesse Jackson on civil rights, liberal Protestant feminists for the Equal Rights Amendment, liberal Jews for a "pro-privatization" of religion, etc.), the violation of the separation of Church and state is conveniently *not* invoked.

The new class, in invoking its particular understanding of the separation of Church and state, had developed its own "divisiveness doctrine" theory.[4] Under this doctrine, Catholics and other religious individuals can lobby for legislation only if they do not win! If, for instance, an orthodox Catholic organization is successful in helping to pass a piece of legislation, the law, it is argued by the new class, is unconstitutional under the Establishment Clause of the First Amendment. This doctrine is clearly an attempt to promote the idea that only non-believers — i.e., secular humanists — have a right to engage in public policy-making. Religious beliefs, for the new class, can be held only "privately." The position of those who are pro-religious, conversely, is that the separation of Church and State means only that no preference to any specific religious institution can be offered by the state; it does *not* mean that religious groups and individuals have no right to lobby for their positions within the democratic framework of the United States.

Proposition Four: Liberal Protestants, liberal Jews, and heterodox Catholics are in a pragmatic alliance with the secular humanist new knowledge class.

The rise of the new knowledge class has seen a rearranging of coalitions in American politics: on the one hand, the creation of a "practical" alliance of orthodox to neo-orthodox Catholics with conservative/traditional Jews and Protestants and, on the other, the coalescing of secular humanists and heterodox Catholics with liberal to radical Jews and Protestants.

Heterodox Catholics tend to identify with secular humanism not because of its anti-religious bias but despite it; matters of a this-worldly economic justice and the exercise of an "individual conscience" that is basically anti-institutional in nature are seen as paramount. Orthodox Catholics tend to sympathize with conservative Protestants and Jews not out of any ecumenical impulse or any desire to create a "common-denominator" religious expression but because a pragmatic alliance is required to guarantee the institutionalization in the United States of the formal or procedural rights necessary to allow the Catholic religion the ability to keep itself alive through successful socialization, identity-maintenance, and evangelization.

Proposition Five: The clear majority of Americans reject the new knowledge class and with it a liberal religiousity in general.

As Benjamin Wattenberg argues in his **The Good News Is The Bad News Is Wrong**, the American population as a whole can be characterized as centrist *politically* and is constantly eschewing the extremes of both the political left and right. According to Wattenberg's logic, the election of Ronald Reagan to the American Presidency in 1980 and 1984 can best be seen as a reaction against the ultra-left wing of the Democratic Party and, as such, a startling rejection of the worldview and policies of the anti-religious new knowledge class. It is important to point out the two-edged nature of Wattenberg's proposition regarding American political life: the American people are about as likely to reject an ultra-conservative political party as they are to reject an ultra-liberal one.

Wattenberg's proposition regarding the political realm is *not,* however, directly analogous to the religious realm. In the latter realm, a persuasive argument has been made by Dean M. Kelley as to why conservative churches are growing while liberal churches are fast losing membership. According to Kelley, those churches that (1) specialize in explaining the ultimate meaning of life and (2) are serious and strict in the application of their dogma, tradition and rules are becoming stronger and more vibrant in American life. It is important to note that Kelley's findings do not indicate that the average parishioner is uninterested in the social activism advocated by the more liberal religions but that these activities must be both derivative of and secondary to the promulgation of a religious worldview. Kelley's logic finds its Catholic analogue in the work of theologian Brian Benestad and educator

Edward A. Wynne who argue that the Church's most important task is, respectively, "evangelization" and "character-development." One can reconcile Wattenberg and Kelley by noting that in the public political realm of activity, Americans want and demand compromise and a display of civility; in the relatively more private religious realm of thought, Americans want and demand sureness and firmness. For this reason, gaining a legislative victory in the national debate over abortion (even among Catholic voters) is, in principle, much harder to achieve than creating the consensus among Catholic voters (and non-Catholic voters, too) that abortion is a sinful violation of God's gift of life. Applying the logic of Kelley, Benestad, and Wynne to the present situation of an ever-more "liberalizing" heterodox Catholic Church in the United States, one can say that the Church, again, is moving fast along the path of her own self-destruction.

Proposition Six: While some elements of a conservative to moderate Protestantism may be in a pragmatic alliance with elements of an orthodox Catholicism, the future of such an alliance is very precarious.

As Congressman Henry J. Hyde notes in "Keeping God in the Closet: Some Thoughts on the Exorcism of Religious Values from Public Life," some of the more moderate elements of conservative Protestantism (along with some orthodox Jews) have moved toward a pragmatic alliance with orthodox Catholicism. Perhaps the single greatest example of this movement is Jerry Falwell and his inter-religious movement, originally termed the "Moral Majority," now the "Freedom Foundation." Falwell early in his career preached a narrow Protestant Biblical fundamentalism with typical anti-Catholic overtones. Of recent years, however, he has advocated a more "civil" approach in the relationship of religious bodies opposed to the secular humanist new knowledge class and their liberal religious allies. The nature of this traditional/conservative Protestant, Catholic, and Jewish alliance is truly "pragmatic" in nature. It is one of "form" and not of "content." The focus is on protecting the "formal" rights of orthodox of all religions to promote their heritages and evangelize their faiths and *not* on the development of any common denominator religious expression. Simply stated, the unifying cement in this alliance is decidedly "negative" in character; the emphasis is on a common opposition to the "anti-religion" forces in the United States. Unlike the secular humanist class which advocates some alleged "universal brotherhood of mankind," orthodox religious, by their very nature, hold claim to "absolute" allegiances which, in a pluralistic context, can be seen to be "particularistic" and "balkanizing" in nature. For this reason, an eventual victory over the new knowledge class may usher in the reappearance — to some degree or another — of more "conventional" religious/political warfare in the United States, i.e., warfare between denominations and not along class lines. The beating back of the new knowledge class could lead to the "closing of the ranks" between a fundamentalist and evangelical Protestantism against Catholicism, assuming that the latter refuses to capitulate its principles along common Protestant themes.

In all fairness, it must be pointed out that present social science research does *not,* at this point at least, signal such a dire scenario. Perhaps the single most important piece of longitudinal research on religion in American life, **All Faithful People: Change and Continuity in Middletown's Religion**, indicates, using a host of empirical indicators, not only that religion in Muncie, Indiana is as vital today as it was at the turn of the century but that today one sees a far greater degree of religious tolerance between Protestants (at least the moderate ones) and Catholics. The empirical work of Theodore Caplow, et. al., on Middletown stands in line with the theoretical work of sociologist Edward A. Shils who in **Centre and Periphery** argues that modern life can sustain much traditional thought and activity while encouraging the spread of civility.

There are, then, two scenarios that the Church can prepare for in the *post* new knowledge class era. The Caplow-Shils scenario sees a large religious "center" consisting of moderate orthodox religions (including, most prominently, Roman Catholicism) in which the line of demarcation would be the dominant "sacramental" churches versus the more "peripheral" and narrowly fundamentalist "puritan" churches. In this most rosy of scenarios, the Catholic Church in the United States would be able to grasp, following the phrase of the Lutheran theologian Richard J. Neuhaus, the "Catholic moment" by providing the United States with an historic compromise, a model of the "via media," synthesizing the best of the traditional and modern worldviews.

The second more ominous scenario sees a Protestant closing of the ranks against Catholicism. In this case, the situation that would face the leadership of today's American Catholic Church would not be unlike that faced by American governmental leadership during World War II. For the latter, the victory of the forces of Fascism commenced the battle against Communism. However, the price of victory over the Fascists cost a great deal (that is, most of eastern Europe) with permanent ramifications for the subsequent battle against the Communists. The leadership of the Catholic Church should be prepared, then, for the possibility that it may have to immediately shift battlefronts. Therefore, it should try to consciously minimize any immediate concessions made to our present allies that might come back to haunt the Church at a later time. There is the possibility that, assuming that the new knowledge class will be defeated, the "real" war may not even have started yet! On the other hand, Catholic Church leadership should be aware of the conscious "fundamentalist baiting" taking place today and lead by such Catholic intellectuals as Father Richard McBrien of the University of Notre Dame. McBrien is obviously trying to take the heat off present day heterodox Catholics by stressing that the real enemy is Protestant fundamentalism and not Catholic modernism.

Proposition Seven: American Catholicism has seen a significant erosion of its vitality and distinctiveness since Vatican II. This erosion is not along lines of out-and-out rejection and an acceptance

of atheism or agnosticism but of an acceptance of many principles
of the Protestant faith.

The State of the American Catholic Church
According to Andrew Greeley

Andrew Greeley's "unauthorized report" **American Catholics Since
the Council** is a valuable work, both because it summarizes most of
Greeley's research findings on the values and demographic conditions
of American Catholics and because it exposes Greeley's own values
and normative understanding of the evolution of the Church. Empirically, Greeley documents a picture that includes a significant weakening in the authority of the institutional Church, especially in the area
of human sexuality, and the call, on the part of a significant percent of
middle-to-upper-middle class professional Catholics, for a more "pastoral," "therapeutic," and "soft" Church at the expense of a Church
that sees for itself the necessity to set high and stern religious and
moral standards.

Methodologically, Greeley's survey-based findings can be criticized on two fronts. First of all, his data about the values and behavior of
the American Catholic population are subject in specific instances to
alternative plausible interpretations. His "facts" in other words are
often "colored" by his "Americanist" worldview. For example, Greeley's
argument (to be analyzed subsequently) that the liberalization of the
American Catholic population would have happened with or without
the selective (mis)interpretation of Vatican II theology can be easily
opposed. Secondly, his data are inadequate as a bases for his conclusions. Greeley, for instance, cavalierly argues that "American Catholics
are not engaging in actions which they take to be sinful but are defying
the Church by sinning against the Church's commands." American
Catholics, he argues, "are saying that the institutional Church is wrong
about such matters" (pp. 89-90). While such serious dissent is no doubt
a reality, the question is the correctness of Greeley inferring this gen-
erality on the basis of a simple and superficial survey questionnaire
(e.g. belief about birth control, divorce, etc.). A "verstenhen" sociological approach tapping the motives and emotions of individuals could
have properly balanced Greeley's positivistic approach. Indeed, to a
significant degree, Greeley purposefully misuses social science as
a form of mystification in order to intimidate unsophisticated readers.
He arrogantly notes that "many readers ... will say that my empirical
data do not take into account all the energies and forces and factors
that are at work. Perhaps they do not. But unless one is to go beyond
the boundaries of empirical evidence and make projections by wetting
one's finger and holding it up into the wind or by investigating the en-
trails of slain chickens, one must do serious data collection and analysis
to confirm that the impressions which contradict the data that I have
gathered are correct (p. 175). The strong suggestion that I offer here is
to call Greeley's bluff: a dissertation by an orthodox Catholic sociologist on "Andrew Greeley's Mystification of Social Science" would prove
to be a fruitful exercise.

It is also essential to make explicit the implicit Protestant theology that informs Greeley's sociological work. For Greeley, it is clear that the Spirit is working within culture and therefore social science is a vital vehicle for uncovering God's message for mankind. He leaves unclear the exact relationship between the "information" provided by the laity with the inspiration afforded the Magisterium of the Church. What *is* obvious, however, is that Greeley sees great promise for Catholicism only if the hierarchy would, again in unspecified ways, catch up to the "people of God" defined, in large part, through Greeley's own, sometimes quite arbitrary, interpretation of survey research findings. I am being only half-facetious when I claim that Greeley sees himself, defacto, as Pope.

Greeley's "findings" in his **American Catholics Since the Council** can be summarized and criticized as follows:

(A) American Catholics have obtained a superior position vis-a-vis most other American groupings in terms of such demographic information as income, education, etc. This finding is accurate, acceptable, and "value-neutral." What is not, however, is Greeley's implicit assumption that the effects of these "gains" are all positive. One can clearly grant, following a logic unsimilar to that taken by St. Thomas, that a certain amount of material, status, and intellectual advance is good in that it allows, in principle, the Christian to be in a position to perform his/her own essential Christian duties. On the other hand, Greeley, like a typical "Americanist," woefully ignores the other side of this development: hedonism, selfishness, and a weakening of the perception of an other-worldly, transcendent reality as the necessary anchor of one's existence. Greeley, thus, speaks of the "anguish" that American Catholic laity went through during the sixties and seventies over the Church's position on sexual and marital relations (p. 215). He assumes honest, soul-searching, prayful, and legitimate dissent. It never occurs to him that some, if not much, of this "dissent" was taken because it was the easy way out; that it was as much the result of selfishness and convenience as anything else. Or, in other cases, that "dissent" simply reflects a profound ignorance of, and lack of acculturation into, the tenets of the Catholic faith.

(B) Greeley's analysis exposes an important shift in the image of God on the part of young American Catholics, an image that he sees as a permanent part of the Catholic landscape in the United States. This change is one from viewing "God as Lord and Master" to one emphasizing "God as Lover." Greeley not only feels that this image is basically an improvement but that it has allowed Catholics who otherwise would reject an institutional and hierarchical Catholicism to continue to go to Church and particpate in the official Catholic religion. Such individuals, Greeley fails to point out, may be "in" but not "of" the institutional church; they routinely "go over the head" of the Magisterium in fine modernist fashion. Finally, Greeley argues that this change in social-psychology is the fruit of a long, painful evolutionary process in which Catholics have struggled bravely and honestly between the authority of the Magisterium on the one hand, and the practical needs of living and of common sense on the other.

The criticisms I have of Greeley here revolve around the issues of (a) *why* the change? and (b) is the change *good* or *bad?* Regarding the first question, I suspect that Greeley is basically wrong. The social-psychological change is at the expense of any true understanding of the Catholic faith and is primarily the result of the internalization of a middle-class American culture that is becoming progressively softer and more self-centered. The change is *not* primarily the result of honest, wrenching debates within a legitimately informed Christian conscience but rather of the easy acceptance of a "therapeutic" mentality — a "Yuppie" mentality that similarly exposes a weakening in the ideals of self-sacrifice, altruism, spirituality, and in the willingness to defend traditional Catholic (and American) ideals against Communist tyranny.

Regarding the second question and despite his explicit disclaimer that he is "only" repeating the "facts," a fair reading of Greeley's volume makes it perfectly clear that he is happy with the change in the imagery of God. He, for instance, makes clear his position that "doctrinal propositions" are secondary to "experience" as foundational to Catholicism or religion-in-general. One can simply disagree with Greeley's normative evaluation on this point which sees Catholicism as primarily an "expressive-experiential" religion. One could argue, as most traditional Catholics do, that doctrine is central to Catholicism and that the institutional Church can and should be forgiving of human finitude and imperfection, but it must also set doctrinal standards upon which morality can be judged. The Church, simply put, can forgive the sinner but never the sin. Sociologically speaking, Greeley's celebration of a purely pastoral Catholicism, if ever fully institutionalized, would exacerbate the selective or "communal" Catholicism that he has frequently praised in many previous works. This raises the logical question as to whether or not Greeley has any true appreciation of the Catholic tradition and whether or not his normative ideal for U.S. Catholicism is that of a flaccid and degenerative liberal Protestantism. Aggrandizing American activist and individualist values, Greeley offers merely a basically this-worldly, middle-class, social Gospel.

(C) Greeley argues that the value changes which he documents would have happened regardless of Vatican II. This argument, again, exposes the hidden values in Greeley's theory. I certainly agree with the formulation that, all things being equal, the socializing influence of the outer society is greater than the socializing influence of a less inclusive unit, in this case, the Catholic Church of the United States. Nonetheless, Greeley tends to ignore, unselfconsciously or otherwise, the reality of what the American sociologist, Talcott Parsons, termed "ambivalent socialization," or simply the fact that in a pluralistic society, there are multiple sources of socialization. Individuals can and are influenced by primary groups that coexist *within* larger secondary groups. Peter Berger and Richard J. Neuhaus have argued for the strengthening of what they term "mediating structures" (family, ethnicity, neighborhood, parish, voluntary associations, etc.) not only to attempt to limit the absolute political power of the state but, likewise, to limit the "socializing" monopoly of America's central value system. Greeley, as such, tends to underplay the ability of a strong, vital, and voluntary Catholic Church in the United States serving as a "brake" to cultural developments in the outer society. One suspects that his "theory," emphasizing the greater socializing power of the outer society, conveniently "fits" his Americanist bias, which sees little threat in the development of an American Catholic Church that has incorporated fully — and with little qualification — such American and Protestant values as individualism, democracy, materialism, and relativism. Greeley, as a matter of fact, defiantly informs the reader that "well-educated Catholic professionals ... (are) ... here to stay and ... (are) not about to leave the Church. But neither (will they) participate in the Church on any other terms but (their) own" (p. 34). Put ever so bluntly, one can agree with Greeley that a significant percentage of middle-to-upper-middle class Catholics have become, in essence, "protestantized" in a liberal way without accepting Greeley's assumption that such a liberalization was either inevitable or positive from the viewpoint of Roman Catholicism.

The Religious Beliefs of Catholic Theologians and Catholic Laity

In a fascinating and important piece of social scientific research entitled "Are There Two Catholicisms," three faculty members of the University of Dayton empirically tested the controversial thesis of Thomas Sheehan's 1984 article "Revolution in the Church."[5] Sheehan argued that there is an enormous and irreconcilable gulf between the traditional Catholicism of the average Catholic-in-the-pews and the radical "liberal consensus" of Catholic theologians. This thesis, interestingly enough, was intuitively acknowledged as correct by both heterodox and orthodox leadership wings of the Church; in the former case, as an indication of the strength of a "progressive" Catholicism among the elite and, in the latter case, as an indication of the scholarly corruption of a now wayward intellectual avante garde.

The findings of Johnson, Barnes, and Dolye indicate significant differences between theologians and parishioners but belie the notion that any irreconcilable chasm exists between the two groupings. Their research compared the survey responses of the membership of the College Theology Society with that of the adult members of Corpus Christi Church (an urban church located in Dayton, Ohio) to ten religious issues. The issues to which responses were solicited were on "Afterlife," "Church Authority," "God," "Exclusivity," "Eucharist," "Divinity of Christ," "Resurrection," "Founding of the Church," "Jesus' Self-Identity," and "Miracles." The authors' findings demonstrated that while Catholic theologians and Catholic parishioners *do* differ significantly on issues of religious belief (with the exception of the issue of the Eucharist), they do *not* indicate the reality of two clearly polarized groupings. Differences were seen to be more a matter of method and degree than they were of substance and quality.

The findings indicate, more specifically, that theologians, showing a considerable amount of diversity, most often tend to offer "nuanced" interpretations of traditional religious belief with "traditional" and "highly liberal" responses usually coming in, respectively, second and third place. Showing somewhat less diversity, parishioners tend, on the other hand, to most often opt for traditional understandings of religious reality. However, a considerable percentage registered a nuanced response, and a small but not insignificant percentage took the highly liberal perspective. In sum, theologians and parishioners do differ on religious beliefs but there is, again, much overlapping of perspectives with neither group taking the highly liberal response as modal. The findings seem to support the understanding, cognitively although not necessarily normatively, of "moderate centrists" like Raymond Brown, Avery Dulles, Francis A. Sullivan, and Lawrence Cunningham. Whether the "nuanced" approach of the theologians and some laity represents a "half-way" house to the eventual complete capitulation of the faith to the secular age or a legitimate adaptation of the faith to the present social context remains to be seen and requires longitudinal analysis. What is clear, however, is that there has been some movement toward "symbolic" and away from "literalist" interpretations of religious reality. The key, again, is whether what Avery Dulles terms the approach of "symbolic *realism*" will eventually degenerate into a pure and simple cultural symbolism, typical of extreme liberal Protestantism.[6]

The Notre Dame Study of Catholic Parish Life — 1981-1988[7]

The Notre Dame study is a major interdisciplinary effort aimed "to understand better the American parish of the 1980's as a dynamic community" (Leege and Gremillion, Report #1, December 1984, p. 2). Despite the fact that much material on Catholic parish life is contained within the study, for purposes of this specific report, *I am concerned only with the values of the so-called "average" parishioners.* The latter material is found primarily in Report Number Seven, "The People, Their Pastors and The Church: Viewpoints on Church Policies and Positions," which sampled 2,667 parishioners from thirty-six selected parishes (March, 1986). A couple of important qualifications, stated in the study itself, are (1) that the findings exclude the U.S. Hispanic Catholic population and (2) that the findings are allegedly more accurate for "core" Catholics, i.e., those people known to be "registered" Catholics within each sample parish than for "inactive" Catholics, i.e., those people who, for whatever reason, seldom connect with parishes. In other words, the Notre Dame findings claim *not* to represent the large percentage of nominal Catholics that would be and are represented in large national surveys in which self-identification is the sole criterion for religious categorization.

The study taps the feelings of Catholic parishioners on a battery of thirteen questions that deal with Church positions and directions. Instead of presenting the findings as percentages of individuals who either support or oppose a particular statement, an index of support was used. This index runs from 1.00 to 4.00, with the lowest figure indicating strongest disagreement and the highest figure indicating strongest support. Thus a score of 2.50 represents the break-even point; a lower score indicates opposition with a higher score indicating agreement. In addition, the researchers tabulated a standard deviation for each question. The standard deviation measures the extent to which there is either diversity or consensus in viewpoints; the lower the standard deviation, the more people share the same viewpoint, the higher the standard deviation, the more they have different viewpoints. The following table is taken from Report Number Seven, page four. Responses by parish leaders, i.e., "volunteers," "professional staff," and "pastors" have been omitted; again the concentration is solely on the "average" parishioner.

TABLE 1
ATTITUDES ON POLICY AND POSITION ISSUES,
BY LEVEL OF INVOLVEMENT IN 36 PARISHES

| | Parishioners | | |
A. Policy Directions	Rank	Mean	Standard Deviation
(a) The Church should become more people-oriented, less concerned about its organizational structure and rules	6	2.97	.81
(b) The Church should stress a personal, spiritual relationship to Christ	1	3.42	.58
(c) The Church should listen more to the voice of ordinary lay Catholics	5	3.03	.77
(d) The Church should put more emphasis on spreading the faith	4	3.07	.62
(e) The Church should make more effort to understand family life	3	3.34	.57
(f) The Church should put less emphasis on lay participation in the Mass or liturgy (reverse)	7	2.08 (2.92)	.85
(g) The Church should follow through more on changes and guidelines that resulted from Vatican II	9	2.81	.66
B. Church Positions			
(h) The Church should remain strong in its opposition to the use of contraceptives	12	2.23	.98
(i) The Church should remain strong in its opposition to abortion	2	3.35	.85
(j) The Church should liberalize its position on divorce	10	2.72	.86
(k) The Church should allow women to become priests	13	2.13	1.03
(l) The Church should allow married men to become priests	11	2.65	1.02
(m) The Church should encourage communion between Catholics and non-Catholic Christians	8	2.82	.89

(The possible range of scores is 1.00 to 4.00 with the highest score indicating strongest agreement. Any score of 2.50 or higher indicates agreement.)

A cursory examination of the finding regarding "Church positions" indicates that opposition to abortion and to women priests remains strong although the large standard deviation in the latter case indicates a small but significant grouping of dissent. A majority oppose the Church's teaching on contraception with, again, a small but significant grouping of consent to the Church's position. The Church's positions on divorce and a married priesthood is opposed by slight majorities, the latter issue receiving more support for the hierarchy than the former.

That most feel that the Church's efforts in evangelization should be strengthened is a very positive indicator. The rest of the parishioner's responses seem innocuous enough, with the exceptions of the responses which indicate significant, although not overwhelming, support for a "softer," less legalistic, more emotional, more ecumenical, and more pastoral Church. From the viewpoint of those who feel that a strong hierarchical, institutional Church is necessary both to protect the faith and to set high standards for individual religious and moral conduct, the findings are not good but neither should they be construed as disastrous. A base that can be strengthened is still in existence.

Of perhaps special note is the question asked regarding abortion.[8] 1% of the parishioners indicated that "abortion is always acceptable," 5% indicated that "abortion is acceptable under most circumstances," 69% stated that "abortion is acceptable under extreme circumstances, like a threat to the mother's life, rape or incest," with 26% stating that "abortion is never acceptable" (Leege and Gremillion, Report #7, March, 1986, p. 7). For Leege and Gremillion, the position of Catholic parishioners is that "abortion is not a matter of free choice or a method of birth control, but abortion is a medical option circumscribed to extreme situations" (Report #7, March, 1986, p. 8).

Two quick methodological caveats should be noted immediately. The first is to remind the reader that Hispanic Americans were excluded from the study. The question is "why is this the case?" Could it be that the expected traditionalist and conservative responses of the Hispanic population might upset "the heterodox picture" with its idealization of the middle-class, professional, "communal" Catholic? The second is to argue that the definition of "core Catholic" used in this study, i.e., "registered" Catholics in any parish, is so loose as to dilute its meaning. The effect of this, contrary to the stated intent of the research, is to blur any meaningful distinction between a "core" and "nominal" Catholic and to make it falsely appear that many positions (presumably those that stress "dissent") are held by Catholics in "good standing." A much better definition of a "core" Catholic would be based on obligatory weekly Mass attendance. To define a Catholic as one who faithfully participates in an "official" Catholicism, it would seem, upsets those who argue for an unchecked Catholic "pluralism."

I have no way of knowing whether these methodological decisions were made in a self-conscious way to distort the findings. What I *do* know is that most of the social scientists involved in the study are affiliated in some way with what may be called the "mid-West" liberal Catholic school of populist, social activists. Those that do not fit such a categorization are liberal Protestants. Indeed, the projects co-director, David C. Leege, like the distinguished Catholic University sociologist, Dean Hoge (who served as a consultant), are liberal Protestants. That no orthodox Catholic social scientists were asked to participate with the Notre Dame Study is hardly a surprise and breeds suspicion, at least, that the study's goals may be as much ideological as social-scientific in nature.

Trends in Catholic Lay Attitudes Since Vatican II On Catholic Life and Leadership

This study by Dean R. Hoge is the fifth and last of a series entitled "Study of Future Church Leadership."[9] It traces out change regarding answers to fifteen identical questions included in nation-wide surveys of lay Catholics in 1963, 1974, and 1985. The fifteen questions are grouped into three sets of five each: 1) *theological attitudes,* 2) *priests today,* and 3) *future vocations.* The responses to these fifteen questions are both given in the aggregate and are broken down by many "background" variables (sex, education, age, ethnicity, etc.). Hoge's findings, in the aggregate, on *theological attitudes* are as follows:

—— less Catholics in 1985 felt it is a sin to miss weekly Mass obligation than they did in 1974 (58% down from 69%) ——

—— *slightly* more Catholics in 1985 (62%) support Papal infallibility than they did in 1974 (60%) ——

—— the large drop between 1963-1974 in the percentage of those who feel that God will punish the evil for eternity basically held between the years 1974-1985 (73%—52%—53%) ——

—— the acceptance of the doctrine of apostolic succession which lost 15 percentage points between 1963-1974, lost an additional 3 percentage points between 1974-1985 (86%—71%—68%) ——

—— openness to change in the liturgy increased slightly between 1963 and 1974 but essentially returned back to 1963 form by 1985 (72%—79%—73%).

Hoge's findings, in aggregate, on the *priesthood* are as follows:

—— ratings of priests in terms of their ability to understand people's practical problems dropped markedly from 1952 to 1974, then improved slightly by 1985 (72%—42%—50%) ——

—— ratings of priests sermons dropped markedly from 1952 to 1974 but improved slightly by 1985 (43%—20%—29%) ——

—— approval ratings for priests went up between 1974 (81%) and 1985 (88%) ——

—— there was no movement between 1974 and 1985 in the question as to whether priests should use the pulpit to discuss social problems. (There was a 50%—50% split in both years) ——

—— there was a continual drop between 1963 and 1985 on the lay perception that most priests don't expect the laity to be leaders but only followers (46%—44%—39%) ——

Hoge's findings, in the aggregate, on *future vocations* are as follows:

—— there was a marked decrease in the acceptance of the idea of having a son become a priest between 1963 and 1974 with a slight rebounding by 1985 (67%—50%—55%) ——

—— the idea, similarly, that becoming a priest is not a good vocation showed no change between 1974 and 1985 (16%—16%) ——

—— between 1963 and 1985 there was a slight and consistent increase in the unhappiness of daughters entering religious communities (17%—25%) ——

—— there was a decrease from 1974 (57%) to 1985 (51%) in the percentage of laity favoring a married priesthood ——

—— there was a significant increase from 1974 (29%) to 1985 (47%) in the percentage of the laity favoring the ordination of women.

The findings from the perspective of those who defend a "hierarchial" Catholicism demonstrate significant slippage since Vatican II with some of the trends being halted or slightly reversed by 1985. The key question is *why* the decline?

Catholic College Students' Religious and Moral Attitudes 1961 to 1982: Effects of the Sixties and Seventies[10]

This study was jointly authored by two distinguished sociologists of religion, David O. Moberg, a Protestant evangelical, and Dean R. Hoge, a liberal Protestant from Catholic University. Two versions of the study were analyzed, the first a conference paper presentation, the second a slightly revised edition published in the *Review of Religious Research.* The purpose of the analysis was to study changes in the opinion of Catholic youth on religious and moral questions between 1961 and 1983. Three nearly identical surveys of Marquette University undergraduates were done in 1961, 1971, and 1982-83.

Given its clarity and usefulness, I will quote at length the findings of the original conference paper:

> In the period from 1961 to 1971, the trends can be interpreted as having three elements: first, the students became much more individualistic regarding religion and morals. They claimed more autonomy for making moral judgements and asserted that Catholics should be as free in intellectual matters as anyone else. This is seen in the decreased concern with "avoiding sin" when they assess moral behavior, in the tendency to think of God less as a judge, and in the increased tolerance of individual judgment in such moral areas as religious devotions, dating non-Catholics, drunkenness, and sexual behavior. Second, their religious doubts increased, and the level of concern about having these doubts increased. Third, Mass attendance rates plummeted to an amazing degree. This suggests the possibility that earlier many students had been regular Mass attenders out of a concern about obligation, sin, or morality. The size of several of the shifts from 1961 to 1971 was immense, unlike anything else found in college student trend research.
>
> The shifts from 1971 to 1982 were different. They can be interpreted as having four elements. First, the amount of thought about religious topics decreased, and concern about religious doubts abated. Second, the earlier demands for autonomy in intellectual matters cooled off, so attitudes in 1982 were less insistent on individualism. Moral judgments on several behaviors reverted toward more traditional values. Third,

whereas Mass attendance did not increase, regular reception of Communion and participation in Catholic organizations did increase, coming to resemble earlier levels. Fourth, there was no reversal of the earlier trend away from traditional views of sexuality — the sexual revolution seemed to be continuing.

Very importantly, Moberg and Hoge continue:

> The great magnitude of the changes from 1961 to 1971 are unique to Catholic students, since they have not been found in any research on non-Catholics. And, indeed, the greatest changes were on topics quite particular to Catholicism itself. The changes from 1971 to 1982, by contrast, are not unique to Catholic students, since other research on non-Catholics has found similar conservative trends; the changes from 1971 to 1982 should be seen as a product of shifts in the overall college climate of America. The peculiarly Catholic element in our data is mainly the enormity of the liberalization and individualization from 1961 to 1971. *Certainly the impact of Vatican II and its aftermath is behind it.* Probably that impact was felt more by young Catholics than older Catholic adults. (p. 26)

The importance of this version of the Moberg-Hoge study, in this reviewer's opinion, *is that it stresses that it was changes "internal" to Catholicism that are more important in accounting for the "post-Vatican II" weakening of the Catholic Church in the United States than were "external" cultural and social forces.* The finding stands in sharp contrast to the argument of people like Andrew Greeley and, on other occasions, Dean Hoge himself. The *published* version of the paper, however, offers a different interpretation of the very same data. As the published version states:

> Many argue that the changes in the 1960's would have occurred even apart from any council, since earthquake-like pressures had been building up for some time in American Catholicism as a result of increasing wealth, education, and both religious and ethnic assimilation. *This argument is convincing to us* (p. 115).

This discrepancy between the two versions offers yet another example of how much latitude exists in the interpretation of the same data. The discrepancy between the two versions may also reflect the biases (consciously or unconsciously held) of the two authors. The first interpretation is much more consistent with the worldview of the evangelical Protestant, David Moberg, with the latter published version much more consistent with the worldview of the Protestant "Americanist," Dean Hoge.

The Baby-Boomers and Religion

The final piece of research to be reviewed is by sociologist John C. Gessner of the College of St. Thomas entitled "Shifting Sands: Some Observations on Religious Responses to the Changing Needs and Lifestyles of the 'Baby Boom' Generation."[11] The paper explores the past and present linkages between the "baby boom" generation and religious organization and behavior with some illustrations on American Catholicism offered. He persuasively argues that any analysis of the relationship between the "baby boom" generation (those born between the years 1947 and 1964) and religion must take into account the following three distinct but interrelated processes:

(1) the "aging effect," i.e., that any cohort passes through the same phases of the life cycle with their respective needs, problems, and interests, both biological and social in nature;

(2) the "cohort effect," i.e., that cohorts experience the same general socialization experiences, thus sharing aspirations, orientations, and styles and develop a group consciousness;

(3) the "period effect," i.e., the same broader historical events envelop a cohort thus providing many of its capacities and frustrations.

Gessner is very wary, appropriately, about making predictions about the relationship over the next forty years of an aging baby-boom generation with organized religion. His first of three possible future scenarios would, however, please religious traditionalists:

> One scenario predicts that the churches should be prepared for an on-slaught of introspectives — probably yearning for the old doctrines, practices, and rituals. This could yield a need for larger facilities again; a source of "new" vocations (middle-aged seminarians and novices); new programs...; the sponsoring of clubs and organizations for adults ...; and ideological retrenchment back to earlier theology (e.g. 1950s style). At an inter-organizational level, there will be proclamations of another 'Great Awakening' or religious revival — with the mainline religions participating again (unlike the alleged resurgency of the 1970s which occurred more on the margins). This scenario would predict those Boomers staying with their re-found religiousity unti death, with their respective denomination "greying" with them. (p. 17)

It is important point out that Gessner's other possible scenarios are not conducive to traditional religious belief and practice (a possible return to the "occult" or to another heady embrace with "secular science" or the creation of a "new" interdenominational religious dimension combining the major faiths of the Biblical orbit) and that his analysis doesn't specifically focus on the Roman Catholic tradition. Putting my own neck out, I will make some observations about the *probable* implications for U.S. Catholicism of an aging Baby Boomer generation using Gessner's framework:

(1) The "aging effect" will most probably work in favor of a traditional Catholicism — as people become older, get married, have children, assume responsibility, their respect for the participation of an "official" Catholicism should markedly increase.

(2) The "cohort effect" will continue to work against an official Catholicism — the baby-boomers were formed during a period of chaos both internally in terms of the Church and externally in terms of society. The Church must not cater to this trend; it should hold, and, indeed, strengthen "the line." The Church will be around long after this generation, with its malcontents, isn't.

(3) The "period effect" will gradually work to the advantage of an "official" Catholicism assuming that the Church immediately starts to "tighten up her ship" and that the present day conservative and stabilizing cultural developments continue unabated.

Proposition Eight: The erosion of American Catholicism was not inevitable in the sense that a full assimilation into the value system of Protestant America was inevitable but it occurred because of the willingness and desire of Catholic America to destroy or at least severely weaken the network of institutions that had protected and maintained its religious and cultural identity.

Sociologists like Andrew Greeley, Dean Hoge and the "early" Peter L. Berger would clearly argue against the above proposition. They, and many other scholars, claim that (1) the outer value system, what the classical European sociologist Emile Durkheim called the "collective conscience," of the United States is opposed to many Catholic beliefs; (2) that the outer value system of the U.S. is too strong and pervasive in its influence to be resisted by the populace short of rearranging Catholicism into a narrow sect-like posture; and (3) that the recent embourgeoisement and middle-classification of the American Catholic population guarantees the inapplicability of such an extreme sect-like stance to the world and, conversely, guarantees a high degree of assimilation into the central value system of the U.S.

Social thinkers like Michael Novak, Richard J. Neuhaus, and the "later" Peter L. Berger would contend, on the contrary, that the degree of influence of the outer society on any sub-group in American society is an empirical question. It is a question that would be answered according to the degree that American society's "mediating structures" or "intermediate institutions" are firmly established. A mediating structure or intermediate institution is a structure or institution that stands between the individual and the state or the "collective conscience" of a nation. Examples of these are the family, neighborhood, religious and ethnic organizations, voluntary associations, or other such "primary group" attachments. To the degree that these structures and institutions are effective, they both politically limit the power of the state and provide meaning and a worldview to those individuals who participate in them, thereby limiting the socializing ability of the outer value system.

If one accepts the sociological theory of those like Greeley and Hoge, Catholicism in the United States can only survive in one of two unsatisfactory ways: (1) by surrendering its integrity and mirroring itself along the beliefs and principles of Protestant America or (2) by reducing itself in size and influence to a small fraction of its present community and assuming a tiny sect-like posture. If one accepts the sociological theory in the work of Novak, Berger, and Neuhaus (as I do), the situation for a significant, vital, large-scale Catholic subcultural reality that neither capitulates to the present age or reduces itself in scope and influence is a realistic possibility.

Between the years 1917 and the opening up of the Vatican II era in the U.S., the American Catholic Church had such a vital and distinctive subcultural reality that it was, in effect, a viable and impressive "mediating structure." One can say this without endorsing every characteristic of this period in American Catholic history. This period was characterized by an interlocking and compatible array of impressive religious institutions that focused on educational, charitable, social, political, etc. matters. In the post-Vatican II era the Catholic Church in the U.S. as a "mediating structure" or "intermediate institution" has clearly been weakened if not destroyed. Why did the Catholic intellectual and political leadership allow this to happen? Sharing an affinity with the sociological theories of Greeley and Hoge, among others, the increasingly dominant liberal or "Americanizer" wing of the Church argue that the destruction of what it invidiously referred to as the Catholic "ghetto" was both necessary and inevitable. It was inevitable given the claim that such a de-institutionalization would have happened with or without the occurrence of Vatican II theology. Vatican II is viewed by the Americanists as the Church's belated response to the themes of modernity. That Vatican II occurred when it did only speeded up an inevitable Americanization/modernization process. Simultaneously speaking out of both sides of their mouths, liberals also argue that the destruction of the "ghetto" was called for by at least the 'spirit" of Vatican II; the ghetto allegedly creating a Catholic mentality at odds with the necessary modern worldview.

Orthodox Catholics see it otherwise and share an affinity with those theorists who stress the importance of primary group attachments and relationships. On the one hand, many "neo-orthodox" Catholics feel no need to aggrandize a pre-Vatican II Catholic America with its provincialness. However, while such thinkers feel that the Catholic "ghetto" should have been "modernized" in light of a *literal* understanding of Vatican II, they believe it should not have been destroyed. Such neo-orthodox feel that whatever authoritarianism there was to the "Catholic right" has now been transferred to an authoritarianism of the "Catholic left." Furthermore, they continue, the establishment of the Catholic left in the United States is tantamount to the capitulation of Catholic values to those secular and liberal Protestant in orientation. Catholic orthodox feel, then, that the destruction of the "ghetto" was neither sociologically inevitable or theologically called for by Vatican II. Indeed, a "correct" understanding of Vatican II requires a cohesive and distinctive subcultural entity in order to fulfill the Catholic task of "Christianizing the temporal sphere."

Proposition Nine: The present and deep crisis that the Catholic Church in the United States faces has attempted to be "covered up" by the conscious activities and strategies of Catholic heterodox. These include a highly selective interpretation of Vatican II and post-Vatican II theology and a view of religious and cultural pluralism that refuses to grant any ultimate or final status to the Magisterium and to the "institutional model" of the Church.

The question has often been raised as to why heterodox Catholics simply don't leave the Church instead of maintaining their stubborn conviction to radically transform both the God-given and historic nature of Catholicism. Perhaps it is the desire to take control over the power, majesty, and legitimacy of a tradition that has "spanned the ages." Or perhaps it results from the knowledge that the most effective way of destroying the last great bastion of Christianity and of tradition is from the "inside out." Whatever the motivation, it is clear that the conscious strategy of the Catholic heterodox is to *deny* that recent developments both inside and outside of the Church represent, in any real sense, a crisis. Rather such developments are variously promoted as "natural," "inevitable," "favorable," "necessary," and "prophetic."

Two heterodox strategies regarding internal Church developments deserve special mention. Both are aimed at redefining the essence of Catholicism. The first is a highly selective and distorted "liberal" interpretation of Vatican II theology. In line with such a selective interpretation, the Church "as the people of God" invalidates the rule of the Magisterium; "collegiality" makes religious authority obsolete; "conscience" replaces tradition; "ecumenicity" and "relativity" substitute for the truthfulness and absoluteness of Catholicism; "this-worldliness" overtakes in importance a sense of transcendent salvation; materialism overtakes spirituality; and culture is seemingly equated with religion. As Cardinal Ratzinger argues in his **Report**, "progressive" Catholics have constructed their own imaginary Vatican *III* in order to legitimate their own public thought and activity. This first strategy has as its goal the redefinition of Catholicism *in its totality.*

A second strategy is superficially less ambitious but perhaps more effective in furthering the goals of the heterodox. The strategy here is not to deny the reality of the Magisterium and of the institutional Church but to weaken it by *relativizing* it. According to the heterodox, there are numerous authentic models of Catholicism and numerous authentic individual interpretations or ways of being Catholic. Regarding the former, while all the five "models of the Church" as discussed by Avery Dulles are useful and needed for a full-bodied and rich Catholicism, the orthodox argument — one that I accept — is that the "institutional model" must be placed at the "command post" of a cybernetic hierarchy and must be granted a "controlling" or ultimate status over the others. Catholic heterodox, to the contrary, are all united in their opposition to the institutional model. This opposition ranges from a total rejection of the institutional model to its subordination to other models. Regarding the latter, Andrew Greeley, in such works as **The Communal Catholics** and **The American Catholic**, has for decades been aggrandizing the selective, highly individualistic approach to Catholicism he terms "communal Catholicism." Examples of Greeley's communal Catholics include those who define their Catholicism *primarily* in terms of, among other things, *political activities* (e.g. liberal social activists, neo-conservative defenders of democratic capitalism); *cultural or socio-economic attachments* (e.g. a middle-class suburban, neighborhood/ethnicity-centered, "lower-class disinherited"); *emotion or experience* (e.g. cursillo, charismatics); and *philosophy or worldview* (e.g. Marxism, Feudalism, Nationalism). On the one hand, it is true that the Catholic faith is necessarily mediated through social forms that correlate with an individual's biographical experience and social location on the map of society; on the other hand, those social forms must be subordinated to the official interpretation of the Magisterium if they are to be considered authentic expressions of the Catholic faith. The typology offered by the "early" Joseph Fichter, for instance, in his **Southern Parish** effectively gauges the degree of Catholic authenticity expressed by individuals. In his parish study, Fichter was able to classify Catholics as either "nuclear," "modal," "marginal," or "dormant" depending on their participation in the prescribed sacraments, rituals, and organizational life of the institutional Church. Since this classification sees the Church in images of successive concentric circles extending from an ecclesiastical center, it is a more useful way to chronicle the official Catholicity of an individual than Greeley's "multi-dimensional" approach which denies the need for any unifying Catholic center.

Twelve Proposals Aimed At Strengthening
The Catholic Church in the United States

In light of our previous discussion, I will now suggest the following proposals aimed at strengthening and then maintaining a vibrant and authentic Catholic presence in the United States:

(1)   The Church must simultaneously attack both the centripetal and centrifugal forces responsible for her weakened condition in the United States, i.e., the outer culture and society and the dissent operating within the existing institutional network of the Church.

(2)   The Church must be prepared to suffer an initial and significant loss in membership as a result of such a strategy. Forced to choose between central values associated with America and Catholicism or liberalism and tradition, many Catholics will leave the Church. The argument here is that, in the longer run, a distinctive Catholicism will attract many conversions (and not necessarily just lapsed or former Catholics). The sociological evidence on this is clear: "conservative" or "traditional" churches (e.g. evangelical Protestantism, Mormonism, orthodox Judaism) are growing, while "liberal" or "modern" churches are shrinking.

(3)   The "major" thrust of the Catholic assault must be launched *internally* for no other reason that it is intra-Church affairs that can be manipulated or reconstructed more easily. Conversely, it is much harder to try to convert or make significant in-roads with the outer American culture and society because of the combination of secular humanistic influence in the elite structures of American society and the Protestant values that permeate the society-at-large. Action geared toward the public sector can most properly be seen as a "holding action" while the Church gets her ship in fighting order.

(4)   Regarding the strategy toward the outer culture and society, there must be a-the strengthening of organizations like The Catholic League for Religious and Civil Rights which protect and represent the legal and formal rights of Catholics in the United States. Simultaneously, there should be the creation of a "Catholic Action" movement in the United States, composed of clergy and laity loyal to the Pope and the Magisterium whose primary task would be the promotion of Catholic interests in the elite economic, cultural, political, social, and intellectual temporal spheres of society.

(5)   Regarding the strategy toward internal reform, the single most

important goal is to have the U.S. Catholic Church reverse her present priorities from those of "social and economic justice" to those of "evangelization" and "character development." The Church must concern herself with the formation of authentic Catholic identities which will in a derivative fashion translate into the appropriate thought and behavior regarding the "social question."

(6)   In order to successfully negotiate the suggested reversal in priorities, the Church must judiciously exercise proper "social control" techniques. Social control can be either formal and involuntary or informal and voluntary. The most successful is clearly the latter, i.e., the informal, voluntary, active, and willing internalization of Catholic values and principles. Less successful but necessary is the use of formal and involuntary sanctions.

(7)   Regarding informal and voluntary social control, primary emphasis must be placed on the successful socialization of the young. The U.S. Catholic Church must immediately reverse her present de-emphasis on Catholic grammar and high schools. Given the probably hopeless situation at many "Catholic" colleges, new elite Catholic liberal arts colleges must be created *de novo.* The Pope may want to create a new Catholic University of the first rank as a "flag ship" of orthodoxy in the United States to compete with the Catholic University of America and the University of Notre Dame.

(8)   At the same time that one can expect a strategy that places primary emphasis on the socialization of the young to reap rewards twenty years from now, the Church must reluctantly use a more overt and formal expression of social control over active and conspicuous dissenters (e.g. firings, demotions, transfers, silencings, reductions, dismantlings, etc.). The exercise of this form of social control must be very judicious and selective with only "leading" figures and symbols being singled out as disciplinary examples. It is important to remember that the goal is to recapture the "lapsed but redeemable middle." Specifically, the following action must be taken:

(a) the activity of the U.S.C.C. must be monitored and reduced in scope.
(b) heterodox Catholic college presidents must be forced to resign.
(c) *dangerously* dissenting Catholic politicians of national scope must be singled out for condemnation.
(d) heterodox Catholic theologians must be silenced or at least clearly labeled as "non-Catholic."
(e) there must be greater, but very selective, use of public excommunications for those who consistently, overwhelmingly, and ostentatiously violate the sacred tenets of the Faith.
(f) there must be a greater use made of public condemnations of certain stances on specific issues (e.g. abortion, euthanasia) that oppose Catholic teaching.

(9)   Regarding the issue of internal reform, there must be a successful articulation of a "theology of legitimate pluralism." Simply put, what are the acceptable parameters in the interpretation of the Catholic faith? Legitimate and illegitimate forms of pluralism must be distinguished with a simultaneous acknowledgment that the Catholic faith is inevitably

mediated through cultural and linguistic forms but that the major criterion of a legitimate Catholic expression is the objective evaluation of the "balance" between a Universal Faith and an always changing culture. Secondarily, the implications of this "tightened" understanding of pluralism for ecumenical relations must be spelled out.

(10) There must be greater clarification of the respective roles of the clergy and laity. When Catholic parishioners go to Church they should get what they need and want, i.e., a mediator to God and a dispenser of His sacraments. Subsidiary functions, like social activism, should be handled by lay people. The Pope ought to consider a "one-shot" deal allowing those priests and sisters unwilling to redefine their roles in such a way to resign through the process of laitization. It is better to have less religious than religious working against the faith from within the system. Simultaneously, deacons and laity, including females, ought to be more fully incorporated into the daily non-sacramental activities of the parish.

(11) Special attention must be placed on the growing Hispanic population in the United States. Unlike the non-Hispanic Catholic population and due, *in part,* to its low socio-economic class position, heterodoxy as a result of assimilation into the themes of Americanization and modernity is not yet a problem for Hispanic Catholics. They are, indeed, a people both respectful of tradition and conservative politically. Generally speaking, however, they do not rank high on Catholic orthodoxy. The contemporary "Hispanic problem" in the Catholic Church of the United States is very similar to that of the Italian immigrants and second-generation Italian-Americans vis-a-vis the Church during the early part of the twentieth century.[12] The "Italian problem" centered primarily around the immigrant's primary attachment to peasant southern Italian culture; the immigrant was quite "religious" but also quite unchurched in the doctrines and practices of the Catholic faith. The fact that the Italian immigrant was non-Catholic in sensibilities attracted the attention of Protestant and Socialist proselytizing but to little avail. Italian-Americans through the generations have remained culturally traditional, politically conservative, but also religiously (in many cases) little more than nominally Catholic.[13] Analogously, one can expect strong conversion attempts geared toward Hispanic Catholics on the part of Pentecostal Protestants and Marxist theology-of-liberationists. While these attempts are likely to be by and large unsuccessful, there is no guarantee that the United States Hispanic population will ever become authentically Catholic. If appropriate attention is given to the U.S. Catholic Hispanic population, there is a distinct possibility that new orthodox leadership and vitality will be infusing the American Catholic Church for years to come.

(12) The emergence and institutionalization of a "neo-orthodox" Catholic center, loyal to the letter of Vatican II, is a presupposition for maintaining the unity, continuity, and universalism of the Catholic Church in the United States. If forced to choose between traditionalist orthodox and modernist heterodox factions of the U.S. Catholic Church, I hope it is clear that this author stands firmly with the former. However, the

chances of saving a larger percentage of the American Catholics from heterodoxy and shortening the upcoming civil war in the U.S. Catholic Church lies in the development of an updated neo-orthodoxy which incorporates modern methods from the social sciences and humanities to defend, propound, and maintain an authentic Catholicism. Such a neo-orthodoxy represents a "via media" between the traditional and modern worldviews and provides Catholics with an intelligent and most persuasive synthesis of faith and reason.

FOOTNOTES

1 The list of American values is taken from Ian Robertson, **Sociology**, (second edition, updated) New York: Worth Publishers, 1981, pp. 62-3.

2 See my review of Dolan's **The American Catholic Experience** in *The American Historical Review,* June, 1986. For some interesting reading, see the following exchange between myself and Dolan in the December, 1986 issue regarding my review. In my reply to Dolan's angry rejoinder, I note the creation of a "neo-orthodox" movement in the United States Catholic Church that will be systematically opposing the further establishment of what liberal Catholicism has degenerated into since Vatican II. Also, see my forthcoming review essay comparing **The Ratzinger Report** with Greeley's **American Catholics Since the Council** in *Religious Studies and Theology,* forthcoming.

3 This section is taken almost literally from my paper, "To Empower Catholics: The Catholic League for Religious and Civil Rights as a 'Mediating Structure'," read at the joint Annual Meeting of the Society for Scientific Study of Religion and The Religious Research Association, Washington, D.C., November 14, 1986.

4 For more on this theme, see the published work of Father Virgil Blum, S.J., founder of The Catholic League for Religious and Civil Rights. I suggest the following: **Quest for Religious Freedom**, Milwaukee, Wisconsin: Catholic League Publications, 1984; "The New Wave of Anti-Catholicism," Supplement to the *Catholic League Newsletter,* Vol. 11, #1, January, 1984 and "Shinto Catholics and the Right to Life," Supplement to the *Catholic League Newsletter,* Vol. 11, #9, September, 1984.

5 For a copy of this fine piece of research, write to Professor Michael H. Barnes, Department of Religious Studies, University of Dayton, 300 College Park, Ohio, 45469-0001.

6 Dulles' concept of "symbolic realism" is discussed in his brilliant book, **Models of Revelation**, N.Y.: Doubleday, 1983. For the record, I personally consider Father Dulles to be within the boundaries of a legitimate orthodoxy, although at the "left-most" boundary.

7 For information about the total study, **Notre Dame Study of Catholic Parish Life**, write the University of Notre Dame, 1201 Memorial Library, Notre Dame, Indiana, 46556.

8 The individual to contact for reliable information and statistics on the abortion issue is Richard Doerflinger, Legislative Assistant, National Conference of Catholic Bishops, Bishops Committee for Pro-Life Activities, 1312 Massachusetts Avenue, N.W., Washington, D.C. 20005.

9 For more information write to Dr. Dean R. Hoge, Department of Sociology, The Catholic University of America, Washington, D.C. 20064.

10 For more information about the conference paper, write to David O. Moberg, Department of Sociology, Marquette University, Milwaukee, Wisconsin 53233.

11 For more information, write Dr. John C. Gessner, Box 4368, College of St. Thomas, St. Paul, MN 55105.

12 cf. Henry J. Browne, "The 'Italian Problem' in the Catholic Church of the United States, 1880-1920," New York: Historical Records and Studies, *The United States Catholic Historical Society,* Vol. XXXV, 1946.

13 cf. Joseph A. Varacalli, "The Changing Nature of the 'Italian Problem' in the Catholic Church of the United States," *Faith and Reason,* Vol. 12, #1, March, 1986.

The Renewal of the Church: Toward the 21st Century

by

Thomas Weinandy, OFM, Cap.

To identify the central issues confronting the world and the Church at the end of the second millennium, I have decided to take my cue from Pope John Paul II. In reading the pope's encyclicals and his weekly audiences and addresses, I have been struck by his numerous references to the approaching Millennial Jubilee. Significantly, John Paul's three major encyclicals on the Trinity — **Redemptor Hominis**, **Dives in Misericordia**, and **Dominum et Vivificantem** — as well as his encyclical on Mary, **Mater Redemptoris**, are set within the context of the approaching 2000 year Jubilee. I have concluded that it would be helpful to examine these encyclicals to see how John Paul speaks of the year 2000 in light of the Church's and the world's needs.

I. Redemptor Hominis

"The Redeemer of man, Jesus Christ, is the center of the universe and of human history" (1). Pope John Paul II, in this opening sentence from his first encyclical, proclaimed that Jesus, as the incarnate Son of God, must be acknowledged as the pre-eminent person in creation and in human history. As John Paul began his pontificate, this truth acquired even greater significance for God had entrusted to him the Chair of Peter at a time "already very close to the year 2000" (1). He conceded that it is difficult to know "what mark that year will leave on the face of human history," but "for the Church, the People of God . . . it will be the year of a great Jubilee" (1).

We uncover here, at the very outset of John Paul's pontificate, the heart of his strategy for the renewal of the Church and for his solicitude toward the world as the year 2000 nears: the centrality and primacy of Jesus and the salvation he brings. The Incarnation marked the high point of God's plan. "God entered the history of humanity and, as a man, became an actor in that history . . ." (1).

Evaluating Vatican II and the previous pontificates of this century, John Paul asked himself: "In what manner should we continue? What should we do, in order that this new advent of the Church connected with the approaching end of the second millennium may bring us closer" to our Father (7)? There is only one answer: "Our spirit is set in one direction, the only direction for our intellect, will and heart, towards Christ our Redeemer, towards Christ, the Redeemer of man. We wish to look towards Him, because there is salvation in no one else but Him, the Son of God . . ." (7). The foremost task of the Church at this juncture in human history is to ensure "that each person may be able to find Christ ..." (13).

With the approach of the third millennium, the world and the Church need Jesus and his salvation more than ever. John Paul insists that this present century is "groaning in travail;" that it is increasingly "subjected to futility." The environmental crisis, numerous and ever-increasing armed conflicts, the threat of nuclear war, social and economic injustice, the disintegration of the marriage and family life, and the contempt for human life (even of the unborn) make this abundantly clear.

Cognizant of this frightful situation, the pope heralded Jesus as the Liberator from this bondage to evil: "Christ, the new Adam, in the very revelation of the mystery of the Father and of his love, *fully reveals man to himself* and brings to light his most high calling." The pope contended that Christ is "himself the perfect man who has restored in the children of Adam that likeness to God which had been disfigured ever since the first sin." (8). Jesus, through the Incarnation, has raised humanity to a new dignity by uniting himself to each person. Only in Christ can we be restored to our rightful rank as reflections of God's image. Only in Christ can we be recreated and made new. Thus, only in Christ can the world find an answer to the present threat of self-annihilation begotten by the wages of sin.

From this perspective, the pope made a concluding reference to the year 2000. Here he spoke not of a time of jubilation, but of an hour for intense prayer in the face of immense problems and difficulties; a moment that could be decisive both for the Church and the world for better or worse:

> Faced with these tasks that appear along the ways for the Church ... we feel all the more our need for a profound link with Christ. ... We feel not only the need but even a categorical imperative for great, intense and growing prayer by all the Church. Only prayer can prevent all these great succeeding tasks and difficulties from becoming a source of crisis and make them instead the occasion and, as it were, the foundation for ever more mature achievements on the People of God's march toward the Promised Land in this state of history approaching the end of the second millennium.

He concluded by asking us to join with Mary's intercession for "humanity's new advent." (22).

II. Dives in Misericordia

If we say that John Paul's second encyclical is just the next installment of his trinitarian trilogy, treating of God the Father, we would be missing its full significance. Yes, it does discuss the Father, but more specifically and importantly it speaks of the Father's mercy. It is this specific attribute which the pope believes the world most needs to experience at this critical time.

The Father's mercy is poured out most abundantly through his Son, Jesus. "It became *visible in Christ and through Christ,* through his actions and his words, and finally through his death on the cross and his resurrection ... [Jesus] *makes it incarnate* and personifies it. *He himself, in a certain sense, is mercy."* (2). The supreme act of mercy is the cross of Jesus. He reconciled us to the Father, making peace through the blood of the cross. He put to death our sinful nature so that we might become the very holiness of God.

Looking at the world, the pope asked whether the fears and tensions within contemporary culture and society have become "less disquieting" since first addressed by the Second Vatican Council:

> It seems not. On the contrary, the tensions and threats that in the Council document seem only to be outlined ... have revealed themselves more clearly in the space of these years; they have in a different way confirmed that danger, and do not permit us to cherish the illusions of the past (10).

He then enumerated the evils, physical and moral, that confront mankind today. Despite the dilemmas that face the world and the Church, human beings have become oblivious and insensitive to God's mercy and, in turn, have hardened themselves against showing mercy to others. Resentment, bitterness, anger, hatred and unforgiveness have gripped and enslaved the entire world. To the pope's mind, humanity is desparate for the mercy of God made manifest through his Son, Jesus Christ. Without this mercy there is no hope. Human strategies and designs for resolving the problems of the word are not suited to the task at hand. Only Jesus is capable of destroying the sin and evil that imperils humanity. Only the power of his cross and Spirit can free human beings from their callous and obstinate hearts and their darkened minds.

He concluded this encyclical with an impassioned call for prayer. "Everything that I have said in the present document on mercy should therefore *be continually transformed into an ardent prayer:* into a cry that implores mercy according to the needs of man in the modern world" (15). Having stated with great intensity the crisis confronting the modern world, he insisted:

> [The mystery of Christ] obliges me to have recourse to that mercy and to beg for it at this difficult, critical phase of the history of the Church and of the world, as we approach the end of the second millennium. In the name of Jesus Christ crucified and risen, in the spirit of his messianic mission, ... *we raise our voices and pray* that the Love which is in the Father may once again be revealed at this stage of history, and that, through the work of the Son and Holy Spirit, it may be shown to be present in our modern world and to be more powerful than evil: more powerful than sin and death (15).

III. Dominum et Vivificantem

More than in any previous encyclical, the pope sets **Dominum Vivificantem** within the context of the approaching 21st century. This emphasis highlights the perilous condition of this present age. Part II of the encyclical, which is its heart, focuses exclusively on the Spirit's mission of convicting people of sin and manifesting the saving and healing work of Christ crucified. Part III applies this work of the Spirit to today's circumstances. John Paul judged that with the close of the this second millennium the Church must be even more committed to "the mission of proclaiming the Spirit" (1).

The first task of the Holy Spirit is to bring to light our sinful nature and the iniquity which flows from it. This work is crucial today. John Paul believes that Pope Pius XII was absolutely correct when he declared that "the sin of the century is the loss of the sense of sin ..." (47).

This accent on sin is not one of pessimism, cynicism or despair. Rather, the pope realizes that sin is our worst enemy. It undermines and destroys the integrity of humanity and fosters hate and animosity both within the Church and the world. Until the Spirit convicts us of sin and leads us to repentance and a change of heart, the plight of the present age will not be abated.

Moreover, only the Spirit convicts us of the righteousness of Jesus and moves us to faith in him. Jesus promised that he would send another Counselor, who would lead us to the fullness of truth. Thus, it is the Holy Spirit who bears witness to Jesus, who is the truth. John Paul declared that *the witness of the Spirit* inspires, guarantees and convalidates the faithful transmission of this revelation ..." (5). He performs his work in the hearts and minds of men and women by bringing them to faith in Jesus. "Here the Spirit is to be man's supreme guide and the light of the human spirit" (6). This faith will make us righteous in the Righteous One — Jesus Christ. In Christ, we become new creations: our lives can actually change.

The convincing of the Spirit "becomes at the same time a convincing *concerning the remission of sins,* in the power of the Spirit ... the gift of the certainty of redemption" (31). This conviction of sin leads to the cross by which our fallen natures are put to death. Through the cross we become new creations in the Spirit (44). "It is in the power of this crucifixion that he [Jesus] says to them [the apostles]: 'Receive the Holy Spirit.' ... There is no sending of the Holy Spirit (after original sin) without the Cross and the Resurrection ..." (24).

The third and final section of the encyclical is an application of the Spirit's work to our millennial age. The coming of Jesus into the world marked the "fullness of time" and "the *great Jubilee* at the close of the second Millennium ..." celebrates both the birth of Jesus and its actualization "by the power of the Holy Spirit" (50). This Spirit who accomplished the act of Incarnation is the same Spirit who prepares us for the coming Jubilee: "The Church cannot *prepare* for the Jubilee in any other way than *in the Holy Spirit.*" Only the Spirit can impart to the Church the saving mystery of Christ in this "new phase of man's history on earth: the year 2000 from the birth of Christ" (51).

As in the previous encyclicals, the pope addressed the critical times in which we live. The real battle is between the flesh and spirit. In our day, the pope asserted, this dispute is more fiercely fought than ever before and "reaches its clearest expression in *materialism ...*" (56). This materialism, this exclusive focusing on man and his sensual passions and egotistical drives to the exclusion of God, has given rise to the great evils of our age — from nuclear war to abortion:

Despite the urgency, of our present age the pope is not without hope: "Yes, we groan, but in an expectation filled with unflagging hope, because it is precisely this human being that God has drawn near to, God who is Spirit" (57). The pope is clear that even though this is a perilous age, there is a power far stronger than sin and evil. The Church fervently clings to and boldly proclaims the gospel as it anticipates the third millennium: "The great Jubilee of the year 2000 thus contains a message of liberation by the power of the Spirit, who alone can help individuals and communities to free themselves from the old and new determinisms, by guiding them with the 'law of the Spirit, which gives life in Christ Jesus' ..." (60).

John Paul concluded by pointing out that in celebrating the Jubilee we are anticipating the second coming. This is ultimately the event for which the Church and the world are preparing and will celebrate for all eternity. The pope asked that we pray: "Come, Lord Jesus!" This prayer not only anticipates Jesus' second coming and the consummation of the world, but at the same time *"this prayer is directed towards a precise moment of history* which highlights the 'fullness of time' marked by the year 2000. The Church wishes *to prepare* for this Jubilee *in the Holy Spirit,* just as the Virgin of Nazareth — in whom the Word was made flesh — was prepared by the Holy Spirit" (66).

IV. Redemptoris Mater

John Paul's fourth encyclical goes beyond being just a treatise on Mary. It proceeds logically (as the above quotation suggests) from his trinitarian encyclicals, not only in Mary's intimate association with the Trinity's work of redemption, but also to her as the exemplar of the Church's proper response to it. Thus, this encyclical is a call to action, an invitation to respond to the gospel in faith as Mary did, a summons to renewal and holiness of life patterned after Mary, a cry to prepare, as she did, for Jesus' coming as we approach the 2000th anniversary of his birth. This insistence on action culminated in John Paul's proclamation of the Marian Year. This year is to be a concrete preparation, in union with Mary, for the approaching Jubilee Year. It is to be a year of intercession and renewal.

Thus Mary is seen as the most faithful respondent to the gospel message as proclaimed in the previous encyclicals. As such, she leads us to a restoration of faith that will not only rejuvenate the faltering Church, but bring salvation to the weary world. "With good reason, then, we Christians who know that the providential plan of the Most Holy Trinity is *the central reality of Revelation and of faith* feel the need to emphasize the unique presence of the Mother of Christ in history, especially during these last years leading up to the year 2000" (3).

The pope wants us to reflect on Mary as she exemplifies the perfect pilgrim of faith: *"The pilgrimage of faith indicates the interior history, that is, the story of souls. But it is also the story of all human beings ..."* (6). As the Church prepares to celebrate the Jubilee year, she looks to Mary who fervently prepared for the coming of her son 2000 years ago:

> Thus by means of this Marian Year *the Church called* not only to remember everything in her past that testifies to the special maternal cooperation of the Mother of God in the work of salvation in Christ the Lord, but also, on her own part, *to prepare* for the future the paths of this cooperation. For the end of the Second Christian Millennium opens up as a new prospect (49).

Not surprisingly, in this Marian encyclical John Paul spoke more extensively about ecumenism, especially between the East and the West, than in the previous encyclicals. Recognizing that Mary is the mother of Jesus, the common life of every Christian denomination, and that she is the exemplar of every Christian's faith, the pope used this occasion to stress that this millennial age is ardently calling the churches to a unity of faith. Division weakens the renewal efforts of every church and likewise gives scandal to non-believers. As Christians grow in unity, their task to revitalize themselves and the world becomes easier and more vigorous:

> The journey of the Church, especially in our own time, is marked by the sign of ecumenism: Christians are seeking ways to restore that unity which Christ implored from the Father ... The unity of Christ's disciples, therefore, is a great sign given in order to kindle faith in the world, while their division constitutes a scandal (29).

Both the encyclical and in the call to faith during this Marian Year, we see again the pontiff's concerns as we near the year 2000. The Church calls out to Mary at this time to "assist your people who have fallen, yet strive to rise again." In light of our fallen nature and its potential of sin the pope wants us to unite us to Mary so that — like her — we might be purified of sin, and commit ourselves to her son, Jesus. He would have us join our prayers with Mary for the transformation of our own hearts, the restoration of Christian unity, and the conversion of the entire world. This Marian Year is primarily a call to repentance and faith, for only through these will the Church, the churches, and the world come to experience the truth expressed in these encyclicals: the mercy of the Father, the redemption of Jesus and the forgiveness and new life in the Spirit. Only in this way can we be truly prepared to joyfully celebrate the Jubilee Year.

V. What Have We Learned?

What have we learned from examining these four papal encyclicals? First, the critical nature of this millennial era is quite apparent. John Paul views it in almost apocalyptic proportions. The world is so entangled in evil and sin that its very life is threatened. Nor is the Church immune from this deadly affliction of confusion, rebellion, and spiritual depression. The world and the Church are confronted with options: the world may be converted to the gospel of Jesus Christ, curing it of the cancerous sin that imperils it, or it can continue on its deadly path to disaster; the Church can renew itself through reconversion to Jesus Christ and become a leaven of life for the world, or it can continue in its weakened condition, thereby contributing to the world's deplorable state. The Church is the future's physician. A renewed Church will be a source of life; a desolate Church will contribute to the world's demise.

Any renewal movement in the Church today must perceive this menacing situation as well as the role which the Church must play to correct it. Individuals and groups within the Church who fail or refuse to acknowledge the precarious nature of our age will be useless. Indeed, such thinking will only contribute to an already unstable condition. Naive prophets of facile optimism are largely responsible for much of the malaise that exists.

Secondly, John Paul is deeply convinced that the only cure capable of reviving the Church and, in turn, the world is the gospel. It alone has the power to excise the sin that has infected the Church and the world and to resurrect men and women to a new and vibrant life. According to the pope, the heart of this gospel consists of the following: (1) the Holy Spirit convicting us of sin, and leading us to repentance; (2) the experience of the mercy of the Father guiding us to faith in Jesus as Savior and Lord; (3) the recognition that only through the death of Jesus has Satan, sin and death been conquered and only through Christ's resurrection can we become new creations in the Spirit, anticipating eternal life. To the world, and even to many in the Church, this remedy appears both unrealistic and mindless. The world considers the gospel impotent in the face of concrete and practical problems. To many in the Church, the gospel is ethereal, pietistic rhetoric. Yet, this is the forceful and anguished message of the encyclicals.

Notice that the pope's solution is not some human program or scheme. It does not involve an elaborate system of conferences, workshops and seminars. The heart of the Church's renewal and of the world's hope is simply the gospel. This alone is what God has given. This is enough. We need nothing else.

Thus, if they are to be credible to a skeptical Church and an unbelieving world, any movements of renewal which are worthy of the name must embody within them vigorous life of the gospel. They must recognize and existentially experience the mercy and love of the Father made manifest in Jesus. This divine mercy must awaken them to their own sinful state and bring them to repentance, faith and new life in Christ.

Thirdly, any renewal movement which is a true work of the Spirit must embrace as its central mission the proclamation of the same gospel by which its members are renewed. This ought to be accomplished in a way that those who become members of the movement, as well as those to whom it ministers, experience the transforming power and life of the gospel — the call to repentance, mature faith in Jesus, and holiness of life.

I have emphasized the lived witness of people, for unless a personal transformation has actually occurred, there is no renewal. John Paul is calling for precisely this type of event within the Church and anticipating this kind of evidence. Only the lived gospel can renew the Church and, in turn, the world. The Marian Year, he believes, can contribute to this perceptible expression of faith life through a recommitment to the gospel after the example and through the intercession of Mary.

VI. Movements of Renewal: The Charismatic Renewal

The Cursillo Movement, the Focolare Movement, Comunione e Liberazione, and Opus Dei all bear witness in distinctive ways and in various degrees to the renewal of the gospel in people's lives. There are probably others. But I believe these are some of the larger movements that are in accord with John Paul's vision for a renewed Church and world. I have purposely left out such movements as Marriage Encounter, Engaged Encounter, and social action groups since their primary focus is not the gospel itself, even though they arise out of gospel concerns.

Because it uniquely qualifies as a work of the Spirit in this critical Millennial Age, I would like to treat one movement of renewal more extensively. That movement is the Charismatic Renewal. Along with Comunione e Liberazione and Opus Dei, John Paul has appointed a representative of the Charismatic Renewal to attend the Synod on the Laity.

The Charismatic Renewal's relationship with the Holy Spirit is obvious. Those in the Renewal point out that Pope John XXIII, in anticipation of Vatican II, prayed for a "new Pentecost." The Renewal's roots, however, are found in Pope Leo XIII's 1897 encyclical on the Holy Spirit, **Divinum Illud Munus**, and in the outbreak of the Pentecostal movement shortly thereafter, within Protestantism. However, the force of Pentecostalism's full potential was only perceived on a denominational and global scale when it emerged within the Catholic Church in the mid-1960's. From a faith perspective, it could be argued that the Holy Spirit for over a century has been preparing the entire Christian Church and the world for the 2000 year Jubilee celebration.

The World Christian Encyclopedia: A Comparative Study of Churches and Religions in the Modern World A.D. 1900-2000, edited by David B. Barrett (published in 1982), states that globally Pentecostalism is the fastest growing movement of the century. At its continued rate of growth, it will have affected more people by the year 2000 (the Jubilee Year) than any other Christian movement of the century. One of its unique features is that it has impacted all Christian denominations. Thus, more than any other renewal movement within the Church, and within Christianity at large, the Charismatic Renewal is, by nature, ecumenical. In his book, **One Lord, One Spirit, One Body**, (Word Among Us Press, Washington, D.C., 1987), Fr. Peter Hocken argues that the ecumenical nature of the Renewal is one its real graces. Without underestimating the real divisions between the various denominations or diluting the truths of the gospel, the Spirit — through the Renewal — has fostered an ecumenism that is founded upon a renewed and vibrant faith in Jesus Christ and his gospel. This is in keeping with John Paul's own parameters and understanding.

The considerable growth of Pentecostal/Charismatic Christianity is evident not only in Europe and North America, but also in Latin America where it is profoundly altering the present religious environment. Its growth in Africa has been slow, partly due to its checkered history among Catholics, but its expansion among the indigenous black Christian churches is extensive. There are vibrant charismatic and Pentacostal groups in Communist countries, even in Russia. Their strength and dynamism are attested to by the fear and persecution they evoke from Communist authorities. Even in China we are discovering that Christianity is not only more alive than previously expected, but that the Pentecostal movement has been notably responsible for its preservation and vitality. This phenomenal growth within Christianity is not presented as the legitimization of the Renewal, but it does call for an appropriate hearing.

Participants in the Renewal are, as a group, acutely aware that the Church is suffering spiritually and is in need of reconversion or revitalization. This awareness stems from the Holy Spirit convicting them of their own desparate state (prior to their renewal) as well as their ongoing weaknesses. They recognize that their former faith was dead or at best nominal; prior to their "conversion," their lives were out of order and enslaved by habitual sin. This personal awareness of sin has heightened their consciousness of the pervasive sin that is destroying the lives of others, of the lethargy and apathy within the Church, and of the world's complete rebellion against God.

This heightened awareness of sin and the need for a renewed life of faith compels Charismatics to bear witness to the transforming power of the gospel of Jesus Christ. The Spirit can bring people to repentance, heal them of sin, and establish a new life with God in Christ. They have seen this in their own lives.

Herein is the basis for misunderstanding and friction between those within the Renewal and those outside it. The charge is sometimes leveled that Charismatics are elitists, who insist, at least implicitly, that all become as they are. Since the Renewal encompasses very large numbers of people, not all of whom are prudent, sophisticated and articulate (not to mention sinless), what is said and done is often not pure, but mixed and even inaccurate. What must be acknowledged, however, is that, despite the negative elements, Charismatics are aware that the faith life of many people in the Church is inadequate and anemic. Those who accuse them of elitism are sometimes the very ones who are self-satisfied and complacent. Moreover, what members of the Renewal want for others is not unique or separatist, but rather the full life of the gospel, something that is available to all through the Holy Spirit. (This is not to imply that Charismatics possess a fully mature faith or are sinless. By no means. What it does mean is that Charismatics realize that the gospel can change people's lives.)

Those within the Renewal testify to the Father's mercy. They are profoundly aware that they were and are sinners whose only hope is in the mercy of God. They recognize, more clearly and personally than most Christians, that without the mercy of God manifested in Christ, they — and the whole human race — deserve nothing less than eternal damnation.

Thus, people within the Charismatic Renewal have a deep appreciation of Jesus and what he has done. They recognize, as the pope has underscored, that the Spirit has renewed and nourished their faith in Jesus. Through the experience of Baptism in the Spirit, they have received an interior and personal revelation of Jesus as the Son of God; that on the cross he alone saved them from sin and death; and that he now is the resurrected Lord of the universe who deserves all honor and praise. Their personal and enthusiastic commitment to Jesus accompanied by their vocal praise and worship of him is often considered the distinguishing mark of the Renewal. But this must be seen as a work of the Spirit. No one can believe and proclaim that Jesus is truly Savior and Lord except by the Holy Spirit.

The enthusiasm of charismatics gives rise to a second common criticism, that of religious fanaticism or emotionalism. Admittedly, there is usually some foundation for every criticism: some charismatics can be overly emotional. Nonetheless, allowing for the immaturity of some, one can still ask: Should not Christians be single minded for Jesus? Should we not devote our minds, hearts, and emotions to him? Does he not deserve our praise, yes, even exuberant vocal praise, just as much or more than the current movie or rock star, or the home team sport's hero? Society tolerates and even encourages enthusiastic endorsement of the newest cars, clothes, music, and trends. On the other hand, it ridicules religious fervor as irrational and fanatical. The Church itself has adopted this attitude. To vocally and enthusiastically praise and worship Jesus, to center one's whole life on him, to live differently from what is perceived as "normal" is often considered as "over-doing it." To criticize the Renewal for religious fanaticism and emotionalism is often more a comment on the sad state of the Church and the world than a valid reproach.

Because of this transforming experience of the Spirit, charismatics want to evangelize and are empowered and compelled to do so. When they have personally experienced the life changing power of the Gospel, they feel impelled to share it with others. They can attest with conviction to the reality of the gospel and its transforming power. Their own lives become the source of their gospel proclamation. Until people are actually transformed by the gospel, it is impossible for them to proclaim it. A true test of the Church's state and of the life of its people is to examine whether and to what extent it is evangelistic. An inability or unwillingness to share one's faith indicates a weak and immature belief.

At the center of the Renewal's promise and vigor is the Holy Spirit. Those involved in the Renewal testify that it was the Spirit who first convicted them of sin, exposed the disorder in their lives, and brought them to repentance. They realize that the Spirit has brought them to new or renewed faith in Jesus, through which their lives have been healed and restored. The exercise of the charismatic gifts — the most distinguishing and visible signs of Renewal — is actually a manifestation of the Spirit's interior achievement.

If what I have said is true, why is it that many ecclesiastics and academics have not taken the Charismatic Renewal more seriously? The fear of elitism, emotionalism, and fanaticism, which I have already mentioned are partially responsible. But there are also a few other reasons.

One is that academics find it difficult to "get a handle on it." Unlike other movements of renewal, the Charismatic Renewal has no human author: it is entirely a spontaneous and sovereign work of the Spirit. No man or woman decided that the Church and the world needed what we find in the Renewal: Baptism in the Spirit and the spiritual gifts. Undeniably there are leaders within the Renewal, but the Renewal was as much a surprise to them as to others. Their understanding of the Spirit's work grew *from* their experience and not *prior* to it.

For this reason, there is no book or treatise outlining the founder's intentions, purposes and spirit. This is in contrast to Focolare or Opus Dei where one has easy access to the founder's ideas and goals. This lack of a preconceived and written plan and program complicates analysis and criticism of the Renewal. To discern the validity of the Renewal is more, then, than an academic affair; it requires an examination of the lives of real people. Moreover, what one is attempting to analyze is the work of God: his supernatural intervention in time and space as it touches the lives of men and women today.

Moreover, because the Renewal has no set program other than the basic gospel message, it is perplexing, especially for Americans. We are a society and culture of methods, programs and systems. If the Renewal had "a program" with specific blueprints and goals for each week, month, and year, complete with instruction books, spread sheets, discussion questions for small groups, etc., its credibility would probably improve noticeably among pastors and teachers. The fact that the Renewal has simply to do with preaching and the appropriation of the gospel, somehow works against it. The suspicion is that there must be a plan, a program, some secret scheme if the gospel is to work. So weak is our faith that, unlike the pope, we do not believe that the gospel can stand on its own and change people's lives. Yet this alone is what Jesus has given us for our salvation. Someone may ask: What about the Life in the Spirit Seminars? Actually, the seminars are just a systematic way of presenting the gospel. They are successful only if the gospel is presented in a clear and convincing manner, and if those participating yield themselves to the work of the Spirit in faith.

Furthermore, because the Renewal is primarily composed of ordinary Christians, scholars can, to a greater or lesser degree, stand aloof and hold it in contempt. Indeed, one of their dominant criticisms is that of fundamentalism. This charge is leveled both against the Renewal's understanding of the gospel and its approach to scripture. This fundamentalism is conceived and nourished, they believe, in the credulous minds of the uneducated.

Again, this charge has a trace of validity. In today's world, anyone who possesses no formal training and little historical sense of how the

Bible has been traditionally read and understood will tend to interpret it literally. Reading the newspaper is the paradigm for all reading. Despite this, a number of points can be made. First, the fact that some charismatics have misinterpreted the Bible is in itself evidence that it is, at least, being read. Better that the Bible be read and occasionally misinterpreted than never read at all. Moreover, the misinterpretations among Catholics usually are not as flagrant nor as frequent as one is led to believe. Secondly, no group of conventional Catholics spend more time and effort reading and studying the Bible than those in the Renewal. Catholic Charismatics, on the whole, are attempting to conquer their ignorance. Any Christian book store owner will verify that Catholic Charismatics are by far the most numerous patrons of Christian literature, especially Biblical studies. The fact that the Renewal has given rise to the two largest Catholic scripturally oriented periodicals: *God's Word Today* (89,000) and *The Word Among Us* (80,000), also demonstrates that the Renewal has done more for critical Biblical scholarship than any other movement. Thirdly, the charge of fundamentalism is frequently made not by men and women of real faith but by those who manifest the spirit of secularism. Accordingly, anyone who affirms anything supernatural is considered a naive fundamentalist who interprets scripture in an uncritical, literalist fashion.

Another area of concern focuses on the fear of some ecclesial authorities that the Renewal weakens people's commitment to the Catholic Church and that other Pentecostal denominations attract and steal Catholics away from the Church, especially the young. Unfortunately, some people have joined Pentecostal denominations. This fear of defection from Catholicism is especially prevalent within the Hispanic Catholic community. The way to attack this problem is not to attack the Renewal or even the Pentecostal denominations, but to recognize that people are hungry for spiritual renewal. The Church has the obligation to provide it and the Church herself must accept the blame for many of the defections.

Lastly, one of the unrecognized reasons that the Renewal is not taken seriously by some pastors and academics is their own spiritual poverty. Whether we are of the theological right or left, our sinfulness can blind us to the Spirit's work. The sinful patterns that enslave us — anger, suspicion, resentment, greed, arrogance, lust, and ambition — deaden and distort our spiritual perception. Our lack of prayer, or its barren routineness, contributes to our failure to see the Spirit's work today or judging it to be of little consequence.

VII. The Call to Sanctity

As the Church nears the end of the second millennium, it does so with the realization that a great task is set before it, viz., that it must renew itself and then the world. John Paul II unquestionably recognizes that preaching and appropriating the gospel is the answer. The Spirit is actively present within the Church today. The Charismatic Renewal is one of the primary ways the Spirit is using to foster renewal in all

Christian denominations. At the core of this Renewal is the gospel alone, the very thing John Paul is so anxious for the Church and the world to seize upon. We must look then, not to some great plan, some new seminar, program, or scheme, but to the constant daily preaching of the gospel, the bringing of people to conversion. This is the real answer for renewal of the Church and the salvation of the world as the third millennium rushes upon us. It is not easily accomplished for it primarily demands the labor of holy men and women. No program, conference, or seminar alone can lead people to holiness, only those who are themselves holy can do so. In the end what the Church must foster and what the world needs most is saints.

This call to sanctity falls most heavily upon us who are pastors and teachers. We can proclaim the gospel and lead people to Jesus only if we ourselves are living that gospel and actually know Jesus. Thus, like our saintly ancestors, we too must pray everyday, despite our hectic schedules and routines. This is John Paul's ardent summons in each encyclical. Prayer is our most potent weapon against sin and evil. It is the source and fount of the Spirit's holiness. We are also called to daily repentance and a living faith in the presence and power of Jesus. Scripture and the Eucharist will nourish our hearts and minds. The Father's will must be our food. Finally, we are commissioned to evangelize our communities, our families, our students, and even our colleagues.

In so doing we will not only be preparing ourselves for the Jubilee Year, we will also be contributing to the jubilation of the whole Body of Christ. The Spirit's ultimate design is to nourish all of God's people, to form the entire community of faith. He does this by conforming the mind of the Church and the minds of all believers to the mind of Christ. As the Spirit accomplishes his task, what will become most central to the Church will be Jesus himself, not the various agendas of assorted theological and political constituencies. Jesus established the Church, not for its own sake, but for himself, to give him glory, to do his will, to serve his purposes. This is the vision that John Paul holds out to us at the dawn of the third millennium, a vision where all men and women are bound together by their faith in and love for Jesus. They desire him alone and wish solely to build his Kingdom. A Church suffused with the Spirit and conformed to the mind of Christ is our only hope.

A Profile of American Catholic Parishioners
by
Father Patrick Egan

In the early 1900s, the American Catholic parish reflected the millions of European Catholic immigrants attracted to this country by an expanding economy. It was a blue collar church situated in the urban working class neighborhoods of the big cities in the economic heartlands of America. More than 70% of the Catholic population lived between the Atlantic coast, the Ohio River Valley and the Mississippi. The South-east was still missionary country, so was the Far West.

During the first half of the 20th century little change took place in the American parish in terms of leadership, liturgy, and religious education. The pastor tended to reign like a monarch — his long tenure reinforcing his considerable position. Devotional Catholicism flourished. In the South-east and Far West the Church developed as the century progressed a more visible presence. But during these decades many social changes were at work which decisively changed the Old World face of American Catholicism.

By the 1920s, immigration from Europe ended, to be followed by a new wave of Hispanics from Mexico, and black Americans from the South. These new immigrants settled in the inner city neighborhoods where the older immigrants lived, and the cities began to expand into the suburbs with many Catholics following suit. By the 1940s, it was clear that American Catholics were becoming more middle-class and more American. Another change profoundly affecting the development of American Catholicism was the growth within the community of a concern for social justice occasioned by the Depression and by Papal Encyclicals.

In the last quarter century, the Catholic population has changed considerably. Catholics now resemble the rest of Americans in terms of birthplace, class and education. Although the majority still live in the old economic heartland, they live in the suburbs rather than in the city. Gone is the public nature of inner city living in an ethnic neighborhood, replaced by the highly privatised suburban life style. A second major influence has been the Second Vatican Council with its emphasis on popular participation. Its theology of the Church as the People of God, its new understanding of the use of authority and its sponsorship of a reformed and vernacular liturgy have had a tremendous impact on parish life. Thirdly, the social revolutions of post World War II America, including increased education, new job opportunities, changing attitudes towards women, the civil rights movement, the Vietnam controversy, and the questioning of traditional authority, have all left their mark on the Church.[1] Dolan concludes his thorough & monumental study:

> A new Catholicism has come to life in the last two decades, and one
> of its most striking features is pluralism. There is no longer one way to do

theology, one way to worship at Mass, to confess sin, or to pray. There are various ways of being Catholic and people are choosing the style that best suits them. Though this is something new for modern Catholicism, it is not something new in the history of the Church. For centuries there have been differing schools of theology, differing liturgical traditions, and differing ways of being Catholic. This inclination towards diversity has been there since the very beginning when the Apostle Paul left Peter in Jerusalem to forge a new Christianity among the Gentiles. Since the 16th century, that ancient tradition of diversity has been lost, as a rage for uniformity and order engulfed Catholicism. Nevertheless, ethnic diversity did give to Catholics in the United States a unique measure of cultural pluralism. A common faith, a common theology and clerical control kept it together. Then, just as the immigrants were becoming united as Americans, the cement that held them together as Catholics crumbled.

With the emergence of a new Catholicism, the immigrant Catholic ethos has changed. A new model of Church and authority is replacing the old, monarchical, clerical concept of church and authority. A new Catholic moral code is replacing the traditional moral code with its exaggerated emphasis on sin and guilt. The sense of the transcendent and the miraculous also remains prominent, especially among evangelical, charismatic Catholics. Though the future shape of the new Catholicism remains uncertain, one thing is clear: the traditions of the past will not always work.[2]

My thesis is that American Catholic parishes, already large, are getting larger, more liberal and less effective at educating the young in traditional Catholic and Christian values.

Section II: Parish Size

Gallup's 1985 study[3] showed that 28% of Americans gave their Church preference as Roman Catholic. This is a rather higher proportion than earlier figures which showed, for instance, 20% in 1940, almost one third less. While the American Catholic population is growing the number of those available to provide pastoral care is decreasing. A significant proportion of these Catholics, 25%, are inactive.[4] There is a preponderance of women and an increasing shortage of clergy. There is a growing number of parishes without a resident priest. Catholic parishes in the U.S. are large and are growing larger. The Notre Dame Study results show that one third of the parishes serve 1,000 or fewer people, about a quarter serve between 1,000 and 2,500 people, one fifth serve between 2,500 and 5,000 people, and the remainder serve more than 5,000 people. Only a small proportion of Protestant congregations approach this size, and it will come as no surprise that some parishes are finding difficulty in developing a sense of Christian fellowship & community.[5] Complaints that they are unable to provide parishioners with a sense of meaningful community have lead to defection from and disaffection with the Church. Yet, if present trends continue, parishes will get larger, not smaller. Parish boundaries continue to orient the church attendance of most U.S. Catholics.

Section III: The Shortage of Clergy

Many parishes have adapted to the shortage of clergy by developing a series of collaborative lay ministries. There has also been a dramatic decline in vocations to the sisterhood. Applicants in the 1980s are 10% of what they were in the Sixties. Current members are older and total at least 1/3 less in number. The decline has not affected all orders equally. Thriving exceptions include Mother Teresa's Missionaries of Charity and the Daughters of St. Paul. Authors cite many different reasons for the decline including entanglement in a pleasure oriented society, chemical dependency, widespread religious doubt, the breakdown of Catholic family life, the media's selective presentation of discontented religious, the erosion of clarity in religious life, the failure of current members to recommend their form of life or wear its distinctive garb, and their failure to show forth Christ in their personal lives.[6] Now unpaid volunteers conduct many important ministries in the parish.[7] In these new collaborative ministries, women clearly predominate. The mind of these volunteers has not been formed by the seminary. Most bring to the Church the values of the world in which they have received their personal and professional formation. Neither are they bound by vows or promises of obedience to the bishop. If they are not part of the solution, they are part of the problem.

Section IV: The Pick 'n Choose Church
The Consistency of American Catholicism

Of the 37 million active American Catholics, many, indeed the vast majority, are very selective in the doctrines they believe, accept and put into practise. Well over 70%, for instance, report that they reject the Church's teaching on birth control.[8] Dissent is widespread. In his study Gallup comments: "Within the pattern of increased attendance of religious services, we find Roman Catholics, the largest single denomination, are coming back to the Church in droves, because more and more of them have come to believe that they can be good Catholics without having to agree with all the teachings of the Vatican."[9]

Selective Catholics are not found among the laity alone. Aumann, writing in a professional clergy journal roundly declares: "The rejection of Church teaching is all the more serious and contagious since clerics and Catholic theologians claim the right to dissent from some of the teachings of the Church. The term "selective Catholics" implies that Catholics now have the right to decide for themselves which religious truths they will accept. They act as if there is no longer any obligation to accept the statements handed down by the teaching authority of the Church."[10]

Social research on American Catholics has demonstrated a phenomenon unique to North America: the co-existence of Church attendance with a secular mind-set. While figures for Church attendance, compared to many other industrialized societies, are still holding up well, this coexists with a massive departure from Christian operating values. The U.S. Catholic Bishops have drawn attention to this "tragic separation of faith and life."[11] When Christians in other societies have succumbed to the values of the world around them and have fallen away from their Christian heritage and way of life, the phenomenon has been called secularization. Large numbers of Catholic Americans have abandoned a Catholic outlook and Catholic obedience, while continuing with Catholic Church attendance. This process can be viewed as a form of mental or *internal secularization.* Gallup reports: "Now American Catholics are content to remain in the Church, even though two-thirds of them favor allowing priests to marry, half support the ordination of women as priests, three-quarters approve the use of contraceptives and only one third think that pre-marital sex is wrong." When he compared American Catholics with their Protestant counterparts, Gallup generally found the Catholic population more liberal on values concerning sex, morality and family life. From this, he concluded:

> 1) Active parishioners do not generally accept the Church's teaching on contraception.
> 2) Active American Catholic laypeople are willing to move further in the direction of liberalism than the Vatican thinks desirable.[12]

These findings are corroborated by the Notre Dame Study which states: "The move towards a lay — rather than a clerical — church reflects the extent to which Americans have assimilated the participatory values found in the American democratic society."[13]

A Cultural Mood: LIBERALISM

James Hitchcock[14] has identified what he calls a "cultural mood" which disposes people to abandon religious commitments. He writes: "Modern culture, for complex reasons of which prolonged prosperity is one of the most important, has inculcated into people the expectation of a relaxed and easy way of life. Anything which appears demanding or difficult, which requires discipline or sacrifice, is not only distasteful; it seems intrinsically illegitimate. Thus many people in the Churches have come to expect that, one by one, all the old restrictions, moral laws, practises like fasting, anything which makes demands on self, will sooner or later be modified or done away with. Their relationship with the Church is largely defined in those terms. They see their role as working continually for the dilution of past absolutes so that present day Christians can feel more comfortable and relaxed."

In 1984, the Center for Pastoral Renewal commissioned an analysis of the figures on divorce and separation gathered by the National Opinion Research Center at the University of Chicago. A particularly striking finding is the sharply rising percentage of Catholics who have been divorced or legally separated. In the decade from 1972-1982 this rose from one in seven to one in every four. Among those ever-married, the percentage of divorced and separated rose in the general population by 50%; among Catholics it rose by 90%. These survey percentages indicate that of the 29 million Catholics in the U.S. who have ever been married, 7 million have obtained a divorce or legal separation; of these 3.5 million are now divorced, 2.5 million are divorced/separated & remarried, 1 million are separated, 1/4 million are now widowed but have been divorced or separated in the past. The authors estimate that Catholic

Church tribunals have granted annulments to less than 10% of the 2.5 million re-married.[15]

However, not all the losses due to internal secularization among active Catholics are to the left. Some are defecting to the right. Recently, *America* magazine devoted a whole issue[16] to the question of Christian fundamentalism. Several of the articles presented alarming figures on the number of Catholics who have joined fundamentalist sects. In May 1986, the Vatican issued a document on sects, cults & religious movements.

Section V: A Young Church

Gallup, comparing American Catholics with their Protestant counterparts, found the Catholic population more liberal on values concerning sex, morality and family life, and rather younger. He also found that the average age of adult Catholics is 42.6 years. The average age of adult Protestants is considerably greater — 46 years. The NDS showed that "core Catholic" parishioners, the "pillars of the parish," are even older, having an average age of 49.3 years. Gallup observes: "Among the factors that help give the American Catholic Church its liberal flavor are its relative youth and the increasing numbers of Catholics with some college education." Population surveys show Catholics having a higher proportion of teenagers and college students than the overall population.[17]

Nearly 30 percent of Catholics are under age 30, while less than 20 percent of Episcopalians, Methodists and Presbyterians fall into that age group. The percentage of Catholics who have attended college, now more than 40 percent, has doubled in the past two decades.[18]

Gallup also notes: "One important factor in determining the proportion of Catholics in the U.S. population in the coming decades will be the success of the Roman Catholic Church in keeping young Catholics in the fold."[19] Quite frankly, this seems highly unlikely. Such data as we possess shows that the "fall-out" among young Catholics to be slightly higher than among mainline Protestants.[20] The lesson is clear: we need, as a Church, to pay particular attention to the needs of young Catholics. Catechetics is of key importance to the future of the American Catholic Church. Moreover, among American Catholics dissent has become so prevalent, and some doctrines are so ignored, that other American Catholics are beginning seriously to question if they have the right to be called Catholic at all.[21] In addition, these children are not all being born into stable families. The divorce statistics are alarming.

Section VI: Socialization (Christian Education)

This section brings us to the key question determining the shape, size and consistency of the future American Catholic Church. Can the affluent, suburbanized, dissenting U.S. Catholic Church of the '80's hold the allegiance of the young? Some of the empirical evidence suggests that Catholics are succumbing to the world around them.[22]

The large-scale Search Survey of 1984[23] shows that Christian moral values are not being successfully transmitted to children. This National Catholic Education Association study of 1,100 fifth through ninth graders from 13 religious groups attests that Catholic students are concerned more than others about academic success and also that they are "more interested and active in the area of sexuality."[26] Manno[27] noted the following differences between the national sample and the Catholics. There may now be a "Catholic work ethic that rivals the Protestant one" which is transmitted from Catholic parents to their children. Catholic parents give a high ranking to "being successful" and "having lots of money" as desired values in life. Catholic students have an "achievement anxiety." Catholic youth "report higher frequencies of thinking about sex and they date more often." They are more likely than the national sample to see abortion as wrong, to use alcohol, smoke cigarettes and attend parties. This survey pointed up these particular areas of concern:

> Nearly 20 percent of Catholic 7th, 8th and 9th graders have experimented with sexual intercourse,
> Many of these are involved with alcohol and marijuana;
> The frequency which these young adolescents express anxiety about nuclear destruction
> The frequency they experience family tension violence & conflict.[28]

The Catholic segment of this study showed that "Catholic youth were more concerned about success and sex" than their Protestant counterparts. This large study involved families with children active in church youth groups belonging to 13 different denominations. Most parents were involved in a church, while mothers (68% attending once a week) tended to be more involved than fathers (52% once a week or more). Mothers were more likely to experience religion as comforting, challenging and liberating. They were also more certain about their beliefs and viewed religion as more important than fathers did. Though institutional religious participation was the norm, religion was not commonly talked about at home. Young adolescents were asked: "How often does your family sit down and talk about God, the Bible or other religious things?" These studies confirmed work done in Maryland in 1976[24] which showed the relationship between parents' values and their teen-aged children's values was generally found to be weak. The study concluded: "Children evidently get their values from the extra-familial culture as much as from their parents." Jennings and Niemi[25] have suggested that possibly other socialization agents, like peer group and media, have such a strong influence that the influence of parents is weak as a result. Commenting on the study a Catholic high school principal wrote:

> Many parents have left religion to the schools and have abdicated their responsibilities. Parishes, too, have often neglected to sponsor youth programs because of the presence of the school. But the schools either lack programs which put into practice what they teach, or fail to demand enough of their students in living what they are taught. In short, each area of the community seems to be pinpointing another to do the job.

I believe that these attitudes are widespread, and constitute a recipe for nothing less than disaster. As Dennis Poyant observes:

The Catholicism of their parents can infect adolescents with materialism. Catholics are supposed to follow the values of Christ, but they have
to live out these values in a dominant consumerist culture, which contradicts these values in many ways. What adults call "inconsistency" in
following these values, teenagers call hypocrisy. When parents offer a
value system to adolescents that has a large discrepancy between the
values professed and the values actually operating, teenagers turn away.
When Catholicism is embraced in a purely cultural and surface sort of
way ... it comes across as a collection of taboos more honored in the
breach than in the observance. The quality of the parents' religious
beliefs, commitment and observance determines how much of their
values get transmitted to their children.[30]

Section VII: Conclusion

The 1984 Bishops Report on American Catholic Parish Life concluded that the pastor, staff and people should work together to articulate a clear sense of mission which should reflect people's needs, provide a basis for setting priorities, and attend to the critical issues of
individual Christian life, family life and the responsibility of the Church
to the world.[31] This may be all very well but Christ has already set his
Church's priorities and high among them is evangelization. Evangelization was the key priority of Vatican II, the reason for its calling. It is
the key to the future of the Church in the Western World, and is one of
the characteristics of the contemporary church.

My thesis has been that if present trends continue, the typical American Catholic Parish will become: (1) larger, (2) more liberal, (3) less
effective at Christian education. Since the parish forms and shapes the
typical American layperson, it follows that the typical American Catholic
will find it harder and harder to reach the Catholic ideal.

The key response to this, which has been developed in Movements
for Spiritual Renewal, is the development of a strong Catholic identity.
Here the Movements for Spiritual Renewal can teach the larger Church.
These are vital issues affecting the very survival of the Church as a
Church; in a time of rapid social transition, Catholics who lack a clear
sense of their identity will continue to be assimilated into the way of the
world around them, and be lost to the Church, to the world they are
intended to illuminate and guide, and maybe even to Salvation itself.

FOOTNOTES

[1] Other established studies on which I have drawn include: (a) George Gallup's Princeton Religious Research Center; (b) Monographs, such as Dolan, **The American Catholic Experience**; (c) Elesser's National Center for Pastoral and Parish Workers
(NAPPA); (d) The Center for Applied Religious Research in Washington (CARA);
(e) *The Journal for the Scientific Study of Religion (JSSR);* (f) *The International Religious Digest;* (g) **The Notre Dame Study** commissioned by the U.S.C.C.

[2] Jay P. Dolan, **The American Catholic Experience**, *op. cit.* p. 442.

[3] Gallup, George E., **"Unchurched Americans"**, 1985, pp. 42-44.

[4] Gallup, George E., 1985, *op. cit.* p. 49.

[5] Pilarczyk, Archbishop Daniel E., *Origins,* Vol. 16, No. 39. rc 1987, "Final Report on a
Visitation of the Cincinnati Archdiocese."

[6] Aumann, Fr. Jordan, O.P., University of St. Thomas, Rome, writing in *The Priest,* March 1987, pg. 5.

[7] **The Notre Dame Study** claimed that beyond the pastor of the parish 83% of the leadership came from laypersons, paid or unpaid. Even among paid staff 57% are lay. Among the unpaid staff 94% are lay. In none of the parishes sampled was leadership provided by the pastor alone; in 36% it was shared by pastor and laity without the involvement of religious, in 64% leadership involved a combination of pastor, religious and laity.

[8] *Detroit Free Press* Readers' Poll, August 19th, 1987, pg. 1.
([8A]) *Time Magazine,* Sept. 17th, 1987, pp. 46 ff, article on "Pope John Paul and His Feisty American Flock."

[9] Gallup, George E., "Religion in America, 50 Years: 1935-1985," *The Gallup Report,* May 1985.

[10] Aumann, *op. cit.* pp. 6, 7.

[11] U.S.C.C., *Pastoral Letter on the Economy,* 1987.

[12] Gallup, George E., **Unchurched Americans**, *op. cit.* pp. 44-49.

[13] **Notre Dame Study**, Report #5.

[14] James Hitchcock, *Pastoral Renewal,* July-August 1982.

[15] Davis, J. E. & Perrotta, K. F., *Pastoral Renewal,* April 1984; **Notre Dame Study**, *op. cit.* Study #5.

[16] *America,* Vol. 156, No. 14, April 11th, 1957: The following causes were cited why Catholics leave the Church to join fundamentalist sects: conflict with, or unjust treatment by a bishop, priest or religious; dissatisfaction with preaching or the liturgy, anaemic prayer life; desire for a more biblical preaching, inability to accept all the teachings of the Church or her authority to teach in the name of Christ.

[17] Gallup, George E., 1985, *op. cit.* pp. 44-49.

[18] Gallup, George E., 1985, *op. cit.* pp. 42-44.

[19] Gallup, George E., 1986, *op. cit.* p. 24.

[20] "Search Survey: Young Adolescents & Their Parents," Search Institute, Minneapolis, 1984, *Our Sunday Visitor,* Nov. 22, 1981, p. 7.

[21] Hoge, Petrillo, Smith, "Transmission of Religious and Social Values from Parents to Teenage Children," *Journal of Marriage and the Family,* August 1982, Vol. 44, No. 3.

[22] **Search Institute,** Minneapolis, 1984, *op. cit.*

[23] **Search Institute,** Minneapolis, 1984, *op. cit.*

[24] Hoge, Petrillo, Smith, *op. cit.*

[25] Manno, Bruce, "Catholic Youth More Concerned About Success, Sex," *Momentum,* February 1984.

[26] Poyant, Dennis R., "Weakness in Church Identity and Service Revealed," *Momentum,* February 1986.

[27] Manno, *op. cit.*

[28] Ianni, "Teen Age Values," excerpted from *Our Sunday Visitor,* March 11, 1987.

[29] "Are America's Catholics Being Protestantised?" *Columbia Magazine,* July 1987 Editorial, p. 2.

[30] Poyant, *op. cit.*

[31] U.S.C.C., "Catholic Parish Life in America," *Origins,* 1984, Vol. 14, 459ff, 670ff.

PART SEVEN:
The Church, Universal and Particular

The Universal Church and Particular Universities
by
Leonard Kennedy, C.S.B.

Last January I received a letter from a professor in one of the smaller Jesuit universities of the United States concerning the relationship between my own university and the bishop of our diocese. As far as I could find out, nothing is written down in our documents about this matter. Up to 25 years ago there was no question that bishops had a great deal of say about the running of Catholic universities. This was taken for granted. Today the situation is different, and it is necessary to spell out the issue. My correspondent made a formal motion before the assembled faculty to have his university's charter recognize the local bishop as the authority in what pertained to the university's Catholicity; *not one other person* supported the motion. I do not know what would happen in my own university if such an issue arose, but it seems quite clear that in most of the Catholic universities in the United States any episcopal control is resented.

This attitude began with the Land O'Lakes document of August 1, 1967, signed by participants from Georgetown, Boston College, Catholic University of America, St. Louis, Fordham, Laval, and Notre Dame. The document claimed that "the Catholic university must have a true autonomy and academic freedom in the face of authority of whatever kind, lay or clerical, external to the academic community itself." This attitude has become so pervasive that it was uttered publicly by Father Byron, the president of the Catholic University of America, at the height of the most celebrated case of the present day (*Envoy,* Spring II, pp. 4-5). And Father Byron is the president of the American bishops' own university!

This claim to independence from the Church is countered by the new **Code of Canon Law** (1983). The **Code** gives bishops the duty and right to see that the principles of Catholic doctrine are faithfully observed in their universities (canon 810), the right to give or refuse mandates for professors of theology (canon 812), the right to bestow or withdraw the designation "Catholic" (canon 808), and the authority to see that teachers lacking integrity of doctrine are removed from office (canon 810).

The basic issue, then, is academic freedom. The Land O'Lakes document, supported fully by the official position of the Association of

Catholic Colleges and Universities, wants a definition of academic freedom in Catholic universities identical with that in secular ones. I have shown in a recent article *(Fidelity,* June, 1987) that the bishops of the United States have supported this position. And so we have a confrontation on this issue between the Universal Church and the Church in America.

Those who love academic freedom should be slow to agree with this position because what is at issue is not a conflict between freedom and authority but a conflict between two freedoms: that of a professor and that of an institution. To develop this point we must first show that it is not possible for a Catholic university to remain Catholic in a meaningful sense if it is forced to adopt the secular university's definition of academic freedom. If it is not able to dismiss faculty who publicly oppose the university's primary purpose, it is forced to teach the contradictory of what is was founded to teach. And indeed we find that Catholic universities which have espoused a secular definition of academic freedom have ceased to be Catholic in reality no matter what they claim in words. Christopher Derrick, in **Flight from Scepticism: Liberal Education as if Truth Mattered** (p. 106), has given us a description of these dead or dying institutions:

> The outlook or philosophy now dominant, assiduously preached by most of the faculty and eagerly embraced by most of the students, will indeed contain certain elements or memories of Catholicism. But it contains much more powerful elements of modernism, of scepticism, of evolutionary relativism, of existentialism, of Marxism, of many another -ism which has become fashionable in the non-Catholic world ....
> Within American higher education today, it is becoming increasingly unreal to apply the adjective "Catholic" to institutions which once claimed it proudly and with good reason. In a number of cases, the college has frankly renounced its claim to have a distinctly Catholic character, usually in return for government money. This was at least honest. But that claim often continues to be made even where it has lost all plausibility.

And, if we grant that a Catholic university can not remain Catholic without a definition of academic freedom in keeping with the **Code of Canon Law**, we grant that the freedom of the institution to exist as Catholic requires this definition. Thus, when a professor publicly and unrepentantly teaches doctrines opposed to the university's beliefs, he is, in the name of *his* freedom, opposing the *university's* freedom. And, since he is a part of the university and knew its beliefs when he was hired, it is clear whose freedom must give way. This becomes even clearer when we realize that the freedom of the university exists for the sake of the students' freedom, their freedom to obtain a Catholic education. The freedom of both the faculty and the university is ordained to the students' freedom.

If an American university wanted to be bilingual and to have all its instruction in, say, French, and deemed that the students needed this in order to become bilingual, the university could reasonably require that the faculty use only French in the classroom. The faculty could not legitimately claim violation of academic freedom because other universities did not have this requirement. One could not imagine an American Jewish university allowing a professor to teach antisemitism, nor could one imagine the American public faulting the university for dismissing the professor.

Of course today we have an ambiguity in the word "Catholic." If an orthodox Catholic looks at the American scene he is saddened. But a dissenting Catholic may look at it and be pleased, as indeed the Association of Catholic Colleges and Universities is. It thus behooves a university to declare itself not only Catholic but faithful to the Magisterium. Indeed, it should state its nature and purpose quite explicitly. And it should state in some detail what is required of faculty by way of assent to the Magisterium, or, at least, by way of not publicly dissenting from it.

Very few of our institutions have such statements. However, St. Joseph's College in Edmonton, Canada, upholds the following in its faculty agreement:

> As an institution under the aegis of the Archdiocese of Edmonton, the College is faithful to the magisterium of the Roman Catholic Church . . . .

And, under the heading "Academic Freedom," the agreement states:

> These freedoms are to be understood within the context of these statutes as a whole. While they allow for a wide range of discussion, they do not, however, give staff members the right to act in a way that challenges or undermines the nature and objectives of the College as set forth in [articles including the one mentioned above].

No doubt some Catholics who want to have a secular definition of academic freedom in a Catholic university do accept the teaching of the Church's magisterium as true. Yet the logic of their position is faulty. The acceptance of truth cannot be an obstacle to a university's progress; on the contrary, it must be a great boon. And the Catholic university recognizes that the teaching of the magisterium is true. Presumably, these Catholics who do not wish to deny their own faith do not mind if a Catholic university denies *its* faith, as it does when its faculty teaches what is contrary to the Church's magisterium.

This diffidence concerning the Catholic university's faith becomes more suspect when we realize that it is tied up with the desire to be accepted by colleagues in secular institutions, as is attested by the documents of the Association of Catholic Colleges and Universities. Certainly the fear of being different is not justification for denying one's faith. And, if our Catholicism doesn't make us different from secularists, what good is it?

Recently the proponents of the freedom of Catholic universities from effective influence by bishops have developed a back-up argument, namely, that a university that is too Catholic will have some government funding denied it. Yet these same proponents argue that our universities are admirably Catholic. They are really facing a dilemma. If the university is too Catholic, funding will be reduced. If they want to retain or increase their funding, they must relinquish their Catholicity, or, at least, deny bishops an effective influence in the university. Yet this influence is necessary for a university to be Catholic, as Canon Law states. These persons are arguing, then, for half-Catholic universities, and, of course, that is what they are getting.

It is interesting that the fear of reduced government funding is not based on recent actions of the government. The argument based on it seems to be an argument contrived to bolster a weak primary argument. It indicates a ready willingness to let the government have the effective influence denied to the bishops. In fact, Kenneth Whitehead, Deputy Assistant Secretary for Higher Education Programs at the United States Department of Education, has shown *(America,* Feb. 7, 1987) that "institutional autonomy is not one of the requirements for federal aid to higher education." Here are some further quotations from Mr. Whitehead:

> ... Catholic institutions of higher education, ... as a condition of receiving any Federal aid, are required to be accredited by an agency "recognized" by the Secretary of Education. ... But it is emphatically *not* the case that either the Federal Government or the accrediting agencies otherwise impose any negative "religious test" on religiously affiliated schools.
>
> ... for religiously affiliated schools to insist upon standards believed to be required by the tenets of their faith has, in fact, never been considered a violation of academic freedom, provided these schools made clear in advance what their particular requirements were with regard to hiring, disciplining, and the like.
>
> ... the idea that churches or denominations can exercise any control over the schools they sponsor only at the risk of jeopardizing their Federal aid is totally at variance with the entire American tradition of higher education. In point of fact, the accrediting associations have long granted full accreditation to schools that are in no way institutionally autonomous.
>
> As things now stand, religious denominations need have no fear of ... losing the Federal aid to which they are entitled by act of Congress. ...

The issue, then, of federal aid being denied to truly Catholic universities is a red herring. And the Church in America, as represented by so many universities and the bishops agreeing with them, has opposed the universal law of the Church while basing its case on a false theoretical argument backed up by a bogus fear.

The Particular and Universal Problem
by
Mary F. Rousseau

The requirements for any community to be a real rather than spurious community are rooted in the metaphysics of being. As the word itself suggests, a community is a "many turned into one without ceasing to be many," a unification of a multitude that does not destroy the multitude. The world itself, then, is a community because its many distinct beings are ordered and unified without detriment to their identities as individual beings. Their principle of unity is their common relationship to the single source of the being: God Who is the giver of existence, and Who is constantly and indivisibly present in each. Yet their common dependence on and union with God leaves beings intact as individuals because the existence with which He endows each being is individualized, uniquely its own. A dog and a tree, then, are two distinct beings. Yet they are united with each other in that the One Indivisible Creator is entirely present in each as the continuous cause of its being.

Human community becomes a reality as we, already members of the community of being, consciously and freely appropriate that community of being for ourselves. The act of that appropriation consists in an act of altruistic love. As Aristotle shows in his treatise on friendship, and as St. Thomas develops Aristotle on his Treatise on Love, the love that unifies, that *is* communion, is the love by which one person takes another, his beloved, as his other self. In order to become one in a properly human way we must identify with some beloved other, make him our other self, and then wish his good to him for his sake. When we do so love, the beloved's good becomes common to us both. In that common possession of a single good, we are unified in real human community without the least detriment to our unique individualities. We are "a many turned into one without ceasing to me many."

The all-important factor for building genuine community, then, is altruistic love. Without such loving identification with another, two or more people may be close to each other in time and space, similar in many physical and psychological ways, perhaps intimates in sharing their thoughts and feelings, but they will not be *existentially* united through the possession of a single good in common.

The altruistic love which unites persons, however, must be rooted in objective reality. That is, if I am to become one with another, the good I wish to him must be his genuine, true good — a good that is specified by his human and individual nature. While to love is to wish some good to some person it is not automatically to wish a good which the beloved wants. Nor is it simply to wish what I want to give. It is to wish a good that is a real, objectively true good for the one loved. Not, e.g., candy to my diabetic child no matter how much each of us would like his enjoyment of the candy. The real objectively true good is his health. When I wish health to my child, then that health becomes a bond which unifies us — a single good that belongs to both of us. The health of my child is obviously his; but it is mine also, though in a different way, because I in my love have freely chosen to make it my good as well. Thus my wish for a diabetic child to have the candy he begs for would not be an act of love. The gift of candy might draw us closer together physically — into an embrace, perhaps — and even bring us into a certain emotional intimacy, but it would not unite us existentially. We could have only an apparent communion with each other, not a real one.

Fundamentally, each act of love focuses, at least implicitly, on the beloved's very existence. By a logic too complicated to trace here and now, whenever I love anyone, I wish to that beloved his very existence, and hence his total reality as a person for his sake. And since that existence is embedded in the network of the entire community of being, *any* act of altruistic love brings me into communion not only with my one beloved but with the entire community of being. Thus, as the saints well knew, to love one is to love all. And to fail to love any one is to fail to love all.

When we look at the universal church in light of this metaphysics of community, we must say that she *is* a community to the degree to which we, her members, love each other altruistically. In loving each other as members of the church, we appropriate the entire community of being. The question, then, as to who is and who is not a member of the church is, at root, a question of who loves and who does not. Since love has to be rooted in objective reality, a further question arises: what, precisely, is the good which we must will to each other for each other's sakes if our unity is to be real and not merely apparent? What is that good whose common possession unifies us so that we constitute the Church universal?

Essentially, it is, of course, our existence in all its fullness. But that existential fullness is specified differently for individuals and for smaller communities within the larger community. To my fellows in the church, I must fundamentally wish their being as sacraments of the Triune God. What Catholics must wish for each other, in short, if the church is to be a genuine existential community, is the ability to love as Jesus did, to keep His commandments, so that He and His Father will come to live in us. And then the world will be evangelized; the world will come to know Jesus as being sent by the Father. We seek, then, in our love for each other, to draw those who are not yet in the church into her life of existential communion with God by wishing to them, for their sakes, the ability to love as Jesus did.

Such love needs guidelines. These guidelines for our sacramental loving are the moral teachings of the church. They are the commandments that come to us through the revelation of Jesus that is recorded in the Scriptures, as that revelation is interpreted by the Magisterium. The moral life of Catholics is neither utilitarian, deontological, or situational. It is a sacramental and mystical life, a life of love, under the guidance of Him Who is the Way, the Truth, and the Life, and the Head of the Mystical Body.

We see, then, the basic requirements for the reality of a particular church within the Church universal. Such a particular church would have to be a group of persons who love altruistically — who seek each other's good for each other's sakes. Its members would have to seek to love and to help each other to love under the guidelines of Him Who, as the Way, the Truth, and the Life, gave us commandments to keep and a teaching office to interpret and apply them. We can have a multitude of communities, of local churches within the universal church as the racial, cultural, political and other differences among people lead to different ways of loving and of enacting love in outward sacramental gestures. But each must enact the love of Jesus, not some other inner attitude. Without common assent to the moral teachings of the Church universal, then, we could not unite in love, nor become one in a joint possession of a common good. Without this guidance, we would risk wishing to others not their good for their sakes, but something inappropriate, perhaps something evil.

However, given the need for such a moral unity, we need not require a rigid, monolithic, static mode of life that would disallow cultural, national, and other differences among particular churches. The moral theory of St. Thomas Aquinas allows great variety and flexibility in the application of basic moral principles to human beings and human situations as these vary from time to time and from place to place. But his principle for such variations guards the unity of the church. The secondary, more specific principles of morality change and develop as people do, but they may not contradict the primary precepts. These remain absolute, universal, and unvarying. Thus all men, of all times and places, must educate their children. That is a primary precept. But some will do so by trekking through the jungle with bows and arrows, while others will do so by installing an Apple computer in the family room of their home. These are secondary precepts. But none may omit education entirely. Similarly, there can be as many particular churches within the universal church as there are ways of living out in varied times and places the commandments of Jesus that guide our sacramental life in the church. But since our only access to those is the Scripture, as formed and interpreted by the Magisterium, we must conclude that assent to the moral Magisterium of the church is an absolute prerequisite for membership in any church. Without that assent, the love which alone enables us to appropriate the community of being, to belong to the Church universal, is bound to go awry.

What, then, of the purported "American Church" which is attracting an inordinate and increasing amount of attention in the media? Can it be a legitimate particular church within the Church universal? Or is it intrinsically condemned to be merely an apparent, not a real, community?

There is one feature of the "American Church" that leads to a negative answer. That feature is the apparent desire to found such a church *on the basis of* dissent from the moral teachings of the Church universal. The proponents of an American Church seem to take as their basic principles secular notions that are utterly opposed to the gospels: the freedom of each individual to define truth for himself; the freedom to create one's own moral values; and the independence of theologians from the Magisterium, indeed, the independence of theology from faith. Dissent from the moral Magisterium, dissent for its own sake, seems to be the common base that would construct the American Church. But if such dissent is itself the basis for a human grouping, that grouping is indeed an illusory community. It rests on precisely a rejection of the guidelines to the love that is required for any community.

For our life in the church, the goods which we must wish to each other if we are to love as Jesus did are the goods specified in His commandments. As these come to us from the Bible through the Magisterium, they constitute the moral dogmas of the Church. Thus for anyone to truly be in the Church and of it, he must love as Jesus did, love as the moral dogmas of the Church command. It follows, then, that moral dissent can never be the ground of a particular church within the Church universal. Such dissenters could never form *any* kind of genuine community. They could be, at best, a mere association, in which unity is apparent and not real, because they lack by their own definition the only principle that can unite persons in genuine community. That principle is the altruistic love which brings two (or more) into the joint possession of a single good. For when the good of a beloved is defined in advance as something other than the real, objective good as defined by the moral Magisterium, it is truly an illusory good. It is candy given to a diabetic child.

As long as the goal of the "American Church" is to "Americanize" the Church from a base of dissent, rather than evangelizing America from a base of assent which is faith, it can be no church at all. It is not, indeed, a community. The "American Church," then is no threat to the unity of the Church universal. It doesn't really exist, never can, never will. It is a metaphysical impossibility, a contradiction in terms, a contradiction in its own freely chosen terms of dissent for the sake of dissent.

The Golden Calf of Inculturation

by

Thomas Langan

At a meeting on "Inculturation" in Tantur, Jerusalem, September 1985, Catholics from eighteen countries seemed much more concerned about making the Gospel message "relevant" to their native cultures and about preserving traditional cultures than about some sort of universality of truth. In its extremest expressions, national cultures at times seemed final goods to be preserved at all costs. At the same time, a wide-spread anti-authoritarianism and a tendency to see Rome only in terms of its "remoteness" and its "failure to understand local conditions" made difficult the task of the few participants concerned about lasting, universal truth and about the unity and integrity of the Church. The local bishop emerged as all important, while the *college* of bishops, under the presidency of the Pope, was scarcely mentioned. You can see why. Once the local "inculturators" have the local bishop thoroughly on their side, the battle is won, and one can start down the road to a national church.

As with all great heresies, vital truths are here being defended, *parts* of the whole truth. The inculturators put forth three propositions which must be retained in any adequate understanding of the Church's situation in the world:

1. The light of the Gospel does have to penetrate and transform local cultures, and to do that, a certain translation is indeed necessary.

2. The local bishop is most familiar with the intricacies of the cultures for which he, as pastor, has responsibility.

3. Each local culture contains its own treasures, which, in so far as they are good, should be retained and should be used to incarnate the Gospel.

Each of these considerations raises complex problems to which the Catholic community must continue to devote study and prayer. In my allotted time, I can do little more than recall the main issues, which is useful in giving direction to future research and reflection.

I. Translating the Gospel Message

It is time to stop repeating the old Harnackian accusations of the "Hellenization" of an essentially "Hebrew" Gospel message, and the anti-Europeans' warnings about the parochial European character of Christian culture and to spend energy instead or securing the epistemological foundations for what we all know: that the truths handed down by the Church and meant for all peoples are believable by persons of all conditions in life and of all cultures.

Philosophical illumination of this experience can be carried out in a sophisticated way, provided one is determined to defend the basic objectivism the universal claims of Christianity demands.

Allow me to outline what must be secured for this defense by adequate philosophical description and argumentation.

Jesus, as all human beings, spoke in a definite cultural setting, expressing Himself in the Palestinian Aramaeic of a certain milieu, and what He did He did in interaction with specific persons in a given setting. But he expressly addressed all mankind, for all ages to come. He spoke of timeless relationships to the Father and the Holy Spirit, of the Kingdom that will have no end, of the salvation of all people.

To express Himself, He both called on the symbols of Holy Scripture, which have to be interpreted as He intended them if we are to know what He meant, and in His parables and other preaching, He used things of the most ordinary human experience, and He taught in terms of a human nature which is accessible in the experience of every human being.

Many of the things Jesus is recorded as having said are not difficult in terms of meaning, and can be readily translated because of the universality of all peoples' access to the things He used to convey His meaning. "Give everything you possess to the poor, and come, follow me!" is all too clear! Others are "hard sayings," as the New Testament puts it, and many of his contemporaries turned away upon hearing them. "Unless you eat the flesh of the Son of Man you shall not have life everlasting" is a hard saying, difficult as to just how we are to take it, and difficult to take altogether in most of its orthodox interpretations. Our incentive for "taking such sayings" at all is Christ's authority, and our guarantee that our interpretation is His interpretation is the authority of the living teaching office of the Church.

The more accessible teachings are the most readily translatable because of their reference to things and human situations which are universal. Objectivist epistemology which examines the experience of the transcendence of linguistic symbol toward real things and situations of intersubjective experience provides the theoretical foundation for the very real possibility of such translation.

The hard sayings and the mighty works which ground the authority on which we accept them demand profound faith in Jesus and in the apostles whom He has sent to witness to this work. They can only be properly interpreted from out of the transmitted lived experience of the apostolic community which provides the context for correct meaning. A connection has to be made, for instance, between the descent of the Holy Spirit in the moment of the Annunciation, His descent at Jesus' baptism, Pentecost, and the experience of the gifts of the Holy Spirit in the apostolic Church and the sacramental reality of the work of the Holy Spirit in the continuing life of the Church. What is meant by "Holy Spirit" is not translatable into the ordinary experience of any community, because it is the fruit of supernatural experience, granted by grace to those joined in the community of the Church.

The problem, then, is not one of finding equivalent words in another language, but of finding a whole fabric of new language that will invite another to take up residence in a community which witnesses, through its Word, its preaching and its life, to the ongoing reality of the Spirit.

For this reason, it is appropriate that the catechumen learn a new language, one for which he is not prepared by the everyday Housa or Tamil, or whatever he may speak. He has to learn a whole tradition, not as a story about the past, but as living reality incarnated in those with whom he has come into contact.

To be sure, those instructing the catechumen can begin to speak to him about some of the simpler, most translatable things in the Gospel. They, for sure, help bring him into the presence of Jesus. But the heart of the matter is the transmission of the Untranslatable.

For these, we *all* need the living apostolic authority of the Church, incarnating the charism of the Holy Spirit, to keep us on the right path in our understanding of them. Hence the importance of the right "ecclesiology."

Do not misunderstand. I am not saying there is no language problem here. Rather, I am pointing out there is no ordinary language for expressing the profound mysteries of the prophetic faith. There is only the traditional treasure of symbols, forged under the guidance of the Holy Spirit, literally God's Words, which are handed on, meditated upon, celebrated in liturgical canticle, and embodied in institutional form. Without the Spirit-filled endeavor to live out the vision they incarnate, these mysteries lose the core of their sense. They are not in their essence about matters of merely national or epochal importance, but about God and His relation with His entire creation. They have to in-form the experience of each new generation.

II. The Charisms of the Church Apostolic

That is why in these matters getting right the nature of the Church's teaching authority is everything. We depend essentially on the on-going charisms, transmitted as Christ intended, as our sole guarantee of being on the right path in our further incarnating these symbols and in our meditations upon their inexhaustible meaning.

The point is not to dispute that the local bishop is the one to know best where to draw the line regarding what is acceptable in translating the truth of Christianity into terms accessible to the local culture, or in striving to preserve local cultural riches. Of course the bishop has a central role of discernment, but he does this as apostle of the universal Christ, in communion with the whole Church, concretely lived out through the college of bishops under the presidency of Peter, whom Christ Himself designated to be the head. The bishop is to be as much concerned with the truth and well-being of the entire Church as with his diocese. The task of in-forming the entire generation in every land of the Spirit's impulsions is that of the whole Church working together under the authoritative guidance of its hierarchy.

III. Preserving Cultural Riches

Catholics should be wary about mixing the fight to preserve cultural autonomy against the overwhelming attack of "modernity" with the quite different challenge of transmitting the faith faithfully. When one begins to bristle against "European culture" to the point of being unwilling to look into the millennial continuity of the tradition transmitting faithfully and richly the central truths of revelation, one is perilously close to sacrificing to the Golden Calf of ethnicity. Of course there are Hebrew, Greek, Roman, Medieval, French and German influences folded into our traditions. But when they are doing their true work, they are there at the service of the central, living expression of what the genius of all times and all places is called on to express and celebrate. Of course, the genius of peoples newer to the faith will be added to the chorus, and that is as it should be. But do not mix up the fight against Europeans and Americans with the question of understanding correctly the gifts the various cultures have made to the tradition.

As national cultures come increasingly under attack by the planetary scale high tech culture, defensive reactions will become more extreme. Under the banner of "inculturation," the Catholicity of truth may come to suffer. Devotion to the center is the one great protection.

An Historian's Perspective: Similarities and Contrasts

by

Father Marvin O'Connell

I should like to make a few observations appropriate to the historian of the Church, with specific reference to the highly publicized strain in relations between the Vatican and the American hierarchy.

First, we should bear in mind that the history of the Church, since the beginning of the Middle Ages, reveals a constant tension between Rome and the various local hierarchies. This is a perfectly healthy and natural state of things, given the realities of governance within an international institution. It does not in itself involve the *doctrine* of the Petrine primacy. Much of it rather results from often petty differences in administrative style.

Secondly, the history of the Church reveals that in some eras Rome's *practical* power has been greater vis-a-vis local hierarchies than in others. The late 19th century witnessed a great increase in decision-making within the Roman curia. Ironically, at the very time, the papacy was losing its thousand year-old civil princedom. There is nothing surprising about this particular process of ecclesiastical centralization; the same thing, **mutatis mutandis,** was going on in all the secular governments of all the developed countries. These processes were made possible by the rapid technological advances in communication and transportation. The pope's writ, like that of a president or prime minister, could be executed relatively quickly and easily.

Thirdly, given the historical record, it is hardly remarkable to find bishops quarreling among themselves. The analogy which immediately comes to mind, in the midst of our present discontents, is the Americanist Controversy, which reached its climax at the turn of the present century. Except in the minds of a tiny number of intellectuals, the disputes had nothing to do with the primacy. They had a great deal to do with what might be called "ecclesiastical home rule," in that the Americanist bishops insisted that the peculiar circumstances of the Church in the United States — primarily the need to amalgamate hordes of European immigrants into their new country which had no tradition of church-state union — called for specifically American policies. There were complaints in this country that the almost exclusively Italian personnel at the Vatican often failed to understand the American situation.

But — and this point I should like to stress — the complaints, with some notable exceptions, were justified more in the abstract than in the concrete. The vast surviving documentation proves that the curial offcials were, by and large, extremely adept, prudent, and even-handed administrators. They never made a serious policy decision without the widest consultation and without hearing all sides of the question. The celebrated Faribault school plan provides an instructive example: the archives of Propaganda fairly bulge with letters, reports, memoranda which reflect all shades of episcopal opinion about this hotly debated matter. In truth, the Americanist crisis (which in fact is rather too strong a word) arose not out of a quarrel between Rome and the American bishops but out of a quarrel between two factions of American bishops who differed about subjects like parochial education, secret societies, the pace at which Catholic immigrants ought to be "Americanized," and the like. Rome acted quite willingly through all these broils as a referee whom both groups of combatants were anxious to employ to bash their local opponents. Intriguing as all this may be, it is hardly startling; this is consistent with the way human institutions usually work.

And Church history, which by its own rules is restricted to viewing the Church in its human dimensions, must teach its lessons accordingly. History moreover does not, despite the homely aphorism, repeat itself. What history has to say about the present never enjoys the status of identity, but is limited to similarity, or analogy, or — often — contrast.

The church historian nevertheless can assert with some confidence that disagreements between the pope and his curia on the one hand and a local bishop or bishops on the other should be viewed with placidity. Such is the nature of the relationship. Certainly there are, in this regard, some amusing similarities between the now and the then. As American bishops ninety years ago — most of them Irish born — complained that Italians could not grasp the essence of the American dream, so American bishops today — *sotto voce,* to be sure, are wont to murmur that a Polish pope and a German grand inquisitor — the latter, incidentally, referred to often, alas, in the most elevated American Catholic circles as a Nazi or a fascist — are beyond understanding the ethos of the United States.

Nor would it be remarkable, from an historian's point of view, if the bishops often disagreed with one another. One would hope indeed that ambitious and strong-minded men would collide in the kind of fierce dialectic which marked the relationship between John Ireland and Michael Corrigan three generations ago. It is therefore a curiosity to me that presently we appear to have a conference of bishops who vote upon issues like nuclear deterrence and the minimum wage (serious matters indeed but surely matters of opinion) with the near-unanimity of the parliament in Pope John Paul's unhappy homeland; a conference which, if press reports are to be believed, sat supinely on its collective hands as several of its members impudently lectured the long-suffering pontiff on his failure to appreciate American values.

The doctrine of collegiality, reemphasized the second Council of the Vatican, is, of course, a two-way street. It means the pope must listen to and support his brother bishops. But it also means the bishops must listen to and support *their* brother, who bears the awful burden of the Petrine office.

And when one speaks of collegiality one thinks of its corollary, the process of episcopal consultation of the lower orders. Here, it seems to me, the contrast between the now and then is largely an illusion.

Let me intrude a shamelessly personal note, one which displays a hubris unworthy perhaps of my cloth and yet one which, as the years run out for me, I have ever less inclination to disguise. I have been engaged for thirty years in the work of American Catholic higher education, in teaching, research, publication, administration, and not without a measure of success. Not once during all that time, never, *numquam,* did a single American successor of the apostles, whether an appointee of Cicognani, of Vagnozzi, of Jadot, of Laghi, ask my opinion on any matter however trivial, related to the one area of contemporary American Catholic life in which I am an expert. I have not even received a questionnaire from Andrew Greeley!

There has clearly arisen in this Catholic community a liberal media and academic complex of which our anointed leaders are so terrified that expert opinion, if it does tow the accepted ideological line, cannot expect even a hearing. What a contrast to John Ireland and Michael Corrigan, ecclesiastical rogues as they surely were in many respects. Yet what among other things endears them to me is that they cheerfully manipulated the press instead of being manipulated by it.

But the most ironic contrast between our current situation and the days of the Americanist controversy is that, having achieved the bourgeois respectability so much coveted by Ireland and Corrigan, the Catholic community, or at least those who have aggregated to themselves the positions of spokespersons for it, often identifies itself with the worst features of American society, without the wit to recognize it. The lady who in San Francisco recently insisted that the pope treat her as "a well-educated adult" had a point: Rome in the past too often has spoken of her "children" around the world more literally than metaphorically. But well-educated? In the United States? This nation, for all its opulence, has the worst educational record in the developed world? It is a nation where cultural as well as functional illiteracy abounds and where policemen routinely patrol the corridors of big city high schools. And, as far as Catholics are concerned, it is a nation where the unique parochial school system is rapidly disappearing and where the most pampered Catholic children in the history of the world do not know what a sacrament is and have never heard of the book of Genesis. These children attend expensive Catholic secondary schools, take courses like Soup Kitchen 101 and Social Awareness 202, and, upon matriculation at prestigious Catholic colleges and universities, learn little else than why **Humanae Vitae** should be ignored and how the bigoted Catholic culture of an earlier time — a redundancy indeed — caused the Holocaust. Well-educated?

The more things change the more they remain the same. That's about as profound as we historians ever get. But we do have another generalization to offer which, when reflected upon, is capable of cheering up these dismal days. *Ecclesia* semper *reformanda est.* The church *always* has to be reformed. *Semper et ubique.* The church always and everywhere has to be reformed. The task is never over, the challenge never finished. We American Catholics have much to offer the universal church, because of our national genius and because much has been given to us. Let us cease the preening and posturing before a hostile communications industry. Let us eschew sham consultation and the irresponsibility of "consensus management." Let us get on with the job of setting our own house in order, even though we realize that that process will never be complete. If we do, we have the assurance — such is the mysterious working of God's providence — that we shall at the same time bear a unqiue service to the larger household of the faith.